Silence to Light

MĀNOA 13:1

UNIVERSITY
OF HAWAI'I
PRESS

HONOLULU

Silence to Light

JAPAN AND THE SHADOWS OF WAR

Frank Stewart
EDITOR

Leza Lowitz
FEATURE EDITOR

Shuzo Uemoto with father, Toshiharu Uemoto (right), and family friend, Miyajima Island, Japan, 1953

Founded in 1988 by Robert Shapard and Frank Stewart.

Mānoa is published twice a year. Subscriptions: individuals—USA and Canada $22 one year, $40 two years; other countries—$25 one year, $45 two years. Institutions—$40 one year, $72 two years. Single copy $20. For air mail add $18 per year. Call toll free 1-888-UHPRESS. We accept checks, money orders, VISA, or MasterCard, payable to University of Hawai'i Press, 2840 Kolowalu Street, Honolulu, HI 96822, USA. Claims for issues not received will be honored until 180 days past the date of publication; thereafter, the single-copy rate will be charged.

Manuscripts may be sent to *Mānoa,* English Department, University of Hawai'i, Honolulu, HI 96822. Please include self-addressed, stamped envelope for return of manuscript or for our reply.

www.hawaii.edu/mjournal
www.hawaii.edu/uhpress/journals/manoa/

CONTENTS

Special Focus ❦ **Japan and the Shadows of War**

Editor's Note

Twice a year, *Mānoa*'s editors gather significant new writing from throughout Oceania, Asia, and the Americas, and focus on a particular country or region. *Silence to Light,* the current volume in the series, features literary and graphic narratives from and about Japan. Some of the pieces illuminate little-known events that occurred during the war that ended in 1945, while others are reminders of the many ways we continue to be affected by the darkness and silence that the war brought about. Fiction, poetry, memoir, and art of the kinds presented here—because they are experiential and immediate—make vivid the truth that, like all wars, World War II was not a political abstraction or a single historical event. Rather, it was the destruction of the everyday lives and ultimate destinies of husbands and wives, daughters and sons by a form of collective madness. Moving and powerful, the pieces in *Silence to Light* leave little doubt that war is the worst failure of human empathy.

For Americans, 2001 is the sixtieth anniversary of the Japanese military strike on Pearl Harbor, which brought the United States into the conflict. But Pearl Harbor was not the beginning of the war. Throughout Asia, the year 2001 is significant as the seventieth anniversary of the war's actual beginning, in 1931. That year, Japan's Kwantung Army seized Mukden, Manchuria, and began Japan's large-scale military expansionism and colonization throughout Asia and beyond. Events during the first ten years of the war are still vivid for many people in Asia, particularly in China—despite the campaign of forgetfulness that has been waged in Japan and, ironically, abetted in the United States, where Pearl Harbor Day continues to be marked without recalling the larger historical context.

Contemporary examples of Japan's continuing denial of responsibility are many. In November 2000, Kajima Corporation, the country's largest general contractor, was forced to begin compensating the families of Chinese who were enslaved in Japanese copper mines during the war. Many of the laborers were beaten and tortured to death, and few survived more than a year. The settlement resulted from a lawsuit that had been bitterly contested in the courts for nearly five years. And although other companies had engaged in practices similar to Kajima's, the settlement marked

Father at desk, Manchuria

the first time that a Japanese firm had compensated any of the approximately 50,000 Chinese taken from their homes by Japanese occupation troops in the 1930s and 1940s and shipped to Japan to work. An additional 10 million Chinese in Manchuria were forced into labor, and an estimated ten percent of them died as a result. Despite the evidence, multibillion-dollar corporations like Kajima maintain they are not responsible for such "unfortunate side effects" of the war.

Of course, it's not surprising that any nation—including the United States—might wish to forget the atrocities perpetrated by its armies during wartime. However, Japan's singular reluctance to accept culpability in the deaths of 20 to 30 million people from 1931 to 1945, to issue clear statements of apology, and to compensate victims and their families continues to cause friction in East Asia.

American novelist James Baldwin, writing about his own country in the 1960s, said that not only are we part of history, but it is also part of us; consequently, he wrote, the denial and repression of past events are ultimately futile. "Until we excavate our history, we will never know who we are," he concluded. Looking back at the twentieth century, many people might agree with Baldwin that individual and national nightmares can only end by exposing them to the light. Through the efforts of citizens of goodwill, this process—which includes listening to the recollections of elders while educating young people about their nation's history—is gaining ground in Japan. Leza Lowitz, the guest editor for *Silence to Light,* writes:

> While many Japanese politicians still refuse to admit any wrongdoing during the conflict, people who were caught in the winds of war are growing old. As they look back, many are engaging in *hansei-suru* (self-reflection). For some, this is a means of understanding and accepting their own actions—seeking answers, if not forgiveness. In such quests for personal truths, buried stories finally come to light.

In this spirit of reflection and understanding, *Silence to Light* focuses on personal truths and stories emerging from the shadows. Tales of individual lives are more complex and troubled than the official histories of nations; they comprise emotions as well as facts, and their telling provides the chance for authentic reparation of human suffering: the healing of hearts and souls across barriers of time and national borders.

Ishii Shinpei's essay, "The Canary That Forgot Its Song," recounts the author's journey to Manchuria in 1991, almost half a century after his brother's death there. In part, his journey was an attempt to understand why 120 Japanese middle-school boys were abandoned by their country during the army's retreat from northeastern China in 1945. Most of the boys and two teachers survived their wartime ordeal—a desperate eleven-day trek of nearly 170 miles that ended with capture and imprisonment by

Soviet troops—but all suffered from the harsh weather and near starvation. Four of the boys died as a result of the flight but could not be properly mourned—an act that Ishii understands to be essential, but that can come only after genuine understanding. "Twenty million people died as a result of a war initiated by Japan," Ishii writes in his essay. "If the weight and meaning of those deaths are not given even scant mention in Japanese classrooms, history will march on and leave behind countless souls lying in the dust."

Similarly, Ishigaki Chōkō's *tanka* sequence, *Requiem,* tells the story of her search for her father, whose identity—and nationality—she did not discover until half a century after her birth. Like Ishii's quest, her search for her absent father took her to China. There, she found her father's grave in an overgrown thicket outside a poor village, and at the age of sixty-four met her Chinese half-sister. Like Ishigaki, her sister had suffered a lifetime of disgrace and self-doubt because of official accounts of her father's role in the war.

Silence to Light also contains pieces that were written during or shortly after the war. Among them is an early, little-known story by Mishima Yukio, "Peonies," published in 1955, when Japan was still recovering from defeat. At that time, neither Japanese nor American authorities wanted to recall or acknowledge in full the atrocities committed in such places as Shanghai and Nanjing. And so, observes translator Anthony H. Chambers, the focus on the so-called Rape of Nanking in "Peonies" is unexpected. The story's Japanese colonel tends to the memory of his crimes as he would a garden. When Mishima wrote the story, he had just begun his phenomenal career as an author. Ahead of him were his advocacy of right-wing nationalism and his ritual suicide at age forty-five.

Among the most remarkable pieces are letters from *kamikaze* pilots to their families, accounts by three Taiwanese women who served at Japanese "comfort" stations, and a collection of testimonials by Japanese schoolgirls who were inducted into the army to serve as nurses during the Battle of Okinawa. Aged fifteen to nineteen, the student nurses carried out their duties valiantly, tending the sick and wounded under the grimmest conditions imaginable. Nevertheless, as the battle reached its climax, Japanese military leaders disbanded the nursing corps, driving the girls out of the few military shelters that remained and into the horrors of that "typhoon of steel" and fire. Defenseless yet forbidden to surrender, nearly all of the schoolgirls who were killed in the battle died between the time the corps was disbanded and the end of the war, two months later.

Lisa Ottiger's literary memoir, *In My Absence,* movingly describes the war in the Philippines from the point of view of the granddaughter of an American POW. When a packet of letters and papers falls into her hands, she is able to reconstruct the ordeal of family members held in Philippine camps and to see that past and present are forever enmeshed. A different captivity is described in the memoirs and diaries of photographer Francis Haar and his wife, Irene; as neutral aliens living in Tokyo, they were arrested after the attack on Pearl Harbor and nearly starved in the Japanese countryside before the war's end. Donald Richie's "Japan Journals" provide striking first-hand impressions of Japan in the early years of the Allied Occupation, a paradoxical time when Japan's cities were mixtures of conquered civilians, stunned by their losses, and ingenuous G.I.s. In Richie's words, Japan had "a beauty and an innocence and a naturalness by which I, from a rigid West, was alternately ravished and enlightened."

Silence to Light also explores the effects of the atomic bombing of Hiroshima and Nagasaki. One of those perspectives is that of documentary filmmaker Ogata Keiichi, whose script for a film about Hiroshima is printed here along with a group of stills. As Ogata studied the city and planned his film, he discovered the story of a young actress, Keiko Sonoi, who was killed by the bomb but whose fragile image was preserved on celluloid. So moved were we by Ogata's "cinepoem"—and so representative of our goals in collecting this material did it seem—that *Silence to Light* takes its title from his meditation on the meaning of light and shadow in a city that epitomizes both.

Hiroshima is also the subject of *Barefoot Gen,* an autobiographical *manga* (cartoon) by Keiji Nakazawa. A seven-year-old child living in Hiroshima with his family when the bomb was dropped, Nakazawa witnessed the deaths and devastation. For the past thirty years, he has told his story through graphic narratives that are masterpieces of the form and deeply sensitive to one of the central holocausts of the last century. Many American readers may not be accustomed to the treatment of such a serious subject in a genre they associate with comic books and fantasy literature for children. However, after what may be an initial cultural shock, they will see why *manga* has powerful literary potential in the hands of someone like Nakazawa, and why he has gained such loyal friends as the translators that comprise Project Gen. Nakazawa's story may seem filled with darkness, but it is a story of hope and survival based on the belief that keeping experiential memory alive, and passing on that memory to young people, may deter us from repeating tragic mistakes.

The shadow cast by the war in Asia fell across America, too. Jeanne Wakatsuki Houston's forthcoming novel *Fire Horse Woman,* excerpted here, is a poignant account of Japanese Americans interned in a concentration camp in the California desert. Best known for coauthoring the memoir *Farewell to Manzanar,* Houston writes from her own childhood—an eyewitness to the imprisonment of American citizens by their own country.

Most of the photographs in *Silence to Light* also describe how the war touched families. In his accompanying essay, "Belated Eulogy," Hawai'i photographer Shuzo Uemoto describes the tangled fate of Japanese nationals and Japanese Americans by telling the story of his own family. The photographs from his family album published here reflect how painful it can be to reconcile memories of half a century ago with the present, to be torn between love and shame, duty and integrity—and to honor loved ones by telling their stories accurately.

HAYASHI KYOKO

Echoes

There's a song my mother used to sing when she was seven or eight years old, part of which goes like this:

Bought rice cakes in Nagasaki
Got some fire in Himi
Cooked them at Yagami
Cooled them off at Koga
Gobbled them up at Kuyama

This fragment from childhood has stayed with her; she sings it even now, gazing into the sky. Perched on the edge of the veranda, her rounded back swaying to the rhythm, she sings, *Gobbled them up at Kuyama.*

She speeds up when she gets to that line, as though she's gobbling up the words. Listening, I can see a traveler popping rice cakes in his mouth before anyone finds out he's got them, and it makes me laugh. My mother laughs with me.

I don't know whether this song was popular throughout the Nagasaki region or just in the Isahaya region along the Honmyo River where my mother grew up. There's no telling how many generations of little girls sang it before it reached my mother and her friends, around 1907 or so, but it seems to have gone out of fashion. Children no longer make balls out of bits of cloth and string and bounce them to the rhythm of old songs, as they did when my mother was a child. Back then, girls would ask their mothers for brightly colored thread left over from sewing and would wrap them around and around a tight wad of old cotton or scraps of cloth until they had a ball. In temple gardens or by the roadside, they'd bounce these balls as they sang. With every line, there was an action to perform, each slightly more difficult than the last. They'd sing, *Gobbled them up,* and quickly roll their balls into the hems or sleeves of their *kimono.* When this move was perfected, they would go on to the next step.

Travelers on the old road from Nagasaki to Isahaya would stop at Himi, Yagami, and Koga on the way. In addition to describing this route, the song depicts their preparations for the midday meal: they would buy rice cakes in Nagasaki before setting out, then stop at a house to ask for some fire from the hearth; after cooking the rice cakes, they'd have to roll them around to cool them off. The distance from Nagasaki to Isahaya was said to be seven *ri* (about seventeen miles), so a traveler starting out from Nagasaki in the morning would reach Koga around noon. The song describes the journey all the way to Isahaya, but my mother only remembers the lyrics for the part up to Kuyama. Now that there's a highway from Nagasaki to Isahaya, how those towns where the travelers used to stop must have changed . . .

But on 13 August 1945, the day turned to dusk along that old road.

Four days after I was exposed to the A-bomb, my mother dragged me by the hand along that route as we fled from my lodging house in Nagasaki to our home in Isahaya.

On 9 August, when I was in my third year at Girls' High School, I was exposed to the A-bomb while working in a munitions factory in Nagasaki. On the evening of 12 August, my mother set out from Isahaya to look for me. In March of that year, we had left Shanghai and returned to Nagasaki. Normally, we would have taken either the *Shanghai Maru* ship or the *Nagasaki Maru*, which made regular trips between the cities they were named for. We'd fall asleep listening to the engine, which sounded like a heartbeat, and in twenty-four hours, we'd be there. But in 1940, both ships had been sunk by American submarines, and there were few vessels left that carried passengers. Day and night, American submarines appeared on our usual route in the East China Sea, sinking any Japanese boat they could find. To get back to Japan safely, we would have to take a boat from Pusan, and there were only two ways to get there: either across China by land, or along the coast by boat to Chingtao and then Dalian, where we would take the train to Mukden and finally to Pusan. At the time of the Shanghai Incident and other battles of the Sino-Japanese War, I had traveled back and forth between Shanghai and Nagasaki by boat with my mother and sisters, enjoying leisurely trips on which we were free to stay on deck and smell the sea air.

That March was different. Citizens of a country about to lose a war, we were escaping back to the motherland. There was a weight limit of thirty kilograms per person, which we had to carry by ourselves. We finally decided on the sea-and-land route, but the boat trip from Shanghai to Dalian alone took five days as we hugged the coast and hid in the shadows of islands. It was an exhausting journey, and soon after we reached our destination, my mother came down with pleurisy. In August, after four months in bed, she was finally well enough to be up and around.

Still weak from her long illness, my mother walked the seven *ri* to Nagasaki and arrived at my lodging house at two o'clock on the morning of the thirteenth. Finding me still alive, she lay down on the *tatami* and rested for just an hour before starting back with me to Isahaya.

And so a weakened mother and her daughter, who since the bombing had been alternately vomiting and having diarrhea, green in color, joined the crowds fleeing from the city toward Himi Pass. The sun rises early in August, but at three o'clock it was still dark. In light so dim the outline of the surrounding mountains was barely visible against the clouds, we couldn't make out either city or people. Only by the noise they made in the dark could we tell there were others escaping with us.

My lodging house was in Junin-cho, a section of Nagasaki on a steep slope; a flight of stone steps led to the business district below. I had lived there for some time, so normally would have known without looking which steps were worn down, and how much, but any semblance of order in the city had been destroyed by the force of the blast. Holding me by the wrist, my mother tested each step carefully with her toes, telling me where there was broken glass or which stones had buckled. But when my strength gave out, I stopped caring about such things and let her half carry me.

When we reached Hotaru-chaya, the city revealed itself: rows of houses in the dawn light. The human shadows we had sensed in the darkness also appeared. After hours of walking through the night, my mother groaned, "How awful," when she saw the hordes of injured in the first rays of morning.

Hotaru-chaya was on the road to Himi. This street also went through Hama-cho and passed by Suwa Shrine in central Nagasaki. In Hotaru-chaya, it began an upward climb towards Himi Pass, which separated the city from the outlying areas of Himi and Yagami. All the streets running through Nagasaki converged at Himi Pass. The tunnel that ran underneath it was like the mouth of a huge sack, and once through it, you saw the scenery change from urban sprawl to countryside. Here there were no munitions factories or military barracks to be targeted by enemy bombs, but only the farming and fishing villages of Himi and Yagami: a natural bay with white sand sparkling in the sun, and hamlets nestled in mountains with groves of mandarin orange and loquat. Not that rural tranquility was a guarantee against attack. But even so, people wanted to escape before the morning sun crawled over the mountains and cast its light on the city in the valley below. Leaflets scattered from American planes announced that on the thirteenth, another of the new bombs would be dropped on the rest of Nagasaki. They gently whispered to us, "Hurry up now—get out while there's still time." And the only way out was through the Himi Tunnel. The Urakami Railway, the other mouth of the sack, had been completely destroyed. It was not an impossible distance to walk, but those who had barely managed to flee the Urakami district with their lives didn't have the courage to return.

The roads to the pass had now merged, and the tunnel loomed before us. My mother's steps quickened. Pulling me by the wrist she said, "I'll let you rest on the other side."

Weeds hung in vines across the gaping mouth of the tunnel. A single, naked lightbulb hung in the entrance. The wind blowing down from the pass swept up grit and sand, hot from the fires of Urakami, which had been burning since the ninth. The lightbulb swayed in the wind and, perhaps due to a poor connection, flickered on and off. Winking as it moved hypnotically back and forth, it looked like a beacon for the dead, but people pressed on toward it, struggling past each other for the lead. Some had put, on sidecars or carts, relatives too badly burned to walk; blankets, pots and pans, and other household goods were piled up beside them. Those with nothing to put their possessions in carried all they could on their backs and tied pots and pans to their waists with ropes. Yet even with their whole bodies clattering and jangling like toy drums, they were dead serious about getting away.

My mother and I were the only ones in sight with nothing but our fire hoods draped around our shoulders.

"With their pots and pans," my mother muttered to herself.

Carried along by the crowd, we entered the tunnel. A cold wind reached us from the other side, blowing up from the sea at Yagami. It was wet, and I inhaled deeply, filling my lungs with the first moist air that I had breathed in a long time. Perhaps relieved now that their bodies were hidden from the sky, the wounded broke their silence and began groaning in pain. The refreshing cold lasted only a moment—gusts of wind carrying the stench of blood and pus mingled with salt air.

As though the smell of other wounds intensified their pain, the burn victims moaned louder. The creaking of cartwheels and clattering of pots and pans bounced off the curved walls of the tunnel, filling it with a din like stones rattling around inside a can. Only the able-bodied were quiet. "The same as the Chinese, like refugees," my mother murmured. "With their pots and pans." Watching her compatriots escape from Nagasaki, my mother was remembering the Chinese driven from Shanghai by the destruction of war. But we weren't *like* refugees; we *were* refugees. My mother couldn't believe that Japanese could actually be running away with pots and pans tied around their waists. She had lived in Shanghai as the citizen of a victorious nation. However humiliating our March journey back to the homeland may have been, we Japanese could still think of ourselves as victors. When the fighting started, it had always been the Chinese who fled with their pots and pans. Living in a country not their own, my mother and her Japanese friends, the conquerors, were free to watch others run away. So in her mind, *Chinese* and *refugees* had come to mean the same thing. This seemed only natural to her because she'd never had to run for her life. The Chinese were used to it. Whenever war came to Shanghai, they'd tie up their worldly possessions with rope, sling them across their shoulders or around their waists, and head for the interior. My mother had laughed when she told us how the Chinese had moved faster than either newspapers or radio during the Shanghai Incident and the Sino-Japanese War. Perhaps because I had grown up listening to her, I also had the simple notion that it was always the Chinese who fled. But unlike my mother, I saw the crowds of people running through the clouds of yellow sand that blew across the city as part of the Chinese landscape. Just as the leaves rustled in the wind, and birds and butterflies flitted through the air with the passing of the seasons, this was a phenomenon that occurred at the beginning of the season called war.

Seasons don't always begin the same way. In Shanghai, 8 December 1941 was different from any seasonal beginning that had come before it. That year, I was in the fifth grade. For two or three years before the Pacific War broke out on 8 December, there had been talk in Shanghai about war between Japan and America. People from all over the world lived there, and except for the most clandestine military operations, international secrets spread through rumors. Not wild speculations, these were based on observations of the movements of people and of changes in the city. When war was about to break out, people from the countries involved left Shanghai for their homelands. Their departures were handled secretly, through embassies or consulates, but when you woke up one morning to find the family that had been living next door suddenly gone, you'd think, This is it. No one was easygoing enough to assume they'd simply moved. Shanghai was an international city: you always felt it, but never more strongly than while watching the boats that entered and left the Whangpoo River.

The flagship of the Japanese navy's so-called Chinese squadron, the *Izumo* was assigned to guard the Whangpoo. A decrepit old ship that had done its part in the Russo-Japanese War, it was heavy and broad-hipped, more like a mother duck than a fighting vessel. It was anchored at the Izumo Pier, on the Hongkew side of the river, which was under Japanese rule. Though the pier was reserved for the Japanese navy, boats belonging to Japanese corporations that had obtained special permission were sometimes anchored there as well. At this point, the river was especially broad; upstream, it curved widely to the left. The Soochow Creek flowed off to the west at the deepest point in the curve; the Garden Bridge crossed it. On the other side was the International Settlement, where the British, Americans, and French lived; the Customs House was a four- or five-minute walk from the bridge.

The *Izumo* was anchored directly across from the Customs House. If you drew a line connecting the ship, the bridge, and the Customs House, you'd have a long, thin triangle with the bridge at the right angle. The side from the Customs House to the *Izumo* slanted across the Whangpoo, and my house was along the straight line between the pier and the bridge. The house where Okiyo had lived was nearby. Okiyo was a Japanese prostitute who had hanged herself. After her suicide, the five or six White Russian prostitutes who lived with her disappeared, and the house was left deserted. In front of Okiyo's house, there was a bench, and while she was alive, she and I sat on it and together watched the boats go by. Even after she died, I'd go there every day to sit and gaze out over the water. Boats from all over the world, of all shapes and colors, came into port. Most didn't stay long, though. I'd go out to see the cargo ship that had come in the day before, painted a shade of green that brought visions of prairies, only to find it already gone. But the *Izumo* never moved. Whenever I went to the river, there it would be, clinging to the pier. As I watched it, I became convinced that certain warships were stuck fast where they were. But then one day, the supposedly immobile *Izumo* vanished.

I was dumbstruck. The mere fact of its absence was surprising enough, but I had never realized what an enormous space it had filled in the river. The pier had lost its master, and the Whangpoo that stretched all the way to the opposite bank was far wider than I had imagined.

The ship that had disappeared without a trace soon became the subject of rumors among my mother's Japanese friends. Wondering if this meant war, they anxiously eyed the storm clouds over America and Japan and waited for the *Izumo* to return. Hearing the grownups talk in hushed tones made me nervous. I couldn't really tell if my fears were rooted in the war that seemed likely to start any moment or in myself, but it was clear that one reason for them was that the ship was no longer there, proudly waving the navy flag.

Until then, I had rarely been conscious of myself as a *Japanese*. I knew very little about life in Japan, and I got along fine with the Chinese children who lived in my neighborhood. We'd play a game with shuttlecocks made from chicken feathers, kicking them high in the air with our toes, and when I lost, we'd fight, screaming at each other in Shanghai dialect. Just as my mother had played with homemade balls, I learned from my Chinese friends how to make shuttlecocks out of brass coins and chicken feathers. I spat like they did, too. Puckering up my mouth like a sea anemone, I would send the spittle flying off my tongue to splatter my victim.

I was a Japanese child, but one who had grown up in China and taken on Chinese ways. Even so, the absence of the *Izumo* made me feel, however vaguely, the insecurity of living in a foreign land.

Then the ship returned to Shanghai. Had it been gone for a month, or only a week? As though nothing had happened, there it was, anchored in front of the pier. The Japanese talked of its having been up the Yangtze River for practice maneuvers. Around the same time, the family recreation committee of M Corporation, where my father worked, was planning a boat trip down the Whangpoo River.

We would be leaving at six in the morning and were to meet on the M Corporation launch, which had special permission to anchor at the pier. The season was early summer, when new growth on the trees that lined the Whangpoo dyed its surface green.

That morning, my sisters and I were on the launch thirty minutes early. There was a thin mist on the water. It deepened with the river's gentle undulations. We heard the oars of junks and sampans, then saw them rise out of the fog and disappear again. Within our limited view, the Whangpoo was lively with morning activity. Then a whistle sounded from the mouth of the river. There was no sign of the ship yet, but judging from the length of the blast, it wasn't a small steamboat like the launch we were on. And yet the blast wasn't so deep that it resounded in the pit of your stomach—like the whistle of a passenger liner or cargo ship. The high-pitched scream sounded threatening. The crew of our launch scattered fore and aft, scanning the river for signs of danger. Someone warned us to hang on to the handrail.

The whistle approached rapidly. The sun was now rising, and the mist turned orange in its light and began to clear. Through it, we saw a ship racing towards us. Bluish and rather small, it had a sharply honed prow sunk deep in the water and spewed out waves on either side as it sped up the river.

Men on nearby junks shouted curses, and we heard the hollow thud of wooden boats knocking against each other. Big waves slapped the metal hull of the launch and then hit the pier. The chain that held the screw to the rudder jangled as it was lowered into the water. When the ship passed the *Izumo,* it let out an especially loud blast—either a warning or a gesture of respect—and then it disappeared, leaving huge waves in its wake. The Stars and Stripes fluttered at its stern. "That was a gunboat," someone said.

The port was full of small boats, so there was a speed limit. If ocean liners came barreling up the river at the speeds they traveled on the high seas, the junks and sampans would capsize. Large vessels sailed upriver quietly so as not to cause whitecaps. Even so, their sheer weight made the surface rough and choppy. The American gunboat had ignored the rules.

On our way home from the excursion that day, we saw the American gunboat anchored in front of the Customs House. Tied to a red buoy in the middle of the river, it sat beside a British gunboat that had arrived before it. Both had their prows pointing towards the *Izumo.*

Our heavy old warship moved once more. It edged away from the pier and into the center of the river, where it turned its cannons towards the two gunboats. The *Izumo* now faced the gunboats at the top of the triangle that connected it to the bridge and the Customs House.

The rumors of war between Japan and America were turning into something more concrete. But this time, the Chinese didn't leave the city. December came, and they calmly stayed in Shanghai. Only the very wealthy left the city to look for refuge.

"War is coming! Shouldn't you be leaving?!" my mother asked our Chinese neighbors, but they just laughed and answered, "No, we're fine." It was strange to see them so complacent. From their behavior, my mother and father concluded that it would be a while before the war started. Contrary to their expectations, the Pacific War broke out on 8 December of that year.

At three or four in the morning of 8 December, Shanghai was awakened by the sound of cannon fire. My mother ran upstairs to our room on the third floor, pulled open our dresser drawers, and got out our best clothes, normally reserved for special occasions. "Put these on," she said, then added, "and stay under the covers." If we had to leave in a hurry, she wanted us to be wearing our most durable clothes. She followed my father up to the roof. Our third-floor roof commanded a view of the entire river. My parents, who had heard the cannons at the time of the Shanghai Incident, figured that this predawn explosion must have come from the *Izumo.* When she came down from the roof, my mother assured us, "Everything's going to be all right. There was no counterattack." She then turned on the radio.

All we heard was the beeping of a broadcast signal. "It must be the *Izumo;* there were bright-red streaks of gunfire going straight up the river," my mother went on, describing what she'd seen. After a while, the news came on. Just as my parents had suspected, the *Izumo* had fired on a warship. The attack had been timed to coincide with the bombing of Pearl Harbor. Shortly before, a military envoy had urged the British and American ships to surrender, but the British had refused. America had yielded. So the warship that had caused such waves as it came into port was now in the hands of the Japanese navy, and the British ship was at the bottom of the Whangpoo.

Does it always rain after a bout of bombing and shelling? On the evening of 9 August, it was drizzling in Nagasaki. The drops were so fine it was like being sprayed with mist; nevertheless, the moisture seeped into our skin, slowly drenching our bodies as we waited in the mountains for the bombing to stop. At dawn I returned to my lodging house and wiped myself off with a dry towel, but my skin was soon moist again.

Rain also fell on the morning of 8 December. The Japanese National Schools held classes as usual. We walked in groups with the children from our assigned neighborhood communities. In mist so fine we didn't need umbrellas, we followed our sixth-grade leader through the tense streets of Shanghai. There was a military cordon on the corner. A naval brigade, rifles with bayonets close at hand, stopped all Chinese whose movements looked suspicious, questioning them one by one. Military guards patrolled the city in groups of four or five. On the surface, things seemed calm enough, but the heavy tread of soldiers' boots echoed through the streets.

When we came to the bridge across the creek near our school, our group leader stopped in front of the soldier on guard and barked, "Forward march!" We stiffened, thrusting our arms and legs out perfectly straight, keeping in step with our whole bodies.

This was where Okiyo, shut out of the Japanese community for simply being a prostitute, had been forced to line up with the Chinese to get her cholera vaccination. But the Japanese now crossing this bridge and stealing nervous glances at the faces of the guards had lost the confidence that had enabled them to drive Okiyo from their midst. The soldiers weren't making exceptions for their compatriots. Anyone they had doubts about was commanded to halt, regardless of nationality. You might say we were showing our loyalty to them by keeping our bodies perfectly rigid as we marched along. Of course, the Chinese crossing the bridge were tense, too. But they were not in a panic as the Japanese were and made no attempt to read the guards' expressions. Though this bridge was packed with Chinese refugees whenever war broke out, hardly anyone was running away this time. The Chinese who stubbornly stayed put and the American warship that had raced defiantly up the river made a far deeper impression on the Japanese than the British ship they had sunk.

Morning assembly was held in the schoolyard as usual. We stood shivering in the rain. Our moustached principal began, "You all heard the cannons this morning, so you already know," then proceeded to inform us of the *Izumo*'s glorious victory. "That explosion will be a most memorable echo in all of your lives. Your homeland, Japan, has embarked on a battle of great significance. With your own ears, you heard the first shots. You yourselves were a part of it." Then he shouted, "Long live the great Japanese empire! *Banzai!*" and stretched his arms towards the rainy heavens. "*Banzai!*" we yelled, raising our arms. "*Banzai! Banzai!*" As our arms pumped up and down, our bodies flushed with excitement.

Then a military march began to play, and we stepped around the playground in time. As I marched, I thought of the cannon fire that had reached my ears before dawn. I had felt it in the pit of my stomach, but what sort of "memorable echo" would it leave in my life? Just as the principal had said, I believed I also had taken part in the battle—partly because I was there when it started. However, the blast itself, stuck fast to the membrane that covered my soft viscera, was beginning to shake me from within.

After passing through Himi and Yagami, we reached Koga past noon. The travelers in my mother's song had sturdier legs and could easily have made the distance in five or six hours, but it took us nine. When we got through the Himi Tunnel, my mother let me rest at the top of the mountain, as she'd promised, but in a mere ten minutes she grabbed my wrist and started off again.

We walked to Koga without a break. My mother seemed as tired as I was. "It's about another hour to Isahaya, so let's stop and rest awhile," she said. She found a farmhouse by the side of the road. The sliding doors facing the road were open, revealing the wooden passageway and a spacious *tatami* room beyond. My mother called to see if anyone was home, and an old woman came out. Clad in striped *monpei* trousers, she bowed her head when she saw me and murmured, "You've been through a lot, poor dear." She told us how on the evening of the ninth, the road through Koga had overflowed with refugees from Nagasaki. From listening to their stories, she knew all about what had happened in Nagasaki.

My mother asked if we could have a drink of water, drawing out the last syllable in the manner of the Isahaya dialect. "They all wanted water. That big flash must've been awfully hot," said the old woman, leading us around back to where the well was.

The old well bucket was dripping, swaying gently back and forth. The pulley creaked as the woman lowered it. Pouring the fresh water into a newer bucket, she said in the Isahaya dialect, "Have all you want." My mother filled the dipper by the side of the well and put it to my lips, saying, "Go ahead, drink." She held it for me while I drained it in one gulp. Gazing into the empty dipper, my mother laughed. "Thank God," she said, and then laughed again.

"They say even the Soviets're in it now," the woman said to my mother, who was soaking a towel in the well water. My mother's hands stopped. "The Soviets, too?" she asked. "That's right," the woman answered. "Everything's gone wrong—it's a horrible mess. Seems they're going to drop one of those new-fangled bombs on Isahaya next, so you be careful." "How far do we have to go to get away?" My mother sighed. "No matter where you try to hide, you'll get burnt to a crisp," the old woman replied, adding, "It's not far to Isahaya. Why don't you stop and rest awhile?" She pointed at the house.

I sat on the wooden floor with my back against a pillar, watching the people escape down the road to Isahaya. Exposed to a noonday sun in a cloudless blue sky, an endless crowd of refugees passed before me. They glanced upwards with frightened eyes; the slightest rumble of an explosion sent them running for the bushes. Leaving their sidecars and carts by the roadside with the wounded still lying on them, those who could walk scurried into ditches or cowered behind trees. In an instant the road would be deserted—only burn victims on carts dotting it here and there. I wondered if this was how the Chinese had escaped. But these refugees were definitely not part of the landscape.

The steps of the people grew heavy. The dragging of wooden clogs and straw sandals filled the air like the scratching of ground beetles gnawing at the roots of trees and grasses. The lazy creaking of cartwheels echoed in the still afternoon. The sounds traveled from the road to the garden of the farmhouse and into my body. And the blast of cannon fire, stored there since childhood, began its dull, regular vibrations.

Translation by Margaret Mitsutani

TAMURA RYUICHI

Four Thousand Days and Nights

For one poem to be born
we must kill
We must kill many things
We shoot, assassinate, poison the many things we love

Look
We shot
the silence of four thousand nights and the glare of
    four thousand days
simply because we wanted the trembling tongue of one small bird
from the sky of four thousand days and nights

Listen
We assassinated
the love of four thousand days and the pity of four thousand nights
simply because we needed the tears of one hungry child
from all the rainy cities and blast furnaces
and the midsummer wharves and the coal mines

Remember
We see things our eyes cannot see
We hear things our ears cannot hear
We poisoned
the power of imagination of four thousand nights
    and the cold memories of four thousand days
simply because we wanted the fear of one stray dog

To give birth to one poem
we must kill the things we love
This is the only road to take to resurrect the dead
This is the road we have to take

Translation by Samuel Grolmes and Tsumura Yumiko

Father, Manchuria

UDA REI

Lukouchiao

Author's Note

On 7 July 1937, when I was seven years old, war broke out between Japan and China. The fighting began near the ancient stone bridge named Lukouchiao (Marco Polo Bridge), on the outskirts of Beijing. The war continued until 15 August 1945. My father, who was in the reserves, was drafted and sent to China.

Because my family had been assisting students from China before the war, I had friendly feelings for Chinese people. I was still a child, but the thought of Japanese and Chinese killing each other made me feel guilty and terribly sad. I remember, when my father came home three years later, how relieved I was to hear that his duties had kept him behind the front lines, so he'd gotten through the war without firing a single bullet.

When the war ended with Japan's defeat, I was fifteen. I liked literature and had already made up my mind to study Chinese literature at university. After graduation, I joined the Chinese Literature Association and began to publish papers on modern and contemporary Chinese poetry. Through my readings of Chinese texts, I discovered that Chinese children had actively participated in the war against Japan. They must have hated Japanese children. I began to feel that I, as a child at that time, had a responsibility to atone for my country's sins.

When I was an adult, my desire to see China with my own eyes grew strong, but Japan had no diplomatic relations with China. Even after relations were restored, China was in the midst of the Great Cultural Revolution, which made a visit impossible. In 1979, when the Great Cultural Revolution was over and stability had at last returned to Chinese society, I received an invitation from the Chinese Institute of Social Sciences. For thirty years I had devoted myself to the study of contemporary Chinese literature without being able to set foot on Chinese soil. Now seven friends and I, all of the same generation, were thrilled to finally be going to Beijing as members of an official "literary research team."

Upon our arrival in Beijing, we listed Lukouchiao as one of the places we wanted to see. At the time, the area around the bridge was off limits to foreigners, but our request was finally granted. While walking slowly across Lukouchiao, I was filled with conflicting emotions. To determine whether or not these thoughts and feelings were simply products of that moment in time, I allowed myself a cooling-off period. Several years later, I wrote the poem "Lukouchiao." The logic and emotions expressed in this poem are personal, of course, but I believe that any

Japanese who was a child during the war has had similar thoughts. I imagine that whenever Japanese my age or slightly older see or hear the name Lukouchiao, they are stricken by the absurdity of war and by a need for expiation.

I walk across Lukouchiao
The riverbed bright with glittering streams
Carved in my mind
This bridge across
All those watching eyes
What do they see in me
What do they see inside
Deep inside of me?
I am neither pebble nor tree nor fish nor bicycle lying on its side
Wanting to run through this deadly silence
I walk across Lukouchiao
Once a long, long bridge
Crossing a distant sea
Stretching out toward me
Was Lukouchiao
Now it crosses straight over me
Over this life now beyond my control
Yet still I am living, so
Starting and stopping, stopping and starting
I walk across Lukouchiao

Translation by Margaret Mitsutani

Father in Teinsing, China

ISHIGAKI CHŌKŌ

from *Requiem*

Editor's Note

In a sequence of 113 *tanka*, *Requiem* explores the author's search for the identity of her father, whom she never met. Throughout Ishigaki Chōkō's childhood, her mother kept her father's name hidden from her, just as she also kept from Ishigaki all photographs, news clippings, and stories about him. Further erasing evidence of her father, Ishigaki's maternal grandparents were officially registered as her parents, and her mother was registered as her older sister.

When Ishigaki was in primary school, she searched the house to see if any photos of her father might be hidden there. Leafing through the books on her mother's shelves, she at last found two photographs of a young man in a Tokyo University uniform and another of the same man standing with her mother in a park. Her mother and the man were smiling happily.

"I took the photographs and put them away in a book of my own," Ishigaki writes in her notes to *Requiem*, "spending days fearing that my act would be discovered. More than ten years passed, and it was not until the night before my wedding that my mother said, 'Can I have those photographs back now?'"

At the age of fifty, Ishigaki began a full-scale search for her origins. Knowing her father had graduated from Tokyo University, she searched for traces of him there and discovered a dissertation written by a graduate student named Liu Xinchun and dated 29 February 1928. The author was her father. From this point, the pieces of the puzzle began to fall into place.

Ishigaki's mother had been an only child, adored by her parents. She entered Jissen Women's Vocational College, one of the country's top educational institutions for women. At the same time, Liu Xinchun was a poor student from northern China studying at Tokyo University on a scholarship from the Japanese-sponsored South Manchurian Railway Company. These two young people happened to live near each other and probably met while commuting on the train. Liu Xinchun was then in the process of becoming a naturalized Japanese citizen.

Events in Manchuria overtook whatever plans the young couple had for a life together. Liu Xinchun was called back to China, and Ishigaki's mother went with him to the provincial capital of Fengtian, now called Shenyang. There, in 1931, she gave birth to Chōkō, just before the outbreak of the Manchurian Incident. Ishigaki would learn many decades later that a half-sister was born three months after her:

the daughter of her father and his legal Chinese wife. The sisters would not meet until 1995, when Ishigaki was sixty-four years old.

Over time, Ishigaki discovered that during the Manchurian Incident, her father had been asked to be an interpreter and accompany a group of Japanese soldiers to Lukouchiao Bridge to negotiate a surrender with Chinese forces. But the negotiations were broken off, and her father was shot, together with all the Japanese soldiers. Their corpses were thrown into the Liao River. The Chinese resistance leader, Lao Beifeng, later returned Liu Xinchun's corpse to his relatives because he was Chinese.

Today in China, Lao Beifeng is an admired anti-Japanese hero while Liu Xinchun is regarded as a traitor. When Ishigaki met her half-sister in 1995, she found that her sister suffered the stigma of being regarded as the daughter of a villain. The two women formed a bond and together visited Lukouchiao Bridge and the grave of their father. Both had suffered a lifetime of grief and secrecy because of the war.

Ishigaki originally intended to write *Requiem* in memory of her father and to have it translated into Chinese, but anti-Japanese feelings in China have made such a translation impossible.

#82

step by step
I cross Lukouchiao
where the long long battle
of the anti-Japanese movement
began

#83

and did
those stone lions
of Lukouchiao
watch the bloodshed
on 7 July 1937?

#84

on the River Liao
where my father died
the ice is thicker
and colder this year,
so the TV reports

#87

father,
once a citizen of China,
were you shot
by a fellow countryman,
and did you sink in River Liao's waters?

#88

has my father's blood
gushing out downstream
stained the river's surface
this chilly November,
this cold Chinese November?

#89

my father's blood
must have flowed to the Sea of Japan
though his corpse
lies buried in the mountain
of his hometown Sanjiazhi

#94

let us think
about the grief and misery of war,
about the binding of each nation
and the pride
and the real meaning of peace

Translation by the author

SAGAWA AKI

Birthmark

When I was very young
I had a small birthmark on my back.
Its shape and place were exactly like
Those of the young man
Who was my mother's elder brother
And died in the southern country.
My mother and grandmother told me so.
In the room where I was born
There was a painting he left
Of a delicate cream-colored rose,
As if wishing to part from his fragility,
He'd gone off to war.

He wrote that he wanted to
Come back to eat his mother's cooked red rice,
But what came back was only a cake of soap.
So we offered the red rice to the soap.
Yes, he was a sad man.
Yet
When I was as old as he was when he died
I knew his slender fingers might have
Shot, stolen from, humiliated, and killed
Those in the southern country.
My birthmark disappeared unnoticed.
Yes, it disappeared.

But in the country where he died—
Beside the river a war memorial hall was built—
A saying is carved.
"We will forgive, but won't forget."
When one has no wish to be forgiven,
Being forgiven is a terrible thing.
When one does not hesitate to forget,
Being remembered against one's will is a terrible thing.

I had the same birthmark as
A young man I've never met.
It gave my life
A shape, and
Made me aware of
Connected time and human beings,
And now I know
I'm also connected.

Translation by Kijima Hajime

Father (left), home on leave from Manchuria, with James Tsujiuchi, Nachi-san shrine, Wakayama Prefecture, Japan

SHUZO UEMOTO

Belated Eulogy: A Family Album

I was born in Hiroshima in 1947 and lived in Japan until I was five. In 1953, our family left Hiroshima on the ocean liner called *President Cleveland* to live in Hawai'i, my mother's birthplace. The war had ended too recently for certain wounds and resentments to have healed, and I was told it was best to stay quiet about the fact that my father had been an officer in the Japanese army. I've kept silent ever since, and only my close friends have known. Now, I'm fifty-three, it's a new millennium, and it feels redemptive to finally acknowledge my father and share openly these photographic memories.

The story could begin with my maternal grandfather, Kamezo Tsujiuchi. Born in Tanomi, Wakayama Prefecture, he had come to Hawai'i in his teens, sent for by his own father. My grandfather became a fisherman, and eventually owned two sampans, which he docked in Kewalo Basin, in Honolulu Harbor. He apparently made a good living fishing for *aku* (tuna) because in 1940 he was able to send his family back to Japan. Others were doing the same, hoping to protect their sons and daughters from a difficult situation in the event that Japan entered into a war with the United States.

There is a family photo taken in Honolulu in 1940 just before my mother and her siblings left for Japan. My mother is the oldest of seven children. Her brother James—the first-born son—is the gaunt young man on the right in the second row. Everyone except James is looking toward the camera. James appears distant and solemn, as though he's not happy about leaving. But my mother says that was his nature, always solemn. She once told me that he kept lyrics to a Hawaiian song in his wallet. I've often wondered which song it was, if he had it with him in this photograph and later too. I wonder what lyrics and melody were so important as to keep in his wallet, and if he kept them in order to remember some place or someone from the Islands.

Born in Hilo, James was just sixteen years old in the 1940 photograph. He and his family were headed to Japan during a time of fast-changing world events. Within a year, circumstances would put him and countless others—on both sides of the war—in harm's way. What was unusual in James's case was that he was both Japanese and American. He had dual cit-

Maternal grandparents, Kamezo and Odai Tsujiuchi, and family, Hawai'i, 1940

Mother's family, Japan
Mother is in the back row, center, next to father. Uncle James is standing on the far right. Grandmother and Great-grandmother are in the front row, center.

izenship, and that's one reason why sending him to Japan did not protect him from the war.

Several years later, just as the war was finishing, James was drafted out of telegraph school into the Japanese army and sent to China. He contracted malaria and ended up in an army hospital. I remember my father telling my mother that he had been in the same vicinity as James but had not known that James was there. Otherwise, Dad could have used his status as an officer to see that James, an enlisted man, had gotten the quinine that would have saved his life. James never left the hospital. He died in August 1945, at the age of twenty. He had been like a younger brother to my father.

There are several photographs of Dad with James. One is a memorable wide-angled shot of the two of them at a shrine at Nachi-san, in Wakayama Prefecture. They are surrounded by immense pine trees, and in the distance stands a *torii,* a gateway marking the entrance to a sacred shrine. Another is of my mother, James, and Dad together. My father is apparently home on leave from the war in China, enjoying the peace and calm of the shrine, several months or years before James would also go to war.

My father, Toshiharu Uemoto, was born in Hiroshima in 1914 to a family of fishermen. While growing up, he loved to swim and practice *kendo.* It was customary for the oldest son to take over the family business and property when he came of age. Because my father was the second son, he was expected to find another career. In the early thirties, he joined the army.

In 1931, the Japanese had attacked and occupied the city of Shenyang (now Mukden), and in 1932, they created the puppet state of Manchukuo from the three provinces of Manchuria. The Japanese military then forced the last Manchu ruler, Emperor Pu-yi, to declare Manchukuo "independent." In reality, Manchuria was turned into an industrial and military base for Japan's expansion in Asia. Within five months, Japanese military personnel occupied all of Manchuria.

It was during this time that my father entered the army and faced the harshness of Japanese military life. He would spend the next twelve years in Manchuria and China. I can only wonder what he saw there and experienced. There's a photo of him in the hospital after being wounded in his right shoulder. Other photos taken in Manchuria show him in rest areas behind the front lines, trying to enjoy normal things: eating watermelon on a hot day, ice skating in the winter, listening to music on a hand-cranked phonograph, and bathing outdoors in a large ceramic pot.

After being promoted to the rank of officer, my father wrote from Manchuria to his parents and asked them to help him find a bride. In time, arrangements were made, and he returned home on leave to meet his prospective wife, Dorothy Yayoi Tsujiuchi. Officers had the privilege of having their wives with them where they were quartered, so after the marriage, my mother crossed the sea to China and then went by rail to

Uncle James Tsujiuchi, nineteen years old, with friend, Japan

Telegraph school, Japan, 1940
James Tsujiuchi is in the last row, third from left.

Wedding portrait of parents, Toshiharu and Yayoi (Dorothy) Uemoto, Japan

Parents, Japan

Father with sword, Manchuria

Manchuria to be with my father. She later said Dad had given her a small, pearl-handled semiautomatic Browning pistol for protection during her journey. My parents would spend almost a year together in Manchuria.

Mother said that during her stay in China, Dad would often send enlisted men to help her do things at their residence. She said he always reminded her to give them a good meal when they were done. Having risen through the ranks, my father knew firsthand that enlisted life is harsh, so he sympathized with them. As the fighting worsened, Dad sent Mom back to Japan for her own safety.

On the Monday of 6 August 1945, Mom witnessed a big flash over the foothills toward Hiroshima. She thought the brilliant light was from an electric plant exploding. Later she would learn that it had been from a thermonuclear bomb. The second bomb fell three days later, at Nagasaki. Soon after, the war would end, and within the month, her brother James would die of malaria in an army hospital in China.

Shortly after the atomic bombs fell, my father's unit surrendered in southern Manchuria, near the Yangtze River. Some of the officers performed their last duty to the emperor rather than surrender. My father returned home to rebuild his life.

Mother's family returned to Hawai'i in 1947, but she stayed in Japan to give birth to me. During that time, she worked as a translator for the American Occupational Forces. A young American soldier named Shuichi Sarae would occasionally visit us in Hiroshima. He was a close family friend from Hawai'i. There's a photo of me with "Uncle" Shuichi, who is wearing an American military uniform; I'm wearing his hat. It must have seemed odd to some of the townspeople to see a Japanese American soldier in postwar Japan.

When he first came to Hawai'i, Dad worked with my maternal grandfather on the sampans in Kewalo Basin. But he wasn't a sea dog like Grandfather. He was a machinist by trade and an excellent craftsman. I still have a set of steel calipers he made in his shop in Japan; and I remember the little wooden sampan he carved for me, and helping him to rig fishing lines and make tuna hooks with feathers as lures. Later, when Grandfather passed away, Dad went into carpentry with some of his Japanese-speaking friends and did this work until he retired; he was in his early seventies then.

Father died eight years ago. Just our immediate family was at the funeral. Mom wanted it that way. Small and intimate. I think it would have been too much for her otherwise. I hired a *shakuhachi* player to play a few songs. He played some *doyo* and *gunka* songs from my father's childhood and some tunes from the forties. That was my eulogy to my father. No one except the priest spoke.

If it had been possible, I'm sure Dad would have reminisced about the early years of my childhood, when we had communicated so well in the same language, both speaking Japanese with ease and familiarity. I still

Shuzo Uemoto, Japan

Leaving Japan for Hawaiʻi: Shuzo Uemoto and mother (foreground), paternal grandmother carrying Naomi Uemoto, family friend in school uniform (far left), paternal aunt

Shuzo and Naomi Uemoto, Hawai'i

think about the conversations we had and could have had. As I was growing up, my mother would sometimes have to translate when we spoke. Our conversations became limited, but I understood many things by the tone of his voice. I remember watching television shows like *Ozzie and Harriet* and *My Three Sons* and sometimes feeling that I was missing something in my relationship with Dad. Even though we had a strong bond and love for each other, I would wonder if that was enough. But I would come to know that I had more than most sons. I have my own children now—Maya, who is fifteen, and Kekua, who's twelve—and I wonder what impression, as a father, I'll leave with them.

My father lived to raise a family and see the birth of his grandchildren. He saw me build a home and was around when his grandchildren started to grow up. Later, he enjoyed a modest retirement with Mom, and together they often went on vacations. He had survived Manchuria and the war, and toward the end of his life, when he had two minor strokes, he managed to come through them as well. But the day arrived when we were all around his bedside as he came out of a coma. I held his strong hands and watched him gaze back at us. Mother stayed beside him in the hospital.

Sometimes I wonder what they said to each other before he passed away. She later told me he said he was tired and wished he could go. I'd like to remember him the way he looked in the Nachi-san shrine photo: he and James are surrounded by immense pines, the *torii* gate at their back, enjoying nature and each other, at the beginning of their young lives.

ISHII SHINPEI

The Canary That Forgot Its Song: A Return to Wartime Manchuria

There's a popular children's song in Japan called "The Canary That Forgot Its Song." The Japanese, with their love of singing along to nostalgic *karaoke* melodies, would never forget a song. But they do forget their history.

Old patriotic war songs continue to be sung within Japan, and perhaps this can be excused. But sometimes these songs are sung by expatriate Japanese in pubs in Korea, China, and Southeast Asia. What must the local people in these places be thinking when they hear a Japanese belting out war songs from half a century ago? Sometimes the singer is simply a cheerful, well-meaning businessman; nevertheless it is disgraceful that he does not know what his country did in Asia during the war. Often, the reason he doesn't know is that he was not taught the truth about modern Japanese history in school; this is a disgrace to the whole nation and not just to a single citizen.

In 1945, my fourteen-year-old brother, Ishii Kohei, was a student at the First Xinjing Middle School in Manchuria, an area of China that had been occupied by Japan for nearly fifteen years. In order to help with the Japanese war effort—which was going badly by then—my brother and 120 of his classmates were sent to do manual labor on a National Service Farm in Dongning, near the then-Soviet border. There, on 9 August, my brother was caught up in the massive Soviet invasion launched to drive the Japanese out of Manchuria.

My brother was one of three million Japanese to die in the war, and as is the case with many Japanese casualties, no one knows the exact circumstances of his death. Many people still do not even know where the remains of their loved ones lie. And so my brother's death is not only a part of my own family's grieving but also a part of our nation's history. In Japan, when someone dies in vain, he is said to have died "a dog's death." If the circumstances that led to my brother's death are not taught in schools—along with the truth of so many other deaths of the war years—his dying will indeed have been no different from that of a cruelly abandoned stray.

The year 2001 marks the sixtieth anniversary of the Japanese attack on Pearl Harbor. For most Americans—especially younger ones—Pearl Harbor represents the beginning of the war that Japan declared on the United States and then lost nearly four years later, after atomic bombs fell on Hiroshima and Nagasaki.

The Japanese, however, sometimes refer to the conflict as the Fifteen-Year War. For us it began on 18 September 1931, when Japan's Kwantung Army blew up a stretch of railroad tracks near Mukden, Manchuria, in order to provoke an international incident. The result of this so-called Manchurian Incident was the seizure of Manchuria by the Japanese military. Many Japanese victories followed, but gradually the war on the Asian continent began to fail, and Japan attempted to find a way out of its problems by bombing Pearl Harbor.

If we compare the Fifteen-Year War to the fifteen days of a sumo tournament, we can say that the attack on Pearl Harbor took place on day twelve. In other words, the United States didn't appear until late in the match. Nevertheless, when Emperor Hirohito formally admitted our country's defeat, he did so at the American embassy; Japan's ceremonial surrender took place on an American battleship; and Americans headed the occupation of Japan and ran the war-crimes trials in Tokyo. A lasting symbol of the end of the war is the famous photograph of General MacArthur towering over the Emperor. That photograph has served to remind the Japanese people that they owed their defeat fundamentally to the power of the United States.

Today, the Japanese media give a great deal of attention to each anniversary of the attack on Pearl Harbor—the portion of the war involving Americans. Meanwhile, almost no attention is paid to the anniversary of the Manchurian Incident, though it marked the beginning of Japan's imperialist aggression in Asia. Why is it that Japan's awareness of its failed war with China is so dim?

During the sixtieth anniversary of the Manchurian Incident, in 1991, I traveled with thirty-seven other Japanese on what we called "A Memorial Journey for Students of the First Xinjing Middle School." Twenty-five members of our group had been students at the school, and thirteen—including myself—were relatives of the boys who were killed in the days following the Soviet invasion of Manchuria. On that August day in 1945, the boys were caught by surprise and fled from the frontlines on foot, finally reaching Dongjing-cheng, south of Mudanjiang, eleven days later. They had managed to flee for 168 miles before Soviet troops captured and imprisoned them. Four of the students were later sent to a field hospital, where they died of malnutrition. One goal of our group's journey to Dongjing-cheng was to discover the burial place of these four students. We also planned to conduct a memorial service at the former Dongjing-cheng

Bayonet practice, Manchuria
Father is seated at lower right.

Japanese military field station, Manchuria

Father with military gear, Manchuria

Settlement Hall, where approximately 110 students had been held captive for two months. Finally, we hoped to understand better the reasons why Japanese authorities had sent these young boys so close to the frontlines, placing them in the teeth of the impending Soviet attack.

Many of the travelers who assembled in the lobby at Narita Airport had been about fourteen in 1945 and now were over sixty. The majority had not seen each other for nearly fifty years. Among those present were the former head teacher at the school, eighty-three-year-old Saito Kiyoshi, and another teacher, seventy-three-year-old Ogawa Yasuharu.

Mudanjiang, Town of Lament

Our 29 May flight out of Tokyo for Dalian took a southern course, circumventing the Korean peninsula for reasons of safety, and arrived after 8 P.M.

Early the following morning, the group boarded three Toyota micro-buses and headed to Mudanjiang, a town that is now principally a distribution center for lumber and grain. While Manchuria had been under Japanese rule, Mudanjiang had been the military capital of the eastern region. The Kwantung Army's Third District Military Headquarters had been located there, and commander General Yamashita Tomoyuki had launched large-scale military operations from the town in order to expand Japanese influence in the region.

During the previous century, when this part of Manchuria had been under the influence of Imperial Russia, the clear waters of the Mudanjiang River had made the town a popular summer resort. Today, the water is still beautiful and the rustic atmosphere remains, enhanced by the bicycles and horse-drawn carriages that pass along the streets. Willows dance in the shimmering light. Low mountains stretch out in the distance, and the entire scene evokes a certain nostalgia—a magical power. One can almost understand why the town's name means "paradise of righteous government" and the region's name means "the place where the five families live in harmony."

Unfortunately, the war turned Mudanjiang into a town of lament. Many Japanese evacuees fleeing Manchuria at the war's end reached Mudanjiang and simply disappeared. After Japan's defeat, radio broadcasts would air the names of persons still missing, in the hopes that some listener might know their whereabouts; a frequently heard description of the missing was "born in Mudanjiang of the Amur region." More recently, Japanese come across the same phrase in lists of orphans who were left behind in China and now, as adults, are traveling to Japan in search of their biological parents.

Our group left Mudanjiang after only one night and headed for Dongning, our final destination. The unpaved road was full of potholes, but our driver, a former transporter for the Chinese People's Liberation Army, kept his foot down on the accelerator. Mr. Chen recklessly dodged bicycles and horse-drawn carriages. The tall ones among us were constantly being bounced off the ceiling of the bus; nevertheless, Mr. Chen charged ahead.

"Look! That mountain is Guoliang Chuankou!" someone suddenly cried out. We were approaching Dongning. A large river came into view. "It's the Suifenhe! Suifenhe!" Everyone was excited. Right before their eyes was the scene the returnees remembered from forty-six years before. All of them took note of the date, 30 May. To these elderly men, this day in 1945 marked the beginning of events that would determine whether they lived or died. They wanted now to reassess their lives in the waning light of those desperate events. The river sparkled under the afternoon sun.

The Kwantung Army Abandons Operations

On 29 May 1945, a group of young students of First Xinjing Middle School—which included members of our delegation—was to head by train for Mudanjiang and then to Dongning. A send-off for the group of 120 boys had been held at a Japanese Shinto shrine in Xinjing (now Chang-chun), Manchuria's capital at the time. The students had lined up in front of the shrine and, following the school principal's lead, shouted three rounds of "Long live the Emperor!"

The students had been urged to do their duty for their country by performing farm labor, and all were scheduled to return home two months later, on 28 July. The whistle drowned out the last, hurried farewells, and the train pulled away. My older brother, Ishii Kohei, was on board. In April, Kohei had transferred to First Xinjing Middle School from a school in Dalian. With no friends among the other boys, he must have anticipated a lonely journey. Because I was only two and a half years old at the time, I have no memories of saying goodbye to him. For my mother, however, it was a parting that she will never forget. She would never see him again. And within a month, her husband would be sent into military service and quickly be captured by the Soviets, ultimately surviving four terrible years as a prisoner in a Siberian internment camp.

During the months before the boys were sent to Dongning, the war had steadily been growing worse for Japan. Tokyo was devastated on the night of 9 March in an air raid that killed an estimated 130,000 people, mostly civilians, and the following nights, American bombers struck with similar intensity the cities of Nagoya, Ōsaka, and Kōbe. Meanwhile, U.S. Marines and naval forces were bombarding Okinawa in a horrific campaign that the Japanese would soon lose, and the southern end of the island chain would be exposed to direct attack.

On 18 March 1945, the Japanese cabinet promulgated the plan known as "Outline of Educational Measures in Preparation for the Decisive Battle." The order closed all schools and mobilized even children to help defend the country. It was in accordance with this plan that the students of First Xinjing Middle School were sent to Dongning as agricultural laborers. But why were they sent 435 miles away when it would have been easier to send the students from Xinghui Middle School, which was much closer to Dongning? Perhaps it was because all of the students at Xinghui apparently had relatives in the Japanese military.

It was not a secret—at least to the Japanese military—that the Soviet border was dangerous. The Imperial headquarters in Tokyo and the Kwantung Army headquarters in Manchuria were both aware that the Soviet Union's entry into the war was imminent. In fact, on 5 April the Soviets had informed Japan that they would not extend the Soviet-Japan Neutrality Pact; furthermore, with Germany's defeat on 7 May, the Soviets had begun deploying large numbers of troops and weapons to Siberia.

On 30 May, the day that the students arrived in Dongning, the Imperial headquarters issued to its forces in the region an order known as "A Strategic Plan Against the Soviets in the Korea-Manchuria Region." The plan called for "abandoning defenses in three-fourths of the entire Manchuria region." There can be little doubt that at precisely the same time that the army was surreptitiously withdrawing from the Soviet border, the middle-school students were being sent to the region as decoys. Furthermore, as part of the army's smokescreen strategy, 290,000 Japanese women and children in this soon-to-be-defenseless region were also being abandoned, with no warning of the impending Soviet offensive. The death count resulting from the Soviet attack would reach 80,000. To add to the tragedy, in a last-ditch effort to save their children's lives, many fleeing Japanese mothers left their children behind in hopes that they would be taken in by the local populace. Today, there are at least 8,000 Japanese war orphans who were raised in China.

It's not surprising that, given the nearly fifteen years that Japan's government conducted its "economic management" of Manchuria, the Chinese people came to despise the Japanese. Nevertheless, it must be noted that when Japanese women and children became refugees, hopelessly wandering through Manchuria, some Chinese came to their aid and did adopt abandoned children.

With these facts in mind, it is indeed time for the history of the Kwantung Army's conduct in Manchuria and Japan's wartime policies toward its own citizens to be investigated by a new generation of researchers.

The Two Teachers

We drove around the vicinity of Dongning until evening, surprised to see that the once-empty plains had been cleared and cultivated into vast farmland. Anti-tank earthworks had been transformed into rice paddies, and forested hills into productive farms. It was hard to believe that this tranquil village had once been a battlefield. Our bus stopped on the bank of the Shifu River. Some people in our group took pictures, and some dipped their hands into the water, remembering the past.

"Ishii Kohei was a good swimmer; he used to swim all the way across this river," my brother's former group leader said to me. With that, I too dipped my hands in the water. I picked up two small stones from the bank and placed them in my pocket.

Our Chinese guide, Mr. Qiu, pointed to a wisp of smoke rising from two chimneys. "That used to be Dongning Station. Now it's a pottery factory," he said. On that fateful day in 1945, the schoolboys had arrived at this station by train. They all expected to return safely home, but in just over two months, on 9 August, the Soviets began their offensive. The area became a battlefield. The boys fled from the farm as soon as they were aware that something was happening. Traveling as fast as they could on foot, they reached the station at two o'clock in the afternoon, but the train reserved for Japanese evacuees had already left.

Sixteen hundred people had boarded that train. They included Japanese families and personnel attached to the regional government, the Manchuria Railway, and the military. Did any of the officials on the train consider the fate of the middle-school students being left behind?

Our guide took us to the aging one-story brick building that had formerly been the train station. In the center was a garden with a fountain. Abruptly, eighty-three-year-old Mr. Saito called for everyone to gather around him. "Students! The last train has left. We will now head toward Daohe on foot. In case we are unable to board a train in Daohe, we will walk to Xinjing—a distance of 435 miles. Not a single person should fall behind. Let's go!" He thus reenacted his exhortation of forty-six years earlier. His former students listened in perfect stillness—perhaps the same way they had listened then.

Also listening was Mr. Ogawa. He had been with the boys at the farm in Dongning, but circumstances had separated him from the frightened group and their fate. On 28 July, the boys' national service was to have ended; everyone had been making arrangements to return to Xinjing. At the last moment, however, a telegram arrived from the Educational Affairs Section in Xinjing telling the teachers to continue in place until further notice. The students and their two teachers were puzzled and concerned. On 6 August, Mr. Ogawa decided to speak directly with the educational authorities in Xinjing in order to have the boys sent home. He had hardly arrived in Xinjing when hostilities broke out. Mr. Ogawa set out at once to return to Dongning, where Mr. Saito and the students were waiting for him. But the train would go no farther than Mudanjiang. At that point, he was forced to return to Xinjing.

Mr. Ogawa was twenty-six years old at the time. He was newly married, and since his wife had just had a baby, she and the infant had taken refuge in Japanese-occupied Korea. Sadly, their baby died there. For a long time after the war ended, Mr. Ogawa was the target of malicious gossip that he had deserted his students on the battlefield.

Our bus left for Daohe the following day, on the very road over which the students had fled, pursued by Soviet tanks and bombarded by artillery shells. "Soon after we had left Dongning," Mr. Saito remembered aloud, "one car passed us on the road. It was the last car out of Dongning—a police car." The winding, hilly road seemed to stretch before us forever. I could only imagine how alone and despairing Mr. Saito must have felt as he led more than a hundred frightened students in a midnight escape.

After an hour we reached Daohe Bridge. One member of our group, Yamamoto Akira, had recorded what the boys had seen there:

> The flow of evacuees has stopped, leaving the area strangely silent. As we approached Daohe Bridge, however, we heard an unearthly voice. A woman, twenty-five or twenty-six years old, was leaning against an embankment on the side of the road and crying. In her arms we could see an infant. Its head drooped down and it appeared already to be dead. The woman's animal-like cries were indescribable. Grief over her dead child, separation from her family, anxiety about her future, fear and exhaustion—all were compressed into those cries that seemed to burst forth from the depths of her being. With the exception of intermittent machine-gun fire in the distance, the road had fallen silent on this afternoon. The woman's wrenching screams pierced the silence, ringing forever in our ears and filling us with sorrow and anxiety as we crossed Daohe Bridge.

Lilacs

On 20 August 1945, the boys were captured and taken prisoner by Soviet troops at Dongjing-cheng. The Soviets assumed the students were Army Youth Corps members since they wore khaki uniforms and arm bands; moreover, on 11 August First Xinjing Middle School had been closed. During the eleven-day flight, there was no way for Mr. Saito and them to have learned that on 15 August, Japan had surrendered unconditionally, that the Soviets had already taken Xinjing, and that the group had been fleeing not away from but directly toward the enemy.

The boys had already endured two months of harsh farm labor as part of their national service and had been on the run for many days over mountain and plain. Now they were prisoners of war, surrounded by barbed wire. Their only meal each day was a small serving of rice gruel; extreme hunger drove them to eat grass and locusts.

Apparently, my brother and a fellow student named Adachi Shoichiro became so emaciated in prison that they were sent to a former military field hospital on the outskirts of Mudanjiang, where they died. The old brick hospital is now a nursing home. The afternoon we got there, the sky was clear blue. Elderly people were being pushed leisurely about in their wheelchairs, and the garden overflowed with lilacs. "When this ground was dug up to construct a new building," the nursing-home director informed us, "a great many human bones appeared." I wonder what those bones might tell us today.

We also set out to visit the remains of another hospital where Japanese evacuees had been treated. The site was now a bustling city street lined with small shops. "According to our investigation," our interpreter explained as we stood before a brick wall, "two Japanese physicians worked here. The hospital was managed by a Japanese in China's Eighth Route Army and was closed in 1948."

Just then, a woman in our group who had lost her younger brother at this hospital took out a candle and incense, lit them, and placed them next to the wall. She put her hands together in prayer, overcome by a place that had lived in her memory for so many years, and knelt before the wall next to the street. Her actions mystified the townspeople who had gathered around us. Our interpreter, Mr. Qiu, went running up to her. "Please stop your memorial service immediately! The local residents will become upset. Let's leave right now!" One of our tour directors suddenly felt that we had spent enough time there. He extinguished the candle and incense, and everyone reluctantly walked toward the bus. Ms. Shimozato, who always wore a white hat, stood alone in the shadow of a telephone pole, silently wiping away her tears.

Three Old Men

Along a sparkling road lined with verdant willows, we drove until our bus reached the village of Shitou, about sixty miles from Mudanjiang. It was Sunday, the day of the thriving open-air market. Vendors hovered near colorful clothing and sundries laid out for sale. Our bus stopped on the grounds of the People's Government of Shiyan (formerly Shitou), in Dongan Prefecture, and we were guided to a second-floor meeting room to be received by the head of the village.

Forty-six years earlier, when the middle-school students of China's enemy arrived on foot from Dongjing-cheng, the people of this village fed them and took them into their homes for the night. For nearly half a century, these former students had wanted to express their gratitude for this kindness, so the village was an especially important stop on our itinerary.

After a few minutes, three old men stepped into the room. Everyone in our group stood up together. A slight stir was soon followed by applause. The interpreter introduced the men. "The old gentleman with the white beard is Mr. Jiang, who is seventy-three years old; Mr. Ma is sixty-four. I understand that all of you remember having stayed in this village." The third old man, who wore the standard gray uniform of the People's Republic of China, was the eighty-five-year-old former chief of Shitou Train Station.

One of our group then spoke, explaining that the purpose of our visit was to express our gratitude. "Winter was approaching," Mr. Jiang replied. "When the students arrived here, they were terribly thin and the villagers felt sorry for them. We didn't have enough food, since the Japanese and Russian armies had commandeered our provisions. But we couldn't just turn our backs on you."

The elder brother of one of the former students stood up and bowed deeply to the men. "I remember being profoundly moved when my brother told me that the family that took him into their home slept on the dirt floor so that he could sleep on the floor's heated section. He later became emaciated in a POW camp and died shortly after returning to Japan, but I would like to express my heartfelt gratitude on his behalf. Thank you very much."

Various gifts from Japan changed hands: an electric clock, a solar-cell calculator, a hand-painted ceramic dish. Then everyone stepped outside for a commemorative photograph, after which we shook hands with the three men and reluctantly bade them farewell. The faces of the former schoolboys softened, and the years seemed to fade away.

Words of Condolence from a Chinese

We had a difficult time finding the remains of our next stop, Dongjing-cheng Settlement Hall, where the students had been kept for two months as prisoners of war. The bus pulled over several times, but each time that we got out and looked around, we found we had been mistaken about the site. One member of our group, when he felt that we had finally found the right place, asked some passersby in Chinese if this was the place where some Japanese boys were interned long ago. They answered that it was, and he called everyone over.

The place was now a lumberyard, with railroad tracks running nearby. A flat-topped mountain stood directly in front of us. The boys used to stare at that mountain and think of their families. As the trains passed, the young prisoners could think only of returning to Xinjing.

Everyone gathered at the entrance to the lumberyard. Just then, an old man walking with a girl of about five suddenly came up to one of the members of our group and started hitting him. Our interpreter ran over; the old man mumbled unintelligibly as the girl tried to pull him in another direction. Our interpreter, doing his best to smooth things over, told us that the man was mentally ill. He suggested that we board the bus immediately, so we were forced to leave. This was the place that had determined life and death for the students. One of the major goals of our entire trip had been to conduct a memorial service here, but suddenly this had become impossible.

Trying to make the best of the situation, we drove to a hill on the outskirts of Dongjing-cheng where we wouldn't attract attention. Out of courtesy, our Chinese interpreter, bus drivers, and staff waited at a distance.

The wind was strong and blew the branches of the nearby willows back and forth. To begin our memorial service, four large pictures—one of each boy who had died—were propped up on the ground. A few members of the group picked wildflowers and placed them in front of the pictures, which frequently blew over in the wind and had to be set upright each time. The pictures consisted of both photographs and painted portraits; none was of particularly good quality. My brother, in the form of an enlarged photograph of what had been a tiny, out-of-focus picture, now sat facing his former teachers and friends for the first time in forty-six years. We placed on the ground an offering of assorted Japanese sweets, and in the center of this memorial a wreath of white butterfly orchids brought from Japan. Ms. Shimozato opened a small bundle wrapped in decorative cloth, took out a student uniform and a pair of sneakers, and placed them in front of her brother's photograph.

Only one Chinese person was present at this memorial service: Mr. Jin, who had accompanied us all the way from Dalian and been a classmate of my brother throughout their elementary-school days in Dalian. Later he taught Japanese for many years at a Chinese teachers' college. Mr. Jin had brought white acacias from Dalian. He now placed these near the pictures. A passing steam engine whistled in the distance.

Mr. Ogawa stood before the pictures and uttered these words: "This is Mr. Ogawa. Here, today, this opportunity to express my deepest regrets leaves me overwhelmed with emotion. At long last, I can commemorate the end of the war."

Mr. Saito spoke next. "I came this distance to meet with you boys. I'm sorry to have taken so long to get here. We brought some sweets for you; I only wish that in those days we could have fed you to your heart's content."

Mr. Jin then stood before my brother's photograph and spoke to him. "Ishii Kohei! I have changed my name to Jin, but this is Hayakawa Mitsuyoshi. We used to sit next to each other at elementary school in Dalian. Do you remember? I have thought of you with fondness over the years, and that is why I am here today. Was it ultimately 'for the Empire' that you boys were deprived of your lives? Was it this impressive pretext that made you die a dog's death? Some people might claim that your deaths played an essential role in laying the foundation for peace. But what can such peace mean to the families who lost their own flesh and blood? There must be a better way of achieving peace." A devout Catholic, Mr. Jin concluded his speech with these words: "Lord, may light always shine upon their heads. Amen."

At just that moment, the setting sun cast its red rays on the very spot where we stood. The altar was then put away and we left. Only the sweets and the white wreath of butterfly orchids remained behind.

That night at our hotel in Mudanjiang, a farewell party was held by members of the China-Japan Friendship Association, which had exerted great efforts to make our trip possible. Countless plates of food—more than we could possibly eat—covered the tables, and toasts were offered throughout the room. Someone began singing some nostalgic Japanese melodies, and the Chinese members followed with some old favorites in their language. Even our interpreter, Mr. Qiu, who is of China's postwar generation, joined in choruses. He had finally completed his nerve-wracking duties and was now smiling brightly at the festivities.

Both Past and Present

In 1931, the League of Nations sent a commission of inquiry under Lord Lytton to warn the Japanese that their invasion of Manchuria would not be tolerated. But Japanese public opinion at the time favored expanding its national interests and special rights on the Asian continent. The mass media fanned the flames. On 19 December 1932, all 132 Japanese newspapers issued a joint declaration: "We, in the name of Japan's organs of public opinion, stand firmly opposed to any policy that would in the slightest way endanger the existence of the Manchurian state." I see this as a clear manifestation of Japan's contempt for China, and I would contend that the lack of attention given to the Manchurian Incident today reflects a continued lack of real interest in China. Where interest does exist, it centers on China as merely an enormous market.

Twenty million people died as a result of a war initiated by Japan. If the weight and meaning of those deaths are not given even scant mention in Japanese classrooms, history will march on and leave behind countless souls lying in the dust, as if they were stray dogs coldly thrown to the elements. Unless our government and citizens earnestly teach students about the war, we will continue to find insensitive Japanese expatriates crooning war songs in pubs in Beijing and Singapore.

I think of the perplexed expression on the face of our interpreter, Mr. Qiu, and am filled with misgivings.

Translation by the author

Irene Haar with Mishima Yukio at Irene's Hungaria restaurant, Tokyo, 1956
Photograph by Francis Haar

Peonies

Translator's Note

"Peonies" ("Botan," 1955) may come as a surprise to readers who are familiar with the later writings of Mishima Yukio (1925–1970) and with his reputation for right-wing political leanings. Though the story is typical of Mishima in some ways—the crisp, precise language; the tone of ironic detachment—it is unexpected in others.

Japan was just beginning to recover from World War II when "Peonies" was written. Reminders of the disaster were everywhere; memories were vivid. The Allied Occupation had ended only a few years before. Mishima had earned enthusiastic notices for *Kamen no kokuhaku* (Confessions of a mask, 1949), with its memorable descriptions of wartime Tokyo, but his career was still young, his political and paramilitary activities still in the future. The implied antiwar, antimilitary message of "Peonies" and its acknowledgement of the realities of war (even today, some members of the Japanese Right deny that the "Rape of Nanking" occurred) come from a youthful Mishima who had not yet assumed the role and persona for which he is most clearly remembered today.—A. H. C.

An unexpected friend came to invite me to an unexpected place. He suggested that we go to see a peony garden. I did not know my friend Kusada's occupation or where he lived; he was rumored to be involved in some political movement or other, but I was not sure. He was small, had sharp eyes and a fine sense of humor, and he knew everything.

We left the house at about two o'clock in the afternoon and, after twice changing trains, boarded a suburban train that I had never ridden before. It was a sunny holiday at the beginning of May.

In front of a small suburban station waited a large bus that would connect passengers to a port city in Kanagawa Prefecture. The bus took a new concrete road, far more splendid than the streets in the city.

"It was built for military use. Just completed," my knowledgeable friend explained tersely. At a pond by the side of the road, a row of picnicking children scooped for tadpoles without a glance at our bus. Their shirts had come untucked from the backs of their little trousers.

At one of the stops we alighted from the bus. A large sign pointed the way to the peony garden. The road meandered between the fields, and, the hour being late, we frequently had to step aside for groups of people on their way home.

Eggplant seedbeds. Onion heads. On the other side of the road was a marsh, where tadpoles, clearly visible as they caught the sunlight, dove through the algae, and last year's frogs, invisible, were croaking here and there. One corner was sectioned off as a place to wash summer radishes. Two farmers in rubber boots that came up to their thighs were energetically washing radishes and stacking them in alternation on a plank to one side.

"This freshly washed whiteness is strangely erotic, isn't it," I said.

"Yes," Kusada replied indifferently as he rushed along the road. He was walking so fast that I lost sight of him in the crowd several times.

The road ascended to a dense grove in which stood a gate. The words KATSURA HILL PEONY GARDEN came into view. Paying our entrance fees, we passed through the gate. The field of vision opened abruptly—sunny beds of peonies lay before us, with a multitude of visitors passing among them in clusters.

Paths separated the flower beds, each of which was bounded with anemone, azalea, or iris. Each peony bush was provided with a label, on which was written an imposing name in Chinese characters.

UNICORN AND PHOENIX
GOLDEN PAVILION
OFFICIAL OF JAPAN
BLOSSOM MINISTER
INEBRIATED FACE
MISTY BARRIER
ETERNAL PLEASURE
COURT MUSIC
BROCADE GLOW
MOON WORLD

Unicorn and Phoenix had a big, reddish-purple, velvet blossom. The pale peach of Eternal Pleasure graduated to a deep scarlet in the center. Most luxurious of all was the large, white Moon World. A visitor knelt before it, aiming a camera, and behind him an artist brandished a sketching pencil.

The peonies were nevertheless past their prime: the crimson petals of the outworn blossoms crinkled as if exposed to flame, their yellow stamens and pistils shriveled. The dry leaves alone retained a sculpturesque elegance in their sharply defined veins. Some plants were only leaves, their flowers having fallen. On some low plants, fresh pale-green sprouts sagged under the weight of huge white blooms, while others were braced with splints and stood a foot tall.

"I wish mine looked like that." The loud voices of two elderly women, probably spinsters, reverberated in my ears.

"One would need to have this much space, I suppose."

"Yes, I must pull out some of mine."

Kusada tapped my shoulder.

I looked in the direction he pointed.

A shabbily dressed old man strolled past us. He wore a patched, striped shirt, narrow-cuffed military trousers, a faded red cap, and the rubber-soled, cloth footwear favored by workmen and gardeners.

The man was solidly built, white stubble glinted on his cheek, and his eyes emitted a glow from their deep sockets. He paid no attention to the sightseers around him. He stopped before each peony, one by one, sometimes squatting, and devoured each with his gaze.

The flower at which he was gazing just then was a crimson peony called New Year's Sunrise. The blossom was fully open and one step short of revealing the first signs of decline. Shadows were wrapped complexly among the petals—shadows that quarreled together as they shifted in the breeze.

"Who is he?" I whispered in Kusada's ear, so gravely was Kusada staring after the old man.

"The owner of this peony garden. His name is Kawamata. He bought the place only two years ago," my friend replied in a low, tense voice. Then he looked up at a tent that had been pitched on a low hill at one edge of the garden. "Hey," he said abruptly, in a cheery voice. "There's a beer stand up there. I've seen enough peonies. Let's have a drink."

Angered by his selfishness, I told him to go ahead and start drinking, because I had not yet seen half of the peonies.

Once my restless guide had left me alone and gone to have his beer, I was free to see the remaining peonies at my leisure.

A peony named Snowy Moon Flower guarded golden pistils and stamens within white crepe petals. Each peony had its own character. When I looked out over the garden, the sightseers standing and squatting here and there obstructed my view; but, nevertheless, the peonies, casting heavy shadows one by one on the black soil, were unlike plants in full bloom at an ordinary flower garden. Each one, encircled by its own allotment of soil, seemed isolated from the rest. The overall impression was one of melancholy. The wide-open blooms, far too large for the squat shrubs they adorned, had an eerie vividness about them, as if they had just blossomed from the rain-dampened soil.

I followed a turn in the path.

The flower beds continued, circling the hill of the beer stand and extending to the foot of the mountains beyond—peonies everywhere.

Feeling thirsty, I relented and started up the stone steps of the hill. A gaudy beach parasol stood outside the tent. Under it, Kusada, a beer bottle and glass on the table before him, raised his hand and called to me.

We emptied two bottles in no time. Kusada wiped the foam from his mouth with his hairy forearm and spoke.

"Do you know how many peonies there are here?"

"There must be a great many."

I gazed down at the peony garden, half of which had been ravished by the evening sun. Many family groups remained. A camera lens catching the setting sun glowed on someone's chest.

"There are five hundred and eighty."

"You're very well informed." Accustomed to Kusada's extensive knowledge, I responded without surprise.

Just then, the old man we had seen before tottered across the center of the peony garden. Stopping before a peony, he stood with his hands folded behind him and stared at the flower's face.

"Five hundred and eighty plants—or five hundred and eighty persons," Kusada said suddenly.

Startled, I lifted my face and looked at Kusada. My knowledgeable friend continued.

"That old man Kawamata used to be the famous Colonel Kawamata. I'm sure you know of him. He's the man who was considered the ringleader of the Rape of Nanking.

"He went into hiding and evaded the war-crimes trials. When it was safe to do so, he reappeared and bought this peony garden.

"According to the war-crimes charges, he's responsible for the massacre of tens of thousands. But the number the Colonel killed with his own hands, gladly and meticulously, was only five hundred and eighty.

"Moreover, they were all women. The Colonel took a personal interest only in killing women.

"After becoming the owner of this place, Kawamata strictly limited the number of peony plants to five hundred and eighty. It's because he cultivated the flowers with his own hands that the peony garden has turned out this well. But what do you make of such a peculiar diversion? I've been thinking about it, and now I believe I've reached the right conclusion.

"He wanted to commemorate, in a secret way, his own evil. He has probably succeeded in fulfilling the evildoer's most compelling need: to exhibit his own indelible evil without endangering himself."

Translation by Anthony H. Chambers

GLADYS SWAN

The Death of the Cat

1

Is it the back room where it begins, through the little passage that once held the table with the dolls' perpetual tea party, cups and saucers Lauren had since come to identify as Japanese willow ware—connecting to the shedlike part that held two great piles, one of kindling, one of coal for the various stoves and fireplaces in the house? For the winter took its toll, and endless fires in the fireplace and woodstove had to be kept stoked to keep life warm enough to get through. Snow. *Falling in great flakes. Sticking to your coat sleeve. Wet wool smell. Snow falling and still falling, piling up to the porch, up to the very eaves, with only the chimneys poking through. Snows of all the years.* She couldn't see over the banks after her father had shoveled the walk: they made a tunnel for her to walk through.

Is the beginning there, in that dark place, where the coal came tumbling in through a chute, roaring and streaming into a pile she wasn't allowed to climb on, for most certainly it would dirty her clothes—though she sneaked back sometimes and took odd-shaped pieces from the kindling heap to pound nails into? *Oh, the cat's been in the coal pile again.* There, where if you went in, you quickly came out and shut the door against the cold and the coal smell and a lingering sense of the unfamiliar; where the snow shovels leaned against the walls in the posture of waiting and the feed stood in bags for the ducks and chickens in the side yard; and where the cat had her kittens. *"I'll put a cardboard box for her in the back room. It's too cold outside. She can have her kittens there."*

Or does she enter the past by the front door, or even the kitchen door off the side porch, by way of the trellis hanging with wisteria, humming with bees and wasps visiting between the wisteria and the climbing rose at the side of the walk leading back to the garden bordered with zinnias? It is a question Lauren has been puzzling over. Her childhood has been locked away for so many years. Somehow forbidden, as in the fairy tales. *You may have all the keys to all the rooms, save this one. This door you must not open.* The key trembles in her hand, different from the others. Glowing now.

Light from the fire has fallen on it like blood. *Fire roaring through the house like time, charring walls and ceilings, leaving black boards and cinders.* Now that there is nothing left, she circles her childhood house. She holds up the key.

To enter by the front door would be easiest, past the porch with its swing and all the places it would go. *Philadelphia, Philadelphia and O-hi-o.* A white house with square, white pillars. She stands there before the porch. An elegant house even though drafty and cold. *Antebellum.* So, then, almost a hundred years old. *Antebellum, antebellum*—the word sang through her childhood and down through the years. Remembered elegance. But how could it have been? Now the town she left fifty years ago sits in the backwaters of no-time, in less than elegant decay—with a modern part trying to pull away like an obstreperous offspring towards the highway sprawl that got her there. Her old neighborhood a slum, no hint of elegance in the houses that remain. Hers is gone—not a trace, razed by a fire, in which a child died. She read this, a little news item in a newspaper published all the way up in Maine, where the family had fled after the fire. Her house is where they lost their child. *Go on now, you have the key. For curiosity is the key. Curiosity killed the cat. But the cat died giving birth.*

So what is there to reclaim? She could try the various ways she'd entered the house—it was a house abounding in doors. But did it matter where you entered or what was there, or even that the cat had died? So much has gone by—in fact, a whole parade of cats. She can't remember now what the cat looked like or even its name. Her father once spoke of a tortoise-shell cat—was that the one? Odd that even then, when she stood sobbing for hours in a grief she had never known, fathomless, as though a chasm had opened under her feet, she had no real image of the cat. Was that why she wept—because she could not see her?

2

It was Christmas, and the house quickened with the season. Not only were the doors and windows all along the street decked with holly wreaths, ending in a downtown strung with lights—so that everywhere you turned it was Christmas—but the tree was up in the living room. Excitement growing about what Santa might bring. And there was to be a party. People coming, breaking into the daily round, the familiar smell of mother-and-father presence. A different rhythm: her mother in the throes of preparation all week, Lauren somehow always underfoot, trying to sneak a candy, or a nut, a bit of icing, a silver ball. Presents to be wrapped, hors d'oeuvres to be created, cakes to be baked. Her mother trying to be everywhere at once. Eggnog—where was the recipe Mamie had given her? And hot punch—to the telephone to call Viola Foley to see if she would lend her punch bowl and cups. Could she get enough meat for the meatballs? For it was wartime, and meat was in short supply.

Bessie, the cleaning woman, came in all that week to help in the kitchen and clean the house from top to bottom, from the upstairs with the arctic bedrooms and the only bathroom in the house—which guests would have to climb the stairs to use—to the downstairs with the living room, dining room, and kitchen. The living room had been refurbished with a whole new set of slipcovers her mother had sewed for months, all in a flower pattern to brighten up the sofa and chairs—it got so dark in the winter. Lights covered the tree—angel hair making green and blue and red and yellow halos around them—and glinted from colored balls and tinsel. Flames danced up from the logs set on the andirons of the fireplace. The room was set aglow—from the mahogany of her father's bookcase, where the Harvard Classics stood like soldiers pitted against the dark, to the crook of the stairs, where the secretary reached up with its glass-fronted shelves, on top of which the cat sometimes surveyed the whole of the living room.

Her father had come home from work a little early the night of the party so that they would have time to eat and he could bathe and dress and build the fire and see to it that there was enough wood to last the evening. He was in one of his rare good moods, making puns that her mother thought deplorable.

Her father was a disappointed man, Lauren now knows. Perhaps it explains why he had to ridicule people, find flaws, bully to have his way. He was supposed to have become someone important—a doctor or a lawyer. But his own father had died when he was young, and he'd had to sacrifice all his ambitions and never done anything more important than become president of the local Kiwanis Club and help with the annual food drive for the underprivileged. Baskets for the poor. He ran a small container factory with his brother, Lauren's Uncle Melbourne, whom she'd seen only once. Her uncle was casual and relaxed, "trying to be a hale fellow well met," her father said with contempt—someone for whom nothing was ever pressing and who left her father all the real work while he ran the sales end in Manhattan.

Most of the time there were quarrels in the house, as when her mother bought an extra pair of shoes or didn't cook something to her father's taste or when he wasn't satisfied with what she did with the household money. Tonight, too, there was a little tiff. "You've got too much lipstick on," her father said.

"Good heavens, Jerome, it's no more than I usually wear."

"And rouge, for God's sake. You look like a French whore."

Her mother so reddened under the comparison that the rouge melted in with the color of her cheeks and little sparkles came to her eyelashes. In a low voice she said, "It's our party. Why are you trying to spoil things?"

"All right, all right—do as you damned please."

Her mother hastily wiped her eyes and went off to the dining room to get out the good dishes and the sterling silver. "They'll be here any minute."

The warmth of expectation closed around the momentary lapse, and in the kitchen Lauren had the giggles and kept dancing on her toes. She had on her patent-leather shoes and a dress of tartan plaid and imagined she was a pony. *Pony, pony, run with the wind.* Then she was a dancer, dancing with the wind. However, she could stay up only long enough to greet the guests; then it was upstairs to bed with her. A promise had been exacted, but she would see. There were solemnly sealed promises and negotiable promises; she had an instinct for the difference.

Then the grown-ups started coming, those great towering figures guarding the portal to the mysterious region they inhabited. First, Miss Gwen in her fur coat and then Dr. Mack, as she knew them, he entering red-faced from more than the cold—oh, that nose of his!—and cheery, shaking her father's hand. "Well hello, hello, Jerome. How's with the old boy? And this lovely girl—growing like a hollyhock, I tell you, and prettier than Shirley Temple." "I'm taking dancing lessons," she told him. "You'll be a marvel," he said and tweaked her nose as Miss Gwen took off her fur coat for Bessie to carry upstairs to the bedroom, and stood splendid in a dark-blue dress that was dotted with rhinestones, like a night sky, and that had one of her famous plunging necklines. "I don't see how she gets away with it," her father would say. "Decolletage to and beyond the pale—and I don't just mean skin. How can they learn anything in front of all that cleavage?" For Miss Gwen was a high-school teacher and taught math. "It's *V* for Victory," he would add with a laugh. She had her hair dyed as well—in Salisbury, twenty miles away, so that it wouldn't be known, but who can keep such a secret?

"The way Mack dotes on her," her mother would say, marveling.

"Like a slave," her father said. "She's tamed him and maimed him. No wonder he drinks."

"Oh, Jerome," her mother protested. "He's like a cavalier. And he knows how to hold his liquor."

"You like his style, eh? Well, don't get any ideas. He's probably too drunk to see what she looks like under all that makeup."

They never went to Dr. Mack for dental work. "I want a man with a steady hand," her father said, "when it comes to working the drill. He could pierce a hole in your eyeball."

But Lauren could only look at Miss Gwen in her stunning dress and take in her dark hair and her rouged cheeks and bright lipstick, all the flavor of her presence deepened by the scent of her perfume. Her heart leapt when Miss Gwen handed her the packages she'd brought, including a small one wrapped in a silvery paper with a splendid bow—the most beautiful package she had ever seen. It had to be hers. She wanted to tear off the wrapping right then, only it wasn't Christmas yet, so it had to go under the tree to keep company with the packages from her aunts. Dull packages with dull things inside. Useful things. Socks and panties and slips. When the aunts visited, they gave her a dime or two to buy a savings stamp to help the war effort and gave her mother advice about how to cook for her father. "Jerome can't stand a tough piece of meat," her Aunt Felicia warned her. "And a sponge cake should never be heavy—you want it to melt in your mouth. It's the extra little effort in beating the eggs."

They opened the door to Mr. Ed, the bachelor, bald as an egg, his little rotund belly tucked under a gray wool vest. She admired the chain of his pocket watch when he took his coat off. It had a seal with an image of a mermaid. His laugh tickled her. "Fussy as a woman" was her father's opinion. "Walks like he has a dime up his ass."

"How can you say things like that?" her mother would protest. "He's the nicest person in the world."

"Pfff. Nice."

Lauren thought so, too, for he collected stamps and gave her his duplicates for her collection. Milman, the optometrist who had a crippled leg, arrived in the company of his beautiful wife, Elizabeth, who came from money, her mother used to say in a low voice, and who helped her husband to a good thing or two. And then Miss Letty, who walked with a cane and kept a parrot.

Bessie took the guests' coats, and her mother led them into the dining room and invited them to try the eggnog or have a cup of punch from Viola Foley's punch bowl. Viola herself wasn't coming—she'd called in the middle of the afternoon but had sent over her maid with the bowl. Jonathan would be there, unless he had a house call.

"I do so hope Jonathan can make it—at least for a little while. Things are so hard for him just now," her mother said.

"You're sweet on him, aren't you?" her father said. "Wish you could have married him, don't you?"

Her mother reddened. "What makes you say things like that, Jerome? Heaven knows I admire him, the way he treated Lauren when she had the grippe. No one could have been more attentive."

"You didn't pay the bill."

Lauren kept running up to the window to be sure to see him first and greet him before her mother did. It had begun to snow again, and she could see a deeper coating on the porch. Icicles hung from the eaves. *How cold it was to put your mouth around one. But so delicious. A slice of cold that sang through your teeth.* Dr. Jonathan still wasn't in sight, but here came Jimmy Calhoun, the tallest man she'd ever seen, who'd once given her father an exploding cigar. He sold insurance. He stomped the snow off his boots.

"Well, look who's here," her father said. "Didn't know you'd been invited. Well, come on in, you inverted exclamation point."

"Are you deliberately insulting me," Jimmy said, holding on to his coat, "or is that your idea of a joke?"

"Better than your idea of one," her father said with a little laugh.

Her mother gave him a look that was both angry and pleading.

"Let me tell you one about an insurance man," Jimmy said glumly.

"Why, Jimmy, honey, we're overjoyed to see you. Now you give me that coat and come in here," her mother said. She had her hand on his arm, and he was somewhat mollified. "I want you to try some of this eggnog. If it's not the best you've ever tasted . . ." And she steered him into the midst of safety.

Her mother hated it when her father insulted people. "You do it all the time," she would say after the party was over. "What is it that gets into you?"

"I can't help it if they're so goddam sensitive. So what if he is a stick—can I help it? I'd just like to have a nickel for every buck he's lost on the ponies."

The party was in full swing and still Dr. Foley hadn't arrived. Sometimes her mother cast a look at the door, frowning slightly. She didn't want to set out the buffet supper until everyone had arrived and had had at least one cup of punch. The eggnog, too, had been suitably spiked. *Spiked is when you pour in the rum.* It seemed smart to know grown-ups did this. People filled the living room and the dining room and even overflowed into the kitchen, where a serious conversation was going on between the dentist and the optometrist. "But Hitler has to be stopped or all of Europe will be destroyed," the dentist said. The optometrist shifted his weight to ease his leg. "It's a bad business, though, our getting into it. All our boys getting killed and wounded." "That's war," said the dentist. "Think of what they say about the Jews, how they've been rounded up. No telling how many dead." "They're nothing to me," said the optometrist. "They've got all the money anyway. Seems like we could do with a few less of them, considering our boys are getting killed."

Dr. Foley finally arrived, stomping his galoshes on the mat and brushing the snow from his hat. "Oh, Jonathan," her mother said as he came in, bringing the cold, "I was afraid you wouldn't be able to come. I'm so sorry about Viola." Her mother put her hand on his arm. "She gets these attacks so often. I haven't seen Viola for such a while."

"Yes," Dr. Foley said. "She's been getting these migraines frequently lately. Rest seems to do the best for her. And a compress on her forehead."

"I'm sorry she has to miss all the fun."

"It's a shame," he said. "I'd hoped a party might do her good." They were quiet and seemed to contemplate the fact that his wife was not the only one deprived. "I won't stay long. I just wanted to say 'Merry Christmas,' Ginny. I have some news, but it can wait a bit."

They stood smiling at one another as her father walked up. "Glad to see you, Doc." The men shook hands. "Good thing you decided to take a little time off from increasing the population. Or maybe decreasing it."

The doctor laughed. "I have only a medical degree—nothing in divinity."

Lauren sashayed back and forth, no one paying any attention to her. Suddenly she ran up and tagged the doctor on the arm.

"Hello, kitten," he said, and whisked her up, held her over his head, and swung her down between his legs. She gave a little shriek of pleasure and begged him to do it again.

"You're still up—it's way past your bedtime," her mother said. "Up to bed immediately."

"Just a little longer," she pleaded. She knew she had an advantage for it was a party and nobody wanted a fuss. She loved it when Dr. Foley came to their house. Once it had been just for her, when she'd had the grippe, but more often now it was for her mother, who had spells of shortness of breath.

"Now to bed," her mother said.

She pushed her advantage and made her bargain. "If I go right up to bed, can I take one present and open it up in my bedroom?"

Her mother vacillated. "Just one," she said finally.

Lauren didn't even go around and say good night to everyone. Forgetting to give her father a kiss, she snatched up the silvery present with the glorious bow Miss Gwen had brought and went upstairs with Bessie, who helped her undress. "What are you getting for Christmas, Bessie?" she wanted to know.

"Lord knows, honey—a chance to rest my feet."

"I hope you can rest your back, too."

"I might try that," Bessie said, laughing deeply. "Good night, honey bun. You sleep well now. Me, I'm going home and get me some supper. I'll be back tomorrow to help with the cleaning up."

From her bed she could hear the noise from the party, but she wasn't thinking about it. She sat with the present in her lap. In its silvery paper, it held its secret. How badly she wanted to open it; but once she opened it, the surprise would be gone. Finally, she worked the paper loose at one end, slipped her hand along the edge, and broke the two halves apart. The silvery paper slipped aside, and there was a little box. How lovely that there was something else to open. Inside, on a lavender satin bed lay a slender flask of blue glass filled with perfume. She unscrewed the gold cap: Miss Gwen's perfume. She inhaled deeply—how fragrant it was. She dabbed a little behind her ears and sniffed it again. She put the cap back on. She wished everything had such a wonderful scent. How lovely it would be, filling the house. She imagined a whole world filled with fragrant scent.

An idea struck her. She slipped out of bed and into the hall. She could see perfectly well. On the table next to her bed burned a small lamp—its base a dog sitting in the opening of a doghouse. The hall light was on, too, and the light in her parents' bedroom, where the coats were piled on the bed.

She took the cap off the perfume bottle and went from coat to coat, dabbing a bit of perfume on each collar till they all smelled lovely. Then she put the cap back on. She heard someone coming upstairs and slipped under the bed, her heart pounding.

"I wish you didn't have to leave so early," her mother said.

"You know how Viola gets." It was the doctor's voice.

In front of her, two pairs of legs came down to the ankles and made feet in shoes. She could have reached out and touched her mother's high-heeled pump or run her fingers across the toe of Dr. Jonathan's heavy man shoes—but she didn't.

"Such a shame," her mother broke in. "I know you suffer."

"Ginny, darling—there is something I must tell you."

There was a pained moment of waiting.

"There's a terrible shortage of doctors and—"

"Oh, Jonathan, you're not going?"

"I must," he said. "It would be on my conscience if I didn't."

"But we need you here. We—"

"Seltz will take over while I'm gone."

"I will miss you terribly."

"You know I love you."

Love you. Love you.

"You *will* write?" her mother asked. "I couldn't bear it if I didn't hear from you—just to know you're all right."

"You know I will. And will you answer?" She heard the doctor slip on his coat. There was another pause, then a low sound, almost a moan from her mother. She heard the creak of floorboards as they left the room and descended the stairs. She slipped out from under the bed and crept back to her own room. She lay in bed awake, the noise of the party louder now. For a while she made caves in the covers and pretended they were inhabited by finger people. Then she rubbed her eyes and watched the little fizzles of color sail across the dark sky of her vision. Then she fell asleep.

3

The cat, she read years later, was worshipped by the Egyptians as a goddess of pleasure. On their visits to the shrines, they bought little cat mummies the way tourists buy postcards.

"When a cat rubs up against you," her father said once, "it's not showing affection for you, but taking its own pleasure. They care for no one, those creatures. Just keep them fed. Independent as hell."

"I don't see it that way," her mother said. "I think they feel an affection if they're treated well."

"Pure sentimentality," her father said. "That's what I love about women —they can't think beyond their feelings. That's why they have no moral history. Can't imagine giving affection to a creature without getting something back."

Her mother looked at him for a long moment. "That would mean frequent disappointment," she said softly.

"Are you contradicting me?"

"Not at all. Or maybe you do get something back in spite of everything."

"Whatever are you talking about?"

Lauren was lying on the floor, letting the cat rub up against her head and nuzzle her face. "Don't get too close to that cat," her mother said. "They have fleas."

"She likes me," Lauren said. She loved the cat. She listened to it purr.

That Christmas she got a small phonograph. You wound it up, put a record on, and set the needle on the edge. Each record played a song. She played the songs over and over.

There was a jolly miller who lived on the River Dee.
He worked and slaved from morn till night,
No lark so blithe as he.
And this the burden of his song
Forever used to be:
I care for nobody, no not I
And nobody cares for me.

She liked it when the phonograph was winding down and the sound was like a gurgle deep in the throat. Years later she remembered the song. Sometimes she wondered if you could take the miller's statement at face value, or was he simply some loveless workaholic so stuck on the dollar that he didn't have any friends and was shunned by everyone. So that he had to pretend he had a good thing. It was a question.

"Lauren, take that phonograph up to your room and play it there."

"Why? Don't you want to hear the music?"

"I can't hear myself think. I need to talk to your mother."

"I want some pretzels."

"Go in the kitchen then."

She got her pretzel and hung about the doorway without showing herself. There was trouble in the house, and she had been the cause. The day after the party, her mother had received a telephone call from Viola Foley. Had her husband been at the party? she wanted to know. And if he was there, what was he doing? Her mother had been taken aback. Why, yes, Jonathan had been at the party, though he didn't stay long. What was the matter? The matter was the scent of perfume on his coat collar. All this was said with people listening in on the party line. Her mother was mystified. Perfume. It was only after she'd spoken with Miss Gwen that things came to light.

"Lauren, do you know anything about Miss Gwen's perfume?"

The bottle was empty but for a tiny drop at the bottom. She'd put it on when she was playing dress-up with Janet Elsley and Suzannah Robertson, and they, too, had dabbed it behind their ears. She'd put some on her dolls. She brought the bottle to her mother. "Why, that was the present for me," her mother said. "Why didn't you ask, honey? Did you put some on Dr. Jonathan's coat?"

"On all the coats. I wanted them to smell nice."

"Oh, getting into mischief, I see," her mother said. Yet she didn't seem angry. "Well, you did make them smell. It's a perfume that lingers. I'll have to call Viola and hope that everybody who listened in the first time is listening now."

"She watches his every move," her mother said to her father the next day. "You see how innocent it all was."

"Where there's smoke, there's fire," her father said.

"What do you mean by that?" her mother said. "There wasn't even any smoke."

"Not here maybe. In any case, fires can burn without it," her father said.

"Really, Jerome, you get on my nerves."

He was determined to pick on her mother. Sometimes he did that. Lauren could tell when he walked in the door that he carried a pick in his hand. Sometimes she hid behind his chair and popped out to surprise him. If he was in a good mood, he said, "Hello, little monkey." But tonight he was peeved and said, "Come out of there. You're getting a little old for that."

Then he said to her mother, "And what do you do in this house while I'm away all day working my ass off?"

"You know perfectly well what I'm doing—I'm cooking and cleaning, and sewing and mending. I'm keeping house and cooking your meals."

"You'd rather be off working in some factory, I suppose—being part of the war effort."

"Maybe I would."

He raised his eyebrows. "Rosie the Riveter," he said. "I can just see it. You there with all the factory girls."

"Some people believe in patriotic duty," she said. He'd put his foot down on her leaving the house and taking a job. It was a sore point both ways. But the doctor had gone.

4

It was bitter cold the night the cat died. The wind whistled around the house and through the cracks. But she didn't know about the cat. Not till she'd kept asking and asking if the cat had had her kittens. She'd been waiting for the kittens. Waiting to see them born. Waiting to see them open their eyes and lap up milk. She could dress them up in doll clothes.

But did it all happen before she and her mother went on the train? One morning her mother had packed a valise and included some of Lauren's clothes as well. She found herself dressed in her woolen skirt and white pullover and dark-blue jacket. The blue beret she hadn't worn before was on her head. They were going somewhere, on the train. Leaving the house. A cab pulled up outside to take them to the train station. Her mother sat in silence as they drove down the main street, past the Sussex Hotel and the A & P and the drugstore. To the place where the stores ended and the houses began—there was the station. Its water tower was set below the street just before the bridge the train went over. You had to take the stairs down. She'd held on to the iron railing. Her mother bought their tickets—to Philadelphia—and they stood waiting on the platform until the train came chuffing in. Those arriving descended. The porter took their valise, and they followed him aboard.

"Why are we going to Philadelphia?"

"To stay with your grandmother."

"When are we coming back?"

"Honey, we're not coming back."

"But what about Daddy? Isn't he coming?"

"No, he's not coming. Daddy will get along just fine."

It was strange. The train was shaking her, taking her away from her daddy and first grade. Trees, houses, people swept past. *No Daddy, no Daddy, no Daddy.* Mama and Daddy—two pillars that held up the front porch. "How come Daddy isn't coming?" Questions. Her mother was looking pale, her eyes watery, and every once in a while she dabbed at them with a handkerchief. Then she took out her compact, applied rouge and lipstick, and powdered her nose. The train kept rushing forward. *No Daddy.*

On the day after the cat died, she was standing in her mother's bedroom watching her put on her face in front of the mirror. She loved to watch her mother dress and her father shave. She liked the little brush he used to put lather all over his face and the way the razor made a clean path through it. She adored the smell of witch hazel. She loved the way her mother brushed her hair and then wound it up into a coil and put combs in it to hold it up. Her mother was going to her Saturday-afternoon bridge game, and Mrs. Langford was coming to stay with her. She didn't like Mrs. Langford because her hands were cold and limp and covered with brown spots. And she never let her do anything.

That morning she wanted to go out to the back porch to see if the cat had had her kittens, but her mother wouldn't let her. She'd whined about it during the day. Why couldn't she see? Where was the cat—why hadn't she come in? She always came inside in the morning.

"Honey," her mother said, turning to her briefly before she began to put on her makeup, "I'm sorry, but there isn't any cat anymore. She died when she was having her kittens."

Died. She didn't know *died.* What was it? She strained towards understanding.

"What happened to her?"

"We don't know—she just died. That means she's gone," her mother said.

"And her kittens?"

"They died, too."

She couldn't believe it. There was no way to take it in, no place prepared. "But where did she go?" The tears were coming then.

"To heaven maybe—somewhere. But now she's gone."

The tears became sobs that took over her whole body—wrenching sobs. "Why is she gone? What happened?" She was sobbing so hard she couldn't breathe. Great wails she didn't know were in her came out. She couldn't stop crying, though her eyes were raw and her nose was running.

Ordinarily her mother would have put her arms around her and soothed her and stroked her hair and wiped her nose with a handkerchief. This time she stood up with strained patience, staring into the mirror. Finally, she turned to her and said with a sternness Lauren didn't recognize, "The cat is gone—that's all there is to it. I want you to stop crying—right now."

5

How long before it happened? She was a year or two older, but the war still raged on. Something was in the air, but she didn't know what it was. First it was manifest in the strained silence that appeared when her father came home from work, in the sudden outbursts from her mother, sometimes of shouting and screaming. And what brought them about was puzzling. Once because she'd forgotten her umbrella at school. Once when she'd broken a glass. Once because she'd lost a dollar on the way to the store. The laughter was worse. Because it wasn't laughter. Just thin scrapings from where the spring had gone dry. It made her put her hands up to her ears. The quarrels had gotten worse: why had she come back and why had he taken her back? What he'd promised and what she'd promised. And what she spent the money on. He wouldn't give her money to run the house—she'd just drink it up. Bessie would do the shopping and the cooking. Shouting and pleading. Or just shouting.

One day there were other voices in the house, other presences. Her aunts, whom she'd seen only the two or three times they came to visit. Now they were installed in the house: the ones to give her breakfast in the morning, to object if she wanted corn flakes instead of soft-boiled eggs. And when she came home from school, they were sitting over their cups of

Constant Comment. Her aunt Felicia, who looked like a spoon, with skinny arms straight as rulers, and her aunt Flo, lumpy as a feed sack. They both looked like her father, but had pale, blonde-white hair instead of black. His nose made for a strong face, but on the two women it left little space for beauty.

They were women who knew the value of a dollar and whose sense of utility was like the starch they gave to their dresses. Bessie was sent away, and the two of them shopped and mopped and cooked and mended and ironed her dresses and plaited her hair. It was as though the day came mounted on a little wheel they had to keep from jumping off the track and crashing in a heap. She learned never to ask about her mother; she continually caught hints of her existence, though seldom of her reality.

I always thought Jerome could have done better. She had a wandering eye, that one.

She didn't know her mother had an eye problem. Her aunt Flo was always telling Lauren to stop squinting and to move over into better light to read.

Jerome said her hand was on the arm of every man she knew. More than friendly. And then, of course, the letters. I hope Jerome burned them.

She didn't know when or how she knew that Dr. Jonathan had been killed in the war: he'd been trying to get to a wounded G.I. during one of the battles in North Africa. Or whether his death had begun or hastened her mother's dissipation. Or where she was left on account of it. She saw less and less of her father, who was now down in Washington, for things were getting worse at the production end of the business. There were shortages of materials, and he was hoping for a government contract.

"What do you want to be when you grow up?" her aunt Flo once asked her.

"A dancer," she said, even though her lessons had been stopped.

"You'd do better to learn some secretarial skills," her aunt said. "Dancers starve to death."

It was her first real experience of hatred. But she never saw things the way her aunts saw them. Certain images she clung to all down the years, stubbornly, as though claimed from the last vestiges of fading sight, where things blur into confusion. She saw her mother sitting in front of the mirror brushing her hair, twisting it into a roll and pinning it up on her head. The rich chestnut color—the way her hair caught the light when she entered a room, as though something inside her had turned it on. Her features she couldn't be certain of. She had only a single photograph: her mother as a young girl, before she was married.

There was another image, perhaps more crucial. She was left with that puzzling moment on the platform after they'd descended from the train. For they never got to Philadelphia, no more than the porch swing had taken her there. They were to change trains at Wilmington. She had hold of her mother's hand and was still asking questions as her mother picked up the valise and they began walking toward the station. They were caught up in a crowd of people, porters bustling around them. It was fearfully noisy. Then the pace of her mother's walk changed, as though intention had left it. She sensed bewilderment or loss of nerve. Her mother paused, opened her purse, and pulled out a train schedule. "Where are we going now?" she asked.

"It's all right," her mother said. "There's another train. We'll get home in time for supper."

A sense of some terrible wrong seized her. More than disappointment. "Why? Why are we going back?"

"Who would be there in that empty house?" her mother said distractedly. "Who would feed the cat?"

Father in Chinese attire, Manchuria

Father smoking at desk, Manchuria

Father bathing in large ceramic pot, Manchuria

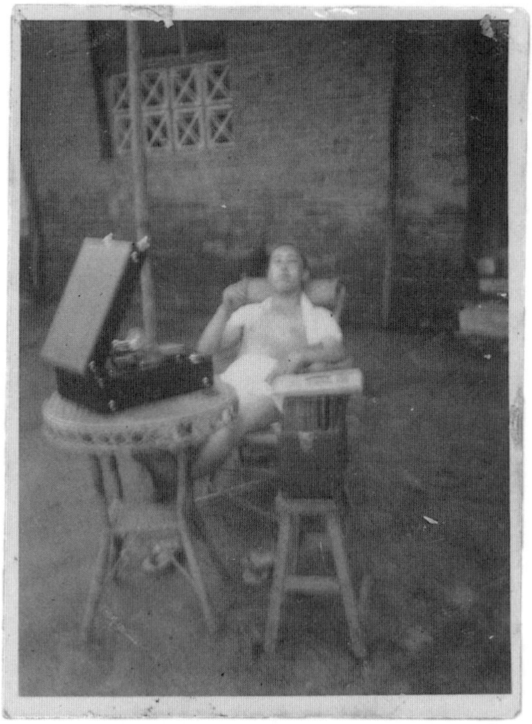

Father with phonograph, Manchuria

Father (back) and friend, Manchuria

December 8

I'm going to take extra care in writing today's entry. I want to describe how one impoverished Nipponese housewife spent 8 December 1941. Then, if this diary of mine should be unearthed in the corner of an old storehouse in a hundred years or so—when Nippon is holding her glorious 2700th birthday celebrations—it may be of some service as a historical reference, showing people what sort of life a housewife of our country was living on this critical day. So, poorly written though it may be, I must at least take care to write nothing but the truth. I don't want it to get all stiff and formal, however. According to my husband, there's nothing to be said for my letters and diary entries and so on except that they're deadly serious; he says they lack feeling. It's true that from the time I was a little girl, I was concerned only with being well mannered, and though I'm not really all that serious deep down inside, I somehow become awkward when I try to express myself and can't seem to loosen up or let down my guard—something I'm forever suffering the consequences for. Maybe it has to do with being too self-centered. I must make an honest effort to reexamine myself, especially now.

Speaking of the year 2700 reminds me of something rather silly that happened the other day. My husband's friend Mr. Ima came to visit for the first time in quite a while, and I had to laugh when I overheard him and my husband talking in the next room.

Mr. Ima said, "You know, this business about the big founding-day celebration has got me worried. It's really bothering me. Are they going to call it the year two thousand seven hundred or the year twenty-seven hundred? It weighs on my mind something awful. Doesn't it bother you?"

"Hmm," my husband said, giving it some serious thought. "It does, yeah, now that you mention it."

"See what I mean?" Mr. Ima, too, was perfectly serious. "It seems they're going to call it the year twenty-seven hundred. That's the impression I get, somehow. But if I could have my way, I'd like it to be two thousand seven hundred. Twenty-seven hundred just won't do. It's indecent, don't you think? I mean, it's not a telephone number or something. I'd like them to say it properly: two thousand seven hundred. I wonder if there isn't something we can do to get people to say it that way when the time comes." He seemed sincerely worried.

"However," my husband said, setting forth his opinion in a horribly pompous tone of voice, "they may have a completely different way of saying it a hundred years from now. Not two thousand seven hundred or twenty-seven hundred, but, for example, *nu-nu* hundred . . ."

That's when I burst out laughing. How absurd can you get? My husband's always engaging in intense discussions with his visitors about things like this—things that don't matter one way or the other. A person with feeling is different from the rest of us, don't you know. My husband writes stories for a living. But it isn't much of a living because he's forever loafing and we just barely get by from day to day. I make a point of not reading his stories, so I have no idea what sorts of things he writes, but apparently they're nothing special.

Whoops. I'm digressing. At this rate, I'll never be able to write something good enough to last till the year 2700. I'd better start over.

Eighth of December. Early this morning, as I lay in bed thinking about all the things I had to do today and nursing Sonoko (our daughter, who was born in June of this year), I clearly heard the words coming from one of the neighbors' radios.

The Imperial Headquarters of the Army and Navy have announced that as of shortly before dawn this morning, 8 December, the Imperial Army and Navy have entered a state of war with British and American forces in the western Pacific.

The words seeped through the slats in the rain shutters and into the darkness of my room with all the strength and vividness of sunlight. In the same crisp, clear voice, the announcement was repeated. As I lay there quietly listening to it, my entire life changed. It was as if I were bathed in a powerful beam of light that left my body transparent. Or as if the Holy Spirit had breathed through me, leaving a single, cold flower petal lodged in my heart. Nippon, too, has changed. From this morning on, it's not the same Nippon.

I called to my husband, who was in the next room, to tell him the news, but no sooner had I spoken than he said, "I know. I know." His voice sounded grim and tense. Well, that's understandable. It was strange, though, that he, who always sleeps in, should have awakened so early. They say artists have strong intuition, so maybe he had a hunch this was going to happen. I was rather impressed. But then he said something so foolish that it completely erased any admiration I might have felt.

"What do you suppose they mean by 'the western Pacific'?" he asked. "The area around San Francisco maybe?"

What a letdown. I don't know why it is, but my husband hasn't the slightest knowledge of geography. Sometimes I'm not even sure he understands what "east" and "west" signify. I really began to wonder about him the other day, when he confessed that the way he'd learned it, the South Pole was the hottest place on earth and the North Pole the coldest. Last year he traveled to Sado Island, and afterwards he told me that when he first saw its outline from the steamship, he thought it was Manchuria. So you see how completely befuddled he is. How did he ever get admitted to university?

"The western Pacific is the side Nippon's on, right?" I said.

"It is?" He sounded disgruntled. After thinking it over for a minute, he said, "Well, that's news to me. So America's in the east and Nippon's in the west? What a revolting idea. Nippon's supposed to be the land of the rising sun. Part of the Far East. I always thought the sun came up from Nippon, and now you're telling me America's to the east of us. What an unpleasant thought. Isn't there some way of looking at it so we can put Nippon east of America?"

He always says the strangest things. I'm afraid he's gone a bit overboard in his patriotism, too. The other day, as he was nibbling on some salted bonito entrails, he suddenly launched into this bizarre boast: "The hairy barbarians, for all their swaggering, would never be able to eat this stuff. But me, I could eat any Western food they set before me."

Anyway, I didn't pay any attention to his oddball grumbling this morning, but got up and quickly opened the rain shutters. It was a fine day. But piercingly cold. The diapers I'd left out hanging under the eaves were frozen stiff, and the garden was covered with frost. The sasanqua were blooming, cold and white. It was so quiet. And to think that, at that very moment, war was on in the Pacific. To the marrow of my bones, I felt gratitude for this land: Nippon. I went out to the well and washed my face, and as I began rinsing Sonoko's diapers, the lady from next door came out. After we'd exchanged greetings, I said, "Well, it's not going to be easy from now on, is it?"

I meant the war, of course, but my neighbor had been elected chief of the neighborhood association just the other day, and apparently she thought I was referring to that.

"Oh, well, there's not much I can do anyway," she said in an embarrassed way. It was a bit awkward for me.

Surely it's not that she isn't concerned about the war, but just anxious about the heavy responsibility of being the chief of the neighborhood association. I felt sorry for her. It really is going to be a difficult job now. If there should be an air raid or something of that sort, the responsibility of the chief is a truly serious matter. At some point I may have to take Sonoko and evacuate to the countryside, which would mean my husband would have to stay behind and protect the house. But he's so incompetent, I hate to think about what would happen. He might not be of any use at all. After all, he still doesn't have a civilian uniform. What's he going to do if worse comes to worst? He's so careless about things like that. If I were to go out and get him a uniform, I'm sure he'd start grumbling, saying something like, "What the hell's this?" Still, he'd probably be inwardly relieved and wear the thing. But he's so long and gangly, it wouldn't do to buy one off the rack. It's a problem.

He, too, got up at about seven this morning and, after a quick breakfast, got right to work. It seems he has a lot of little jobs to finish this month.

At breakfast I said, "Do you think Nippon will be all right?" It just slipped out.

"If not, we wouldn't have done it. Victory is certain," he said, sounding very formal. My husband is forever telling lies, so you can't trust anything he says. However, I decided that these particular words of his were ones I would take to heart.

While I was cleaning up in the kitchen afterwards, I thought about all sorts of things. Is it just the fact that the colors of their eyes and hair are different that makes me feel such hostility toward them? I want to see them beaten to a pulp. It's a completely different feeling from when we went to war with China. Just the thought of those callous, animal-like American soldiers dragging their feet over the noble soil of Nippon is unbearable to me. Take one step on this sacred ground, you beasts, and your feet will rot out from under you. You're not worthy. To the lovely soldiers of Nippon I say this: Wipe the enemy out! From here on in, we at home may have to endure shortages of various kinds, but you needn't worry about us. We don't mind. We won't feel the least bit indisposed. None of us regrets having been born in such difficult times. On the contrary, it's almost as if the times have given purpose to our lives. I, for one, am glad to have been born in this generation. Ah, I'd like to talk with someone about the war to my heart's content. *Well, we did it, didn't we? It's finally started.* Like that.

From morning on, the radio broadcast one war song after another, giving it their all. One right after another until finally—I don't know if they'd begun to run out of songs to play or what—they started broadcasting those ancient ones like "Though the enemy are tens of thousands." I had to laugh to myself. It was really quite charming. My husband doesn't like radios, so we've never had one in the house. And I can't say I've ever wanted one all that badly myself. I do wish we had one now, though. I want to hear lots and lots of news. I'll talk it over with him. I have a feeling he'll let me get a radio now.

Along towards noon there was a flurry of important announcements. I couldn't sit still, so I picked up Sonoko and went out to stand under the neighbors' maple tree and listen to their radio. Surprise invasion of the Malay Peninsula . . . the attack on Hong Kong . . . the Imperial Proclamation of War. As I stood there listening with Sonoko in my arms, the tears started coming and I didn't know what to do. I went back in the house, where my husband was still working, and told him all the news I'd just heard. All he did was smile and say, "Is that right?" Then he stood up, and sat back down again. He seemed kind of distraught.

Shortly after noon, having apparently finished one of the pieces he had to write, he grabbed the manuscript and dashed out. I suppose he was taking it to the magazine publisher's office, but judging from the way he flew off, as if making a getaway, I knew he wouldn't be home until late. He always returns late after fleeing the house like that. Not that I mind, of course, as long as he doesn't stay out the entire night.

After saying goodbye, I roasted dried sardines for a simple lunch, and then I strapped Sonoko to my back and went off toward the station to do some shopping. I stopped at the Kameis' house on the way. We'd received a big box of apples from my husband's hometown in the country, so I'd wrapped a few to give to Yuno-*chan* (the Kameis' pretty little five-year-old daughter). Yuno-*chan* was standing at the front gate when we arrived. As soon as she saw us, she ran to the door and called her mother, saying, "Sonoko-*chan*'s here!" Apparently Sonoko gave Mr. and Mrs. Kamei a big smile from over my shoulder because Mrs. Kamei made an awful fuss over her, saying how darling she was. Looking quite manly and valiant in work clothes and a jumper, Mr. Kamei explained that he'd been laying straw mats under the veranda.

"I tell you," he said, "crawling around under the veranda is a task comparable to landing on enemy shores. You'll have to excuse this filthy getup."

I wonder why he was spreading out straw mats under the veranda. Does he intend to crawl down there if there's an air raid? It's strange.

But I envy Mrs. Kamei. Her husband, unlike mine, really loves his family. I understand he used to dote on them even more than he does now, but after we moved into the neighborhood, my husband began initiating him into the mysteries of alcohol and whatnot. He's not quite the man he was. No doubt Mrs. Kamei bears a grudge against my husband. It makes me feel a bit guilty.

All sorts of tools were lined up by the Kameis' gate: a flame beater, an odd-looking sort of rake, and so on. There's nothing like that at our house. But what can you expect with a husband as lazy as mine?

"My, you're certainly well prepared," I said.

Mr. Kamei smiled and said, "Well, after all, I am the chief of our neighborhood association."

Mrs. Kamei corrected him, saying in a soft voice that he's actually the assistant chief, but the real chief is such an old person that Mr. Kamei has to do most of the work. Well, there's no denying that Mr. Kamei is a hardworking person—he and my husband are as different as night and day.

I excused myself and said I had to be going, and they gave me some sweets to take home.

I went to the post office to pick up a payment of sixty-five *yen* from the magazine *New Tides,* and after that I went to the marketplace. As usual, there wasn't much to buy. I had no choice but to get cuttlefish and dried sardines again. Forty *sen* for two cuttlefish and twenty *sen* for a bundle of sardines. I heard more radio announcements at the market.

Big news flashes, one after the other. Aerial attacks on the Philippines and Guam. The bombing of Hawaii. Total destruction of the American fleet. Official announcements by the Imperial Government. I felt so grateful to everyone, I couldn't stop shaking. It was embarrassing. As I was standing there listening, two or three ladies stopped beside me, saying, "Let's hear the news before we go." Those two or three became four or five, and soon there were nearly ten people standing around me.

I left the marketplace and headed for the kiosk at the station to buy my husband's cigarettes. There was nothing different about downtown at all. A big sheet of paper with the radio news written on it was posted in front of the greengrocer's, but the storefronts and the conversations of people were more or less the same as always. I found this calmness reassuring. Since I had a little more money than usual, I went ahead and bought myself a pair of sandals. I had no idea that, starting this month, there was a twenty-percent tax on anything over three *yen.* I should have bought them at the end of last month. But then again, I think hoarding is despicable. The sandals cost me six *yen,* sixty *sen.* Before heading home, I also bought some cream for thirty-five *sen* and some envelopes for twenty-one *sen.*

Shortly after I got back, young Mr. Sato from Waseda University came by to say that, now he'd graduated, he'd decided to enlist in the army. It's too bad my husband wasn't there. I bowed deeply to him and said a prayer for his safety. No sooner had he left than Mr. Tsutsumi from the Imperial University showed up. He, too, had graduated, but though he'd taken his physical for the draft, he'd been deferred. Both of these young men had always worn their hair rather long, but now their heads were shaved clean. It made a deep impression on me. Not even students have an easy road ahead of them now. It really was a shame my husband wasn't home because late in the afternoon, Mr. Kon came by for the first time in a long while, twirling his walking stick. Having gone to the trouble to make the trip all the way here, to the outskirts of Mitaka, he had no choice but to turn around and go back without seeing my husband. Just thinking about how he must have felt on his way home was enough to make even me gloomy.

As I was beginning to prepare dinner, the lady from next door came over and said that the *sake* ration coupons for December had arrived, but there were only six coupons to be divided between the nine households in the neighborhood association. What should we do? I thought perhaps we should ration the *sake* on a first-come, first-served basis, but it seems all the families wanted some. We finally decided to split the six bottles into nine equal portions, which meant gathering some extra empty bottles and going straight off to Isegen to buy the *sake.* Since I was in the middle of preparing dinner, I was excused from helping. But once I'd gotten the meal under control, I put Sonoko on my back and went to see how things were going. The neighbors were arriving one by one, each carrying a bottle or two, and when I joined them, someone gave me a bottle. Then, on the porch of the association chief's house, we started dividing the *sake.* We lined up nine bottles and carefully measured the volume by eye until they were all even. It isn't easy dividing six bottles of *sake* into nine.

Later, the evening paper came. It was four pages long, instead of the usual two, and how big the headline was! EMPIRE DECLARES WAR ON U.S. AND GREAT BRITAIN. It was more or less the same news I'd heard on the radio, but I still read every word and got worked up all over again.

I ate dinner alone, then put Sonoko on my back and headed for the baths. Getting in the bath with Sonoko is the greatest pleasure of my life. She loves it, and when I put her in the water, she gets very quiet and still. She curls her hands and feet and peers up at my face. I suppose she wonders what's going on. Other people also seem to find their own babies irresistibly adorable—you see them hugging them to their cheeks and kissing them and so on. Sonoko's belly is as perfectly round as if it were drawn with a compass, and it's as white and soft as a new rubber ball. It's almost hard to believe that there's really a little stomach and intestines and everything inside there. And then, just below the center, is her tiny belly button, like a peach blossom. Her feet, her hands, everything about her is so lovely, so darling that I just can't help but go into raptures. There isn't a *kimono* in the world you could put on her that would match the beauty of her birthday suit. When we get out of the bath and I dress her, I always feel a sense of regret. I always wish I could hold her naked body just a little while longer.

It was still light out when we went to the baths, but by the time we started for home, it was completely dark. Blackout. And now it's not just a drill. I felt a strange tightening in my chest. I took one step at a time, sort of feeling my way, but it's a long walk and before long I was getting a bit panicky. Coming out of the field and into the cedar grove was really something. It was truly pitch dark. It reminded me of how frightened I was when I was a student and crossed from Nozawa Hot Springs to Kijima on skis in a snowstorm. Instead of a rucksack, though, I had Sonoko on my back—sleeping, unaware of anything. Suddenly, from somewhere behind me, I heard a man singing "Summoned by-y-y my em-m-peror" completely out of tune, and walking with rough, shambling steps. Then he coughed in a certain way, and I knew who it was.

"This isn't easy for Sonoko," I said, and he answered in a loud voice.

"What the hell. You people don't have any faith—that's why you find it hard to walk on a dark road like this. Me, I've got faith. For a man with faith, walking down this road is the same as walking in broad daylight. Follow me," he said and then plodded ahead.

My husband. There's no telling to what extent he's really in his right mind.

Translation by R. F. McCarthy

Mother, Hiroshima

The blast, visible over the hills,
Sakamachi, Hiroshima

JEANNE WAKATSUKI HOUSTON

from *Fire Horse Woman*

Sayo

In late spring 1942, the biting wind of California's high desert blew harder than anyone could remember. Howling and tearing up sagebrush, it sent skeletal tumbleweeds cartwheeling like drunken clowns over the sandy flatlands. Churned-up dust gathered in clouds so thick they blotted out the noon sun, causing people to speculate about an unscheduled eclipse. Some explained that dark spring as the time when the Great Wind Gods of the Four Directions had met to display their wrath—or perhaps sorrow—at some mysterious event.

Were the Gods speaking to the ghosts of desert Indians who once populated the land? The Owens Valley Paiutes, driven out long before the Los Angeles Water District stole the river's water, were now scattered throughout the nation. Like windblown smoke, their villages disappeared from this elevated land so close to the sky, a land once alive with wild geese, deer, and elk, a rich land nurtured by the light of a constant sun—brilliant even in winter—and pure waters from the Sierra Nevada Mountains.

The Paiutes might have explained that the balance of power between Grandfather Mountain and Grandmother Valley had been corrupted when Los Angeles engineers carved canals in the earth, lined them with cement, and channeled life-giving waters to the south. They might have explained how Grandfather drew snow to the granite peaks of his shoulders and sent it as liquid crystal down his body, directing it to the valley floor, where Grandmother received it into her breasts. Trickling rivulets and gurgling creeks fanned out from her bosom, feeding the surrounding land.

What caused the Wind Gods to converge that spring? Was it exasperation at the condition of the ravaged land? Sorrow for the disappearance of its stewards, the Paiutes? Or could it have been a warning? An omen of things to come?

Coincidentally, something strange was happening in Owens Valley. Between the towns of Independence and Lone Pine, a hurriedly constructed compound of black tar-papered barracks rose in the parched desert. Surrounded by barbed-wire fencing, a square-mile area teemed with thousands of dark-headed bodies—people dressed in somber clothes, huddling in groups for protection from the raging wind. Soldiers with rifles marched around the perimeter. The American flag fluttered at the camp's entrance. What was this mysterious encampment, which sprouted up suddenly in the barren valley?

Roaming aimlessly amid piles of suitcases, bundles, and boxes, the people waited to greet newcomers arriving in buses. Their faces were Asiatic, complexions ruddy brown, warm tan, and pale ivory. Almond-shaped eyes, some almost round and others thin and narrow, watered and turned red from the stinging sand. They looked Indian. Could these be the scattered Paiutes now returning to the homeland? Was the droning "*Namu amida butsu,*" chanted by Buddhist devotees, an Indian incantation?

No. These were not Indians—although some genetic particle of the blood running through their veins may have coursed through those of Mongolian nomads who, eons ago, crossed the Aleutians from Asia and later migrated down the frozen tundra to the lush North American continent. These were Japanese Americans—immigrants—and their children and grandchildren. And Japan was at war with America.

Dressed in a dark-green *kimono*, salt-and-pepper hair swept up into a pompadour, a striking older woman stood alone, apart from the milling crowd. She faced west, towards Mount Williamson, her black onyx eyes glittering a liquid light that may have come from tears—or perhaps inspiration. Those steep peaks soaring toward heaven could have drawn from her the undisguised strength that set her apart from others. Or possibly, her eyes were simply looking west over the mountains and past the Central Valley, to the coastlands, and beyond them, to the Pacific Ocean and Japan, where she had lived until coming to America at the turn of the century.

Matsubara Sayo wondered if her life was to end in this desert. Years of surviving in America had given her an invincibility and a wisdom that allowed her to accept hardship, tragedy, and betrayal and see them simply as the underbelly of freedom. Was this prison camp another underbelly? Or was her journey in *bii koku* (the beautiful land), begun in Hiroshima thirty-nine years before, to end in this wasteland? Was she to ascend to the River of Souls in the Clouds humiliated and defeated, cast out of the country by White Ghosts, who saw all persons with Japanese blood as the enemy?

Matsubara Sayo refused that sentence. She, after all, was a Fire Horse Woman. Hadn't she defied the portents surrounding this birth sign, transforming morbid omens into qualities of courage, imagination, and splendor? Her history would not end here. Nor would she have it begin for those to be born within the barbed-wire fence. Like the *kabuki* stories she had learned in Japan—tales rivaling soap operas of the day—she knew legends would arise from this insult.

Let the winds rave, the sun scorch, frost and snow congeal. She would persevere, as she had these many years. She would harness their *kami* power and transmute it into compassion and beauty.

Thus, this proud woman welcomed the darkened sky and gritty sand blown in her ears and mouth. She stood tall and alone and imagined the sounds of clacking wood in the wind. They were the sounds of wood blocks striking each other, the brittle clacks that heralded the beginning of a drama. A legend was being born. A history begun across the ocean on a volcanic island chain called Japan had arrived at an internment camp in California's high desert country.

Teruko

Manzanar, California, 1942

Terri waits in line for the typhoid shot. She has never had an injection and dreads the needle, thin as silk thread, poised to penetrate the upper arms of internees before her. Mysterious fluid forces children to scream and adults to squint eyes. She leans back against Obāchan, finding comfort in the incense smell always emanating from her grandmother's *kimono.* Obāchan's musky smell. Pine forests, mushrooms, ancient moss. A damp smell that cools the dust-laden desert air.

"Don't look at the needle," Obāchan says in Japanese. "Turn your face away and think of its bite as an insect's kiss." Her arms drape around Terri's neck, long cotton sleeves flowing down over her granddaughter's thin chest, where developing breasts raise the *kimono*'s circular pattern into two small mounds.

"Why do we need to get these shots?" asks Terri in English. "I heard they make you sick."

Sayo understands the American language but rarely speaks it. What she does not do well she refuses to do at all. She would rather appear mute than foolish, and thus refrains from speaking pidgin, the singsong half-English most elders in camp speak. Terri honors this. Even though she hated learning Japanese when she was younger, she is now grateful for the closeness to her grandmother that comes with understanding the language. Like the silky sound of water trickling over worn rocks, Obāchan's voice smoothes the barbed edges of the unknown.

"We won't get sick," says Obāchan. "I have some good herbs I brought from home."

As the line inches forward, Terri keeps her face averted from the white cloth-covered table where two young internee volunteers are jabbing waiting arms. Exposed and vulnerable, the naked flesh surrenders to the needle's swift violation. Swab. Prick, swab.

Terri smells alcohol wafting up from the cotton and needle trays. She steals a glance at her torturer and sees lidless snake eyes gleaming from a smooth, impassive face, unlined as a *mochi* moon cake, thin lips creased in a downward curve. With horror, she watches the needle approach, unable to look away from its piercing attack. *Ping!* Surprised, she feels no pain, only a strange tickle, as if a feather has gently brushed against her. Only when cotton is pressed against the puncture does she feel a slight burning.

"Next," the volunteer says, thin lips cracking open.

She watches Obāchan roll up her *kimono* sleeve slowly and deliberately, undaunted by the young woman's coldness. Obāchan turns, lowering her eyes. With one arm extended and face tilted, she looks like a dancer in the musical stories she teaches. Terri imagines her grandmother fluttering a gold-gilt fan against her cheek and hears *shamisen* music plinking in the background. With a stamp of the foot, Obāchan commands flower petals to shower down from the yellow sky. Like purple snow, blossoms float over them, replacing the sharp medicinal smell with a sweet plum fragrance.

They leave the mess-hall area. Terri's arm now aches, and she holds it tightly with her other hand. The afternoon wind has begun to blow, churning up gusts of sand that prickle her face as they walk toward their barracks. Obāchan glides beside her, wooden *geta* skimming over the gravelly dirt road. She is slim and willowy, bending like a marsh reed in the wind. It is hard to believe she is sixty-four, a fact that gives Terri great pleasure whenever she has the chance to reveal it and witness the widened eyes of disbelief.

Obāchan is tall for a Japanese woman and has skin the color and texture of unblemished ivory. Always erect, her back as strong and straight as a temple spire, she looks taller than she is and commands respect wherever she goes. Terri has seen even the haughtiest of persons, such as the block manager, shrivel in deference to her.

Terri is sometimes embarrassed watching the reactions, suspicious glances of women—especially wives of the *issei,* the first-generation immigrants who had avoided the federal prisons and were interned in camps with their families. *Issei* men seem to like Obāchan and treat her differently from other women, even their own wives.

Terri remembers the incident with Mr. and Mrs. Tani—who live in the barracks next door—when they first came to camp. Arriving earlier, Terri's family had eagerly awaited the new neighbors, hoping they would be from Los Angeles and would bring some word from the outside. But they came from Bainbridge, near Seattle, and had no news except that the train trip was very long and their daughters threw up continuously from Washington State to California.

A few days later Mrs. Tani—who looks about Obāchan's age but is probably younger—was struggling to lift a roll of linoleum given to them by the authorities for covering the rough wooden floors. In his shiny black boots, old man Tani stood and watched with gnarled hands on hips. Obāchan, who had been observing discreetly from her small cubicle, floated over, *kimono* sleeves flapping like sails. Passing Tani-*san* without a glance, she offered help to Mrs. Tani. Rubber-boots, unaware he had been spied on, seemed shaken by her sudden appearance. He began berating his wife, shouting, "*Baka!* You are such a slow-witted donkey!" She and Obāchan stood holding the heavy linoleum roll between them, and tears welled in Mrs. Tani's eyes. Her face turned as red as the crimson lacquered bowl Obāchan keeps on her altar.

Still, Rubber-boots refrained from offering a hand. Then—just as Terri began walking over to help—she saw her grandmother swing her end of the roll like a giant baseball bat and smash it down with great force on Tani-*san*'s oversized boot!

She wheeled around, grabbing Terri's hand, and pulled her back to their barracks. Terri knew her grandmother was furious, slamming the door and causing plank walls to shake as if an earthquake had struck. She noticed her grandmother's face was pale and her hand trembled as she brushed a gray wisp of hair from her forehead.

Remaining silent, Terri sat on the floor. She knew better than to draw attention to herself until her grandmother had recovered her poise. She sat with legs folded beneath her buttocks, as she had been taught—to sit in calm repose for hours until her legs turned to wood.

Finally, Obāchan spoke. "Teruko-*chan*, you must promise something." The Japanese words tinkled like wind chimes. But Terri knew the chimes could change in an instant into clashing steel gongs, ringing with a resonance that could topple temples. She had witnessed enough of her grandmother's unpredictable explosions to know the unruffled exterior was an illusion—not so much deception as powerful strategy. Dazed, some of Obāchan's challengers never knew what hit them.

"Yes, I promise."

"Never . . . never allow a man to speak to you like that."

Allowing the words to float between them, Terri did not answer immediately. She knew Obāchan considered the silence between words more important than the words themselves.

"Why was old Rubber-boots cursing his wife?" she finally asked. "What made him so mad?"

"I humiliated him. But he couldn't attack me, so he cursed his wife!" She smiled slyly. "I don't think he expected some smashed toes!"

"How come Mrs. Tani lets him talk to her like that? She was acting like *she* did something wrong."

"She did! She allowed him to treat her like a dog!"

Then Terri felt her grandmother's intense eyes, jet black, piercing, drawing out some reflection from her own, a reflection she herself did not know. Pulled by surging currents into this mysterious and bottomless underwater world, Terri tried to enter Obāchan's vision. But she only perceived two shiny abalone pendants where her grandmother's eyes should have been.

"Remember, Rubber-boots is not a man . . . a *big* man," Obāchan said. "He needs those boots to hold him up." She began to chuckle. "He needs those boots because his feet are so small they would poke holes in the ground when he walked!" No longer able to hold back laughter, she fell over on her side, covering her face with a *kimono* sleeve.

Terri laughed heartily, imagining Tani-*san* sinking into the ground with each step, two rubber peg legs stabbing and thrusting as he walked.

Terri had learned early that Obāchan's lessons—especially the serious ones—end with images so crazily humorous they seem to make no sense. But she had long given up trying to interpret her grandmother's visions. Listening with an open mind, she anticipates the endings like the punchlines of good jokes—hardly as deep admonitions carved in stone. And almost always, they both end up laughing, laughing so hard that Terri rarely forgets what Obāchan is teaching in her unusual way.

Walking over the sandy firebreak between block 16—where their barracks is—and block 17's mess hall, they meet Hana. Terri noticed her earlier, a lone figure approaching from a distance, wavering in heat lines rising up from the dusty firebreak. Terri knows it is her mother. Not only because of her height—she is taller than Obāchan—but also because of her bearing: the way she slumps forward, curving her upper back into a tortoise shell that encircles the chest, enclosing and safeguarding a heart, Terri feels, that is heavy and sinking. She wishes her mother's posture were more like the erect, challenging one of Obāchan.

Hana's head is covered with a navy-and-white polka-dotted kerchief, knotted under her chin like a babushka. She wears tan-colored slacks, full legged with a pleat, and a white short-sleeved blouse. Tucked under a slim arm is a thick crocheted purse with wooden clasps. Terri wonders why her mother always carries a purse when there is no use for money in camp.

"Where's everyone else?" Terri asks, showing her mother the injection on her arm.

Hana inspects it silently. Terri doesn't expect much of a response. Her mother always dispenses words rather stingily, as if she were measuring crumbs from a leftover cake.

"No mark," Hana says, more to Obāchan than to Terri.

Obāchan asks, "Why are you alone? Aren't Tadao and the rest getting shots?"

"Getting them at block 22. Fewer people there. I came looking for you two." She speaks English, and her words are crisp and clean.

Terri thinks her mother should have been a nurse or doctor instead of a seamstress. She had seen movies with Claudette Colbert and Carole Lombard playing nurses, and they spoke just like her.

"Well, we're finished." Obāchan asks, "Do you want us to go back and keep you company?"

"Oh, no. I'll go home with you now and get my shot tomorrow," she answers in Japanese, turning around to walk back with them to their barracks. "They're doing it again at block 22."

As they saunter across the firebreak, a whirlwind twists toward them. The funnel of stinging sand whistles ominously, wildly spinning dried sagebrush and twigs like debris from a huge explosion. Before coming to camp, Terri never had known, or ever imagined, wind of such ferocity and fickleness. A windstorm could materialize in seconds, blowing sheets of sand that turned day into night. In the few weeks since the family's uprooting from its home on the coast, Terri had already encountered at least a dozen whirlwinds, the first one frightening her so badly that she remained inside the barracks for a whole day, refusing to leave even for meals at the mess hall.

The three figures run from the approaching funnel. Terri, grasping her aching arm, flails long, thin legs that jut from red shorts. She is in front of Obāchan, who clatters in *geta*, one hand holding down her flapping *kimono*, the other hanging on to Hana, who is bent over like a sickle, pant legs fluttering. They lurch against the wind, unable to escape its wrath. It whistles by, flinging tiny stones and bits of wood like a jilted lover spitting out bitter accusations. But as suddenly as it appeared, it dissipates. The silence is heavy, more like the pall before a storm than the aftermath of a whirlwind. Trudging toward their not-yet-familiar barracks-home, the three stride together, each with her own thoughts.

Terri does not fully understand why her family now lives in this foreign land, this glaring, naked expanse of sand, surrounded by barbed wire and rattlesnakes and Indian ghosts. She doesn't want to think about it. She just hopes Obāchan is right, and the injection, which now throbs heavily in her arm, does not give her typhoid fever, as gossip has reported it will.

Hana

Manzanar, Summer, 1942

Today is Hana's thirty-sixth birthday. She sits alone in the shaggy planked room, wondering if the family has remembered. She doesn't expect them to. After all, this internment has been a shock. Who has the calm and presence of mind to think of such frivolous things as birthdays? Even after two months, she still is disoriented. Never comfortable with intimacy, she finds the whole family living together in one room the same size as their living room back home too stifling.

She is relieved to have the room to herself for a few hours. Although the room is stuffy and hot, she declines to open the door. It's known that everyone is curious to see how others have arranged their space, and when doors are left open, it is an invitation to view the interior, even to enter and exchange pleasantries—something Hana hates to do.

Savoring the solitude, she prefers to sweat. The air reeks of vomit. Who would have thought the shots given at block 22 would make the kids sick? She hears rumors the injections were too strong, giving them a slight case of typhoid. Terri and Obāchan escaped because they received shots at block 17, where the medical team was more experienced. She nursed Mac and Carmen as well as she could, but she had no ice to cool them, no pails or basins to catch the bile they retched for days. She had to borrow pans from the mess hall, since so many were sick and other families had no receptacles to lend.

She thinks of her children. Mac, eighteen and big, bigger than most *nihon-jin*. The only son, he is restless, bored, feeling their confinement more deeply than the others. On the straw mattress, he was a vulnerable child again, allowing her to sponge his steaming body with cool wet cloths. Carmen, the middle one, suffered in silence. She reminds Hana of herself: somewhat covert, secretive, so in control of her exterior. Yet, beneath the stillness, Hana knows turbulence rumbles, threatening to crack that smooth surface. She sees it in her daughter's eyes—the way the black shimmering pools suddenly turn opaque, frozen, as if an icy wind has passed through her mind. Hana has felt her own eyes freeze and knows it is fear, fear of revealing true feelings—especially desire—that deadens the eyes.

Terri is the youngest, the long-legged brown nymph whose wild imagination often gives Hana cause to wonder if she suffers from mental illness. She knows there is no history of insanity on her mother's side. Sayo is the most intelligent person she has ever known. If there is an abnormality, she is sure it comes from her husband's family. Terri's open, inquisitive nature, her lack of inhibition make Hana uncomfortable. She does not admit to anyone, hardly to herself, that she is relieved Sayo chose Terri to be her favorite. Even now, she feels guilty that Terri lives next door with Obāchan, in a small cubicle her mother managed to wrangle from the block manager. Like everyone else, they had been assigned one room for the whole family. Sayo, who always had her own room—even when she lived with Hana—convinced the manager that the apartment next to theirs was too small for any family and thus should be used for the tea ceremony.

"The people will need *ocha-ya* to transcend the humiliation of this place," she had advised the manager, who, wanting to appear worthy of his appointment and compassionate to the needs of his block's internees, agreed with her. He then graciously allowed her the use of the space after she informed him that she herself taught the ancient art.

"But you must live there, too," he said. "The authorities would not like having an empty room used for something other than living in. They might get suspicious the space was being used for ritual . . . you know, *shinto*. And you know, *shinto* worship is forbidden."

Hana sits on the straw-stuffed mattress bed. It crackles and hisses as she shifts her sweating buttocks. Her cotton skirt is damp. A circle of perspiration has darkened the blanket under her. Blankets hang from ropes stretched across the room, providing partitions between sleeping spaces. Mushy walls. Wool walls swollen and heavy, absorbing the day's heat like a sponge. At night they release their weight in sweltering waves, undulating as if fanned by a wind. She hates the steamy nights, the feel of wool beneath her. How she yearns for smooth cool sheets. To slide her thighs and calves against their silkiness.

Suddenly she lurches toward the closed door. Flinging it open, she steps outside, squinting in the afternoon brilliance. The sun is high in a cloudless sky. Another scorching day. The door to the Tani apartment across from theirs is open. She sees a silhouette sitting back away from the opening, a slumped figure gently fanning herself. She knows it is Mrs. Tani. Sad Mrs. Tani. Hana feels sorry for her, even though everyone sees her husband as the culprit and she the long-suffering good wife, the block victim, perhaps a symbol of everyone's impotence in the face of uncontrollable forces. Old Rubber Boots struts around the block yelling at his wife and daughters, glaring disdainfully at other internees. Except Sayo. Around her he is meek, almost obsequious. Rumors fly that he has a crush on her, that perhaps the two might even be having an affair. Hana laughs at this. She knows her mother despises the old man, but wonders if she does not know the true reason why. Her mother would never act impolitely toward anyone unless there was good cause, and she has seen Sayo pointedly snub him.

Before Hana can reenter the apartment, she sees her husband round the corner, approaching with hurried steps. He seems preoccupied but manages a smile, revealing straight white teeth. With refined features and thick, curly hair, he is handsome in a Japanese movie-star way. Unlike his short and stocky mother, he is lean and of medium height, resembling his father, who immigrated from Kumamoto. His mother, Kashi-*san,* came from Kagoshima, the southernmost province of Kyūshū Island, and spoke a dialect even Sayo found difficult to understand. Her husband's people were strangers to Hana, more unknowable than the white Americans she had grown up with in Watsonville. Sometimes she feels her husband is a stranger, too.

"Hi, Tad," she says, forcing a smile. "Aren't you helping roof the new barracks in block 32?"

"I am, but I forgot my hat. This sun burns you bald-headed, it's so damned strong."

He steps inside. Hana follows, disappointed her time alone has been disrupted.

"Jesus! This place is stuffy!" His handsome face is scowling. "Did you close the door again, Hana?"

"No," she lies. "It's been open since lunch, since you all left."

"It stinks like puke. I can't figure out why you always keep the goddamned door shut." His voice is loud. "Keep the door open, and air this fucking place out!"

She remains silent, sensing he is irritated about something else and has chosen to take it out on her. After twenty years of marriage, she has learned to make herself small and unnoticed when he is frustrated. He is the oldest son, and as Kashi-*san* and tradition had decreed, the first-born male can do no wrong. He must be indulged, placated, and praised. Then harmony prevails in the home. It was up to her to see that his needs were met, and it was her duty to know without his having to say what those needs were.

He rummages in the closet, which is a stack of large boxes constructed from packing crates he collected when the camp hospital was being built. Finding a heavy canvas hat, he seems to relax. He sits on their bed, a double-sized one they have created by pushing two cots together. He motions for her to join him. Obediently, she sits down, almost wishing he were still angry. She knows he wants to make love. It's too hot, and she had been hoping for this time by herself. Privacy in camp is almost nonexistent. The drab olive blankets provide slim partitions between sleeping spaces and hardly cloak the sounds of constrained lovemaking, confined to the middle of the night when others sleep—or during a chance time in the day when the apartment is empty.

He strokes her arm. She is perspiring, and his palm glides over the hairless skin.

"What if someone comes home?" she asks, feeling only the debilitating heat, which makes her body soggy.

"I'll lock the door." He jumps up and latches it.

"Don't you think it's too hot . . . on these wool blankets?" she murmurs lamely, smoothing the blanket-covered mattress.

"We'll do it on the floor." He is now fully aroused and has begun to shed his clothes. "Hurry, take off your dress."

She removes her blouse and skirt. She wears no brassiere.

"Here . . . on this cool spot on the floor." He has removed his shorts and now lies naked on the linoleum, his penis taut and pointing upward like a giant shaking finger reminding Hana of her duty.

She takes off her underpants and lies beside him. The linoleum is slick and cool.

"See, it's not so hot down here." His hands explore her body.

Surprised, she feels herself aroused by the linoleum's oily slipperiness under her buttocks and thighs, more stimulating than Tad's stroking hands. He is sweating now, emitting a familiar salty smell.

Sayo's voice booms outside. "Would you care to have tea with me, Tani-*san?*"

Tad mounts Hana immediately. Disquieted by her mother's voice, she can barely respond to his furtiveness. But he is determined not to be denied this moment. His excitement builds to its explosive peak. Hana feels his pounding heart against her breasts, relieved he has climaxed so swiftly.

They get dressed. His mood now cheerful, he puts on the canvas hat, adjusting the brim before the small, round mirror on the wall.

"Not so bad, this hat. The other guys wear baseball caps. But this looks a little more dressy, don't you think?" He tries to be funny, pulling the brim down over his ears.

Hana unlatches the door, hoping her mother and Mrs. Tani are gone. The sandy space between barracks is empty, and the shadowy figure has disappeared from the Tani apartment, whose door remains open. Tad shouts back to Hana as he heads for block 32, "See you at the mess hall for dinner!"

Her spirits lift. If none of the kids return, she will have at least three hours to herself. She reenters the apartment, now heavy with a sweaty pungence, and closes the door.

American soldier with Naomi Uemoto, sister, Hiroshima, 1950

MARY YUKARI WATERS

Aftermath

In Imamiya Park the boys are playing dodge ball, a new American game. Behind them tall poplars rise up through the low-lying dusk, intercepting the last of the sun's rays, which dazzle the leaves with white and gold.

Makiko can hardly believe her son, Toshi, belongs with these older boys. Seven years old! Once, his growth had seemed commensurate with the passage of time. These last few years, however, with the war and surrender, the changes have come too fast, skimming her consciousness like pebbles skipped over water.

Makiko is grateful the war is over. But she cannot ignore a nagging sense that Japan's surrender has spawned a new threat—one more subtle, more diffuse. She can barely articulate it, even to herself; feels unmoored, buffeted among invisible forces surging all around her. As if caught up in these energies, her son's thin body is rapidly lengthening. Look! Within that circle in the dirt he is dodging, he is feinting; his body twists with an unfamiliar grace, foreshadowing that of a young man.

Toshi's growth is abetted by a new lunch program at school that is subsidized by the American government, which has switched, with dizzying speed, from enemy to ally. Each day her son comes home with alien food in his stomach: bread, cheese, bottled milk. Last week, in the pocket of his shorts, Makiko found a cube of condensed peanut butter—an American dessert, Toshi explained—which he had meant to save for later. It was coated with lint from his pocket, which he brushed off, ignoring her plea to "get rid of that dirty thing."

And each day, Toshi comes home with questions she cannot answer: Who was Magellan? How do you say "My name is Toshi" in English? How do you play baseball?

Makiko shows him the ball games her own mother taught her. She bounces an imaginary ball, chanting a ditty passed down from the Edo period:

yellow topknots
of the Portuguese wives

spiraled like seashells
and stuck atop their heads

hold one up, to your ear
shake it up and down

a little shrunken brain
is rattling inside

In the old days, she tells him, they used to put something inside the rubber balls—maybe a scrap of iron, she wasn't sure—that made a rattling noise. Toshi, too old now for this sort of amusement, sighs with impatience.

Just four years ago, Toshi's head had been too big for his body—endearingly out of proportion, like the head of a stuffed animal. Even then he had a manly, square-jawed face, not unlike that of a certain city-council candidate appearing on election posters at the time. Her husband, Yoshitsune, nicknamed his son "Mr. Magistrate." Before going off to war, Yoshitsune had developed a little routine with their son. "*Oi,* Toshi! Are you a man?" Yoshitsune would prompt in his droll tone, using the word *otoko,* with its connotations of male bravery, strength, and honor. He would ask this question several times a day, often before neighbors and friends.

"*Hai,* Father! I am a man!" little Toshi would cry, stiffening at soldierly attention as he had been coached, trembling with eagerness to please. His short legs, splayed out from the knees as if buckling under the weight of his head, were still dimpled with baby fat.

"*Maaa!* An excellent, manly answer!" the grownups praised, through peals of laughter.

Makiko had laughed, too, a faint constriction in her throat, for Yoshitsune had remarked to her, "When I'm out fighting in the Pacific, that's how I'm going to remember him." After that, she began watching their child closely, trying to memorize what Yoshitsune was memorizing. Later, when her husband was gone, it comforted her to think that the same images swam in both their minds at night. Even today, Toshi's three-year-old figure is vivid in her mind. On the other hand, she has not fully absorbed the war years, still shrinks from those memories and all that has followed.

Foreigners, for instance, are now a familiar sight. American army jeeps with beefy red arms dangling out the windows roar down Kagane Boulevard, the main thoroughfare just east of Toshi's school. "Keep your young women indoors," the neighbors say. Occasionally, Makiko has seen a soldier offering chocolates or peanuts to little children, squatting down to their level, holding out the treat—it seems to her they all have hairy arms—as if to a timid cat. Just yesterday Toshi came home, smiling broadly and carrying chocolates—not one square but three. Bile had surged up in Makiko's throat, and before she knew it, she had struck them right out of his hand and onto the kitchen floor. "How could you?!" she choked as Toshi, stunned, burst into sobs. "How could you?! Those men killed your *father!*"

This evening, Makiko has come to the park with a small box of caramels, bought on the black market with some of the money she was hoarding to buy winter yarn. "In the future," she will tell him, "if you want something so badly, you come to me. *Ne?* Not to them."

On a bench in the toddlers' section, now deserted, she waits for her son to finish his game with the other boys. All the other mothers have gone home to cook dinner. The playground equipment has not been maintained since the beginning of the war. The swing set is peeling with rust; the freestanding animals—the ram, the pig, the rooster—have broken-down springs, and their carnival paint has washed away, exposing more rusted steel.

Ara maaa! Her Toshi has finally been hit! Makiko feels a mother's pang. He is crossing the line to the other side now, carrying the ball. Makiko notes the ease with which the fallen one seems to switch roles in this game, heaving the ball at his former teammates without the slightest trace of disloyalty.

This year, Makiko is allowing Toshi to light the incense each evening before the family altar. He seems to enjoy prayer time much more now that he can use matches. She also regularly changes which photograph of her husband is displayed beside the miniature gong. This month's photograph shows Yoshitsune in a cotton *yukata,* smoking under the ginkgo tree in the garden. Sometimes, in place of a photograph, she displays an old letter or one of his silk scent bags, still fragrant after a bit of massaging. To keep Toshi interested, Makiko presents his father in the light of constant renewal.

"Just talk to him inside your mind," she tells her son. "He wants to know what you're learning in school, what games you're playing. Just like any other father, *ne?* Don't leave him behind, don't ignore him, just because he's dead." She wonders if Toshi secretly considers his father a burden, making demands from the altar, like a cripple from a wheelchair.

"Your father's very handsome in this picture, *ne?*" she says tonight. Within the lacquered frame, her son's father glances up from lighting a cigarette, a bemused half smile on his face, as if he is waiting to make a wry comment.

Toshi nods absently. Frowning, he slashes at the matchbox with the expert flourish of a second-grade boy. The match rips into flames.

"Answer properly! You're not a little baby anymore."

"*Hai,* Mother." Toshi sighs with a weary, accommodating air, squaring his shoulders in a semblance of respectful attention. Makiko remembers with sorrow the big head, the splayed legs of her baby boy.

It amazes her that Toshi has no memory of the routine he once performed with his father. "What *do* you remember of him?" she prods every so often, hoping to dislodge some new memory. But all that Toshi remembers of his father is being carried on one arm before a sunny window.

"*Maaa,* what a wonderful memory!" Makiko encourages him each time. "It must have been a very happy moment!"

When would this have taken place: which year, which month? Would even Yoshitsune have remembered it, this throwaway moment that, inexplicably, has outlasted all the others in their son's mind? She tries conjuring it up, as if the memory is her own. For some reason she imagines autumn, the season Yoshitsune sailed away: October 1942. How the afternoon sun would seep in through the nursery window, golden, almost amber, advancing with the viscous quality of Hiezan honey or of nostalgia, overtaking sluggish dust motes and even sound. She wishes Toshi could remember the old view from that upstairs window: a sea of gray tiled roofs drowsing in the autumn haze, as yet unravaged by the fires of war.

"I'm done," Toshi says.

"What! Already? Are you sure?"

"*Hai,* Mother." Already heading for the dining room, where supper lies waiting on the low table, he slides back the *shoji* door in such a hurry that it grates on the grooves. Makiko considers calling him back—his prayers are getting shorter and shorter—but the incident with the chocolates is still too recent for another reprimand.

She follows him into the dining room. "A man who forgets his past," she quotes as she scoops rice into his bowl, "stays at the level of an animal." Toshi meets her eyes with a guilty, resentful glance. "Go on," she says blandly, "eat it while it's hot."

Toshi falls to. In order to supplement their meager rice ration, Makiko continues to mix in chopped *kabura* radishes—which at least resemble rice in color—as she did during the war. Sometimes she switches to chopped turnips. At first, before the rationing became strict, Toshi would hunch over his rice bowl with his chopsticks, fastidiously picking out one bit of vegetable after another and discarding it on another plate. Now, he eats with gusto. It cuts her, the things he has grown used to. As a grown man he will reminisce over all the wrong things, things that should never have been a part of his childhood: this shameful pauper food; a block of peanut paste covered with lint; enemy soldiers amusing themselves by tossing chocolate and peanuts to children.

Later, Toshi ventures a question. Makiko has noticed that nighttime—the black emptiness outside, the hovering silence—still cows him a little, stripping him of his daytime cockiness. After his goodnight bow, Toshi remains kneeling on the *tatami* floor. He says, "I was thinking, Mama, about how I'm seven—and how I only remember things that happened after I was three. So that means I've forgotten a whole half of my life—right?"

"That's right," Makiko says. He is looking up at her, his brows puckered in a look of doleful concentration, which reminds her of his younger days. "But it's perfectly normal, Toshi-*kun.* It's to be expected."

He is still thinking. "So when I get older," he says, "am I going to keep on forgetting? Am I going to forget you, too?"

Makiko reaches out and strokes his prickly crewcut. "From this age on," she says, "you'll remember everything, Toshi-*kun.* Nothing more will ever be lost."

In the middle of the night, Makiko awakens from a dream in which Yoshitsune is hitting her with a fly swatter. She lies paralyzed under her *futon,* outrage buzzing in her chest. Details from the dream wash back into her mind: Yoshitsune's smile, distant and amused; the insolent way he wielded the swatter, as if she were hardly worth the effort.

A blue sheet of moonlight, slipping in through the space between two sliding panels, glows in the dark.

In the first year or two after his death, this sort of thing would happen often, and not always in the form of dreams. There were times—but hardly ever anymore; why tonight?—when, in the middle of washing the dishes or sweeping the alley, some small injustice from her past, long forgotten, would rise up in her mind, blocking out all else till her heart beat hard and fast. Like that time, scarcely a month after their wedding, when Yoshitsune had run into his old girlfriend at Nanjin Station and made such a fuss: his absurd, rapt gaze; the intimate timbre of his voice as he inquired after her welfare.

And there was the time—the only time in their entire marriage—when Yoshitsune had grabbed Makiko by the shoulders and shaken her hard. He'd let go immediately, but not before she had felt the anger in his powerful hands and her throat had choked up with fear. That, too, was early on in the marriage, before Makiko learned to tolerate his sending sizable sums of money to his mother each month.

What is to be done with such memories?

They get scattered, left behind. Over the past few years, more pleasant recollections have taken the lead, informing all the rest, like a flock of birds, heading as one body along an altered course of nostalgia.

She has tried so hard to remain true to the past. But the weight of her need must have been too great: her need to be comforted, her need to provide a legacy for a small, fatherless boy. Tonight she senses how far beneath the surface her own past has sunk, its outline distorted by deceptively clear waters.

Toshi has been counting the days till Tanabata Day. A small festival is being held at the riverbank—the first since the war. It will be a meager affair, of course, nothing like it used to be: no goldfish scooping, no *soba* noodles, no fancy fireworks. However, according to the housewives at the open-air market, there will be a limited number of sparklers—the nicest kind, Makiko tells her son—and traditional corn grilled with *shoyu,* which can be purchased out of each family's food allowance.

Because of an after-dark incident near Kubota Temple involving an American soldier and a young girl, Makiko's younger brother has come by this evening to accompany them to the festival. Noboru is a second-year student at the local university.

"*Ne,* Big Sister! Are you ready yet?" he keeps calling from the living room. Makiko is inspecting Toshi's nails and the back of his collar.

"Big Sister," Noboru says, looking up as Makiko finally appears in the doorway, "your house is too immaculate. I get nervous every time I come here!" He is sitting stiffly on a floor cushion, sipping homemade persimmon tea.

"Well," Makiko answers, "I hate dirt." She has switched, like most women, to Western dresses—they require less fabric—but it makes her irritable, having to expose her bare calves in public. She tugs down her knee-length dress.

"*Aaa,*" says young Noboru from his floor cushion, "but I, for one, am fascinated by it. The idea of it, I mean. What's that old saying—'Nothing grows in a sterile pond'? Just think, Big Sister, of the things that come out of dirty water. A lotus, for example. Or a pearl. Just think: a pearl's nothing more than a grain of dirt covered up by an oyster! And life itself, Big Sister, billions of years ago—emerging from the primordial muck!"

"*Maa maa,* Nobo-*kun.*" She sighs, double-checking her handbag for coin purse, ration tickets, and handkerchief. "You seem to be learning some very interesting concepts at the university."

Toshi is waiting by the front door in shorts and a collared shirt, impatiently pulling the door open and then shut, open and then shut.

Finally, they are on their way, strolling down the narrow alley in the still, muggy evening. The setting sun angles down on the east side of the alley, casting a pink and orange glow on the charred wooden lattices, where shadows stretch, like the long heads of snails, from the slightest of protrusions. In the shadowed side of the alley, one of the bucktoothed Kimura daughters ladles water from a bucket onto the asphalt around her door, pausing, with a good-evening bow, to let them pass. The water, colliding with warm asphalt, has released a smell of many layers: asphalt, earth, scorched wood, tangy dragon's beard moss over a mellower base of tree foliage; prayer incense and *tatami* straw, coming from the Kimuras' half-open door; and mixed in with it all, some scent far back from Makiko's own childhood that falls just short of definition.

"We Japanese," Noboru is saying, "must reinvent ourselves. We must change to fit the modern world. We mustn't remain an occupied nation." He talks of the new constitution, of the new trade agreements. Makiko has little knowledge of politics. She is amused—disquieted, too—by this academic young man, who before the war was a mere boy loping past her window with a butterfly net over his shoulder.

"Fundamental shifts . . . ," Noboru is saying, ". . . outdated pyramidal structures." He has just begun wearing hair pomade with an acrid metallic scent. It seems to suggest fervor, fundamental shifts.

"Toshi-*kun!*" Makiko calls. "Don't go too far." The boy stops running. He walks, taking each new step in exaggerated slow motion.

"So much change!" she says to Noboru as she tugs at her cotton dress. "And so fast. Other countries had centuries to do it in."

"*Sō, sō,* Big Sister!" Noboru says. "*Sō, sō.* But we have no choice—that's a fact. You jettison from a sinking ship if you want to survive."

The pair approach Mr. Watanabe watering his potted morning glories in the twilight. Holding his watering can in one hand, the old man gives them a genteel bow over his cane. "Yoshitsune-*san,*" he murmurs politely, "Makiko-*san.*" He then turns back to his morning glories, bending over them with the tenderness of a mother with a newborn.

"Poor Watanabe-*san, ne?*" Noboru whispers. "He gets more and more confused every time we see him."

Yes, poor Mr. Watanabe, Makiko thinks. Bit by bit he is being pulled back in, like a slowing planet, toward some core, some necessary center of his past. Laden with memory, his mind will never catch up to Noboru's new constitution or those trade agreements, or even the implications of that billboard with English characters—instructions for arriving soldiers? —rising above the blackened rooftops and blocking his view of the Hiezan hills.

Oddly, Mr. Watanabe's greeting has triggered a memory from the past: Makiko is strolling with Yoshitsune on a summer evening. For one heartbeat she experiences exactly how things used to be—their commonplace existence, before later events imposed their nostalgia—with a stab of physical recognition that is indefinable, impossible to call up again. Then it is gone, like the gleam of a fish, having stirred up all the waters around her.

They walk on in silence. "Toshi-*kun!*" she calls out again. "Slow down." Toshi pauses, waiting for them; he swings at the air with an imaginary bat. *"Striku! Striku!"* he hisses.

It occurs to Makiko how artificial this war has been, suspending people in the same, unsustainable state of solidarity. For a while, everyone had clung together in the bomb shelter off Nijiya Street, thinking the same thoughts, breathing in the same damp earth and the same warm, uneasy currents made by bodies at close range. But that is over now.

Makiko thinks of her future. She is still full of life and momentum. There is no doubt that she will pass through this period and into whatever lies beyond it, but at a gradually slowing pace; a part of her, she knows, will lag behind in the honeyed light of pre-war years.

"Toshi-*kun!*" she cries. "Wait!" Her son is racing ahead, his long shadow sweeping the sun-lit fence as sparrows flutter up from charred palings.

Makiko stands out on the veranda, fanning herself with a paper *uchiwa.* Toshi is already asleep. The night garden is muggy; the mosquitoes are out in full force. She can hear their ominous whine from the hydrangea bush, in between the rasping of crickets, but they no longer target her as they did in her youth. She is thinner now, her skin harder from the sun, her blood watered down from all the rationing.

It was a wonderful festival. Shadowy adults bent over their children, helping them to hold sparklers over the glassy water. The sparklers sputtered softly in the dark, shedding white flakes of light. Makiko had watched from a distance; Toshi was old enough, he had insisted, to do it by himself. She had remarked to Noboru how there is something in everyone that responds to fireworks: so fleeting, so lovely in the dark.

It was a fine night for Toshi. "This corn is so *good, ne,* Mama?" he kept saying, looking up from his rationed four centimeters of corncob. "This sure tastes *good, ne?*" The joy on his face, caught in the glow of red paper lanterns, brought a lump to her throat.

Tonight there is a full moon. Earlier, at dusk, it was opaque and insubstantial. Now, through shifting moisture in the air, it glows bright and strong, awash with light.

For Makiko, the festival owed its luster to all that lay beneath, to all those other evenings of her life and their lingering phosphorescence. Which long-ago evenings exactly? They are slowly losing shape, merging together in her consciousness.

Perhaps Toshi will remember this night. Perhaps it will rise up again once he is grown. Some smell, some glint of light will bring texture and emotion to a future summer evening. As will his memory of praying before his father's picture or being carried by his father before an open window.

Francis and Irene Haar, with
Mount Fuji in background, 1940

FRANCIS AND IRENE HAAR

A Lifetime of Images: The War Years in Japan

A year and a half after our arrival in Japan, war suddenly caught up with us. All foreigners were ordered to leave Tokyo. Nationals belonging to the Allies had to leave Japan or be interned in a prison camp near Kōbe. Those from Nazi Germany and Fascist Italy were sent to a place near Mount Fuji. Because Hungary was not considered an enemy nation Irene and I, with our two babies, were sent to the resort town of Karuizawa along with citizens of other neutral nations, including Swiss, Turks, and South Americans. Our first child, Thomas, had been born in 1941, and our second child, Veronica, was born the following year. We evacuated to Karuizawa in the spring of 1943.

Karuizawa is a town in the mountains northwest of Tokyo, a plush summer vacation spot popular both with wealthy Japanese and foreigners. We had been there twice before to escape the midsummer heat in Tokyo. We managed to rent the same house we had used before, but this time we had to prepare for the long, cold winter. Although it was a two-story house, basically we lived in one small room on the first floor, which was heated by a small wood-burning stove that we fed with dry branches collected from the nearby woods.

We were fortunate to have a Japanese maid, who helped take care of the children while Irene and I gathered firewood and did the domestic chores necessary to survive. Shizuko had been with us in Tokyo, but when war broke out and we had to leave the capital, we regretfully told her we would have to let her go because we would no longer have an income to pay her wages. She dismissed the idea and insisted she would stay with us. Because she had worked for us so long, she felt she was part of the family. Shizuko stayed with us in Karuizawa through three and a half years of hardship, until the end of the war.

Once the youth of Japan had been mobilized, food was rationed and soon became scarce. We received about a pound of bread a week for the whole family. Our main problem was finding a way to get milk for the children and food for us. I made a small vegetable garden beside the house, but this did not yield enough to get us through the long winter months. Fortunately, a small stream ran near our house with a lot of watercress growing in it, and this is what saved us, as it grew even in wintertime. Irene used it

Irene Haar holding son, Thomas, Karuizawa, Japan, circa 1941
Photograph by Francis Haar

in many ingenious ways—sautéed in soup, or raw as a salad. We lived almost on watercress alone.

We managed to buy from a Japanese farmer a milking goat, which we fed with cut branches and leftovers from the kitchen. Irene milked it daily for the two young children, and for a while things seemed to improve.

We had our goat mated, and it gave birth to one kid. In the summer, when the kid was big enough to eat leaves, I would cut branches for both of them. One day, I tethered the kid with a rope around its neck at the side of the stream, where it could eat the grass growing there. A couple of hours later, when I went back to check on it, I was shocked to discover the kid had slipped into the stream and hung itself on the rope. When I touched it, it was motionless but still warm. I ran back to the kitchen, picked up a sharp knife, returned to the stream, and cut the throat of the small creature to let the blood out. This way we could eat meat, something we hadn't tasted for months. After the hide was dried, I made boots for both of our children. The soles were made from a piece of wooden board. We had to be inventive in those limited circumstances.

Money lost its value. We could only exchange our belongings for food with farmers at neighboring villages. In this manner we got two goats and some rabbits and chickens. The farmer showed me how to feed and take care of the livestock and how to milk the milking goat. This was something new to me, and I was nervous and clumsy at first; fortunately, the goat was patient, and after a few attempts, I succeeded. I was so proud of myself. Goat's milk was very nourishing but had a peculiar strong odor and flavor, and I had to dilute it for our children. I even made some really good cheese from it.

Winter in Karuizawa was long and cold, which made it difficult to grow vegetables throughout the year. Fortunately, there was a small stream nearby where watercress grew—a valuable food, which I used in many ways. I also became a diligent follower of horses, in order to gather their manure to enrich the vegetable garden.

We practically lived in one room in the winter, the room with the stove. We warmed up next to the stove and ran upstairs to bed. For our two small children, we made boots from goatskin and coats from rabbit fur. We got our nutrition from miso *(soybean paste), which was on our menu three times a day. Sometimes I traveled to faraway villages for apples, walnuts, and flour in exchange for clothing. We managed to survive.*

The incident with the goat was a real tragedy for us, since it was a milking goat. Eventually, Francis became ill from malnutrition and was bedridden. I had to work and shop for food. I remember one bitter cold winter morning standing in line at five o'clock at the butcher shop to get some soup bones. We were all numb from the cold. All of a sudden, the woman in front of me just turned and walked away. As I approached the counter, I found out the reason why: the butcher had run out of soup bones.

Real hardship came after two years, when our reserves of money ran out. There was only one thing left to do—barter our possessions for food from Japanese farmers. Our clothing was reduced to a minimum (by the end of the war, I owned only one pair of pants and one shirt). Next, we exchanged one of my cameras for a large sack of potatoes and some vegetables. It wasn't such a big sacrifice because I couldn't use the camera anyway. As a foreign photographer, I was considered a potential spy, and we were constantly watched by the Kempeitai, the military police.

But shortage of food had its effect. After about three years in Karuizawa, an inflammation developed all over my body, a sure sign of malnutrition. The doctor in our community was unable to help me, and I became weaker and weaker until I had no choice but to stay in bed, where I remained for several months. Tokyo was being bombed, and while I was bedridden I often thought about the sacks of photo negatives in my studio there. I was too weak to retrieve them, however, and lost many of my irreplaceable old negatives and glass plates when the studio was destroyed by the bombing.

Soon after the Tokyo bombing, we received an order from the police saying we would no longer be allowed to communicate with Japanese people. We weren't even allowed to greet each other on the street. Our neighbor used to collect the garbage from her kitchen and bring it over to us to feed our goats. The day after the new restriction was introduced, she left her container on the street in front of our house instead of bringing it to our door. An hour later, the military police were at her house, warning her to stop this kind of contact with foreigners or face imprisonment. We were watched all the time.

Although we didn't really understand the reason for this restriction, we guessed it had been caused by events on the war front. The military police wanted to prevent the Japanese from hearing any rumors about the course of the war.

We could hear the bombs exploding nearby, night and day. The earth was shaking and everybody was scared. The windows were covered with black paper to prevent any light from shining out at night. No one seemed to know what was happening. There was a rumor that the Americans would invade Japan and everyone should fight with whatever they could lay their hands on or escape to the mountains. We filled our backpacks with a few cans of food, rolled up blankets, and put on as many layers of clothing as we could and waited—but for what, we did not know.

A complete stillness awoke us on the morning of 15 August [1945], a beautifully bright sunny day. It was so still that it was frightening. About ten o'clock that morning a good friend from the Swiss Embassy came running into our garden. Her face was flushed and tears were rolling down her cheeks. She hugged me and whispered into my ear, "The war is over, the war is over, MacArthur is in the Philippines!" Before I could say anything, off she went, carrying the good news to other friends.

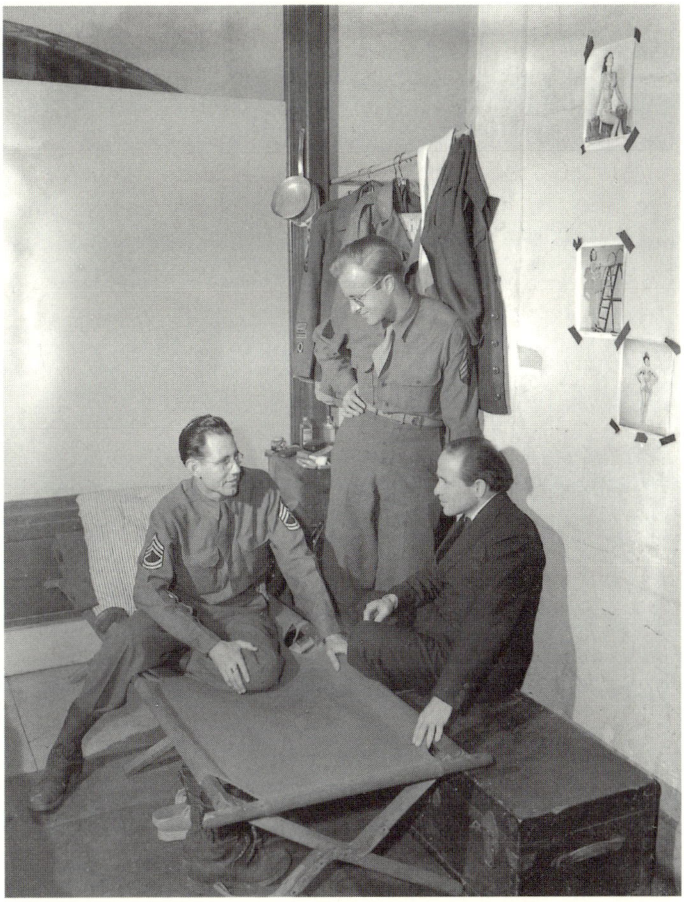

Francis Haar (far right) with staff of
Yank *magazine, Japan, 1945*

Then the police went around with loudspeakers telling everyone to listen to the radio at noon to hear the Emperor speak to the nation. When the time came, our maid went to the neighbors' to listen to the radio. When she returned, she was crying. "Hiroshima and Nagasaki were bombed and are in ruins. Japan has surrendered!"

The surrender was a great shock for the Japanese people. It was the first military defeat they had experienced in the country's long history. Several military officers committed suicide, unable to accept the humiliation. For us, however, it meant the end of our misery, and we were overwhelmed with joy. From this time on, all the restrictions we had been forced to face disappeared. We heard from a foreign diplomat that the Americans would be arriving in Japan. In a few weeks, Foreign Minister Shigemitsu signed the surrender document and a peace treaty with General MacArthur aboard the battleship *Missouri.*

Some foreigners, including one of our friends, managed to obtain special permission to visit Tokyo. We waited anxiously for his return to hear news of what happened to Tokyo. He returned very late at night, utterly exhausted from the trip. "The train was so crowded that I could barely stand," he began in an excited voice. "The city was in ruins except for some large buildings." As he was speaking, he began to shake out the contents of his backpack. "The large buildings are being taken over by the American Occupation Forces as headquarters." Out poured chewing gum, cube sugar, K-rations, a can of ham, and even a couple bars of chocolate. We couldn't believe the things we were seeing.

In a few days, American jeeps were running on the roads. Two American soldiers were guided to our home by the English-speaking young son of a family friend of ours. They were correspondents for the military magazine Yank, *and they were looking for a photographer to work with them. They brought with them some K-rations, and we had a festive dinner together. The baked beans and chopped ham tasted heavenly. Francis got the job, and the two Americans asked him to join them in Tokyo. They became instant friends.*

Within a week or so, I felt strong enough to go down to Tokyo with the American reporters. There I was examined by an American doctor, who attributed the inflammation on my body to malnourishment and lack of vitamins. He gave me some injections and pills and saw to it that I received good, nutritious food. Three weeks later, I was ready to begin work.

DONALD RICHIE

from *Japan Journals*

1947

It was winter—cold, crisp, and clear—and Mount Fuji stood sharp on the horizon, growing purple, then indigo in the fading light. I was standing at the main crossing at Ginza 4-*chōme*.

There was no smoke because there were few factories, no fumes because the few cars were charcoal-burning. Fuji looked much as it had for Hokusai and Hiroshige.

Then the sky darkened and the stars appeared—bright, near. The horizon stayed white in the winter light after the sun had vanished and Fuji had turned a solid black.

The Ginza was illuminated by acetylene torches of the night stalls and by the passing headlights of Occupation jeeps and trucks. In the darkness, Fuji remained visible, a jagged shadow fading into the winter night.

Most of the buildings were cinder. It was a wasteland. And from the crossing, Japan's familiar peak was seen as it had not been seen since Edo times and as it would not be again until another catastrophe.

At the crossing, there were only two large buildings still standing. One was the Ginza branch of Mitsukoshi Department Store. But it was gutted, hit by a firebomb, and even the window frames had been twisted by the heat. Across the street was the white stone Hattori Building with its clock tower. It was much as it had always been, once the clock itself was repaired. With its curved front window, cornices, and pediments, it remained from the prewar Ginza.

South there was not much, nor east, where the standing ruins of the burned-out Kabukiza constituted the view. West were the round, red, drumlike Nichigeki and the Asahi Building. At Hibiya there were a few buildings, some theaters. There were the Sanshin Building, still standing; the Asahi Saimei Building, where the military-police offices were; the Tokyo Takarazuka Theater, then called the Ernie Pyle; and the Hibiya and Yurakuza motion picture theaters—these last destroyed later, as was so much else, by peace, affluence, and the high price of land.

The view was block after block of rubble. The wooden buildings had not survived. The buildings that still stood were made of stone or brick. Yet already among these large, fire-blackened structures, there was the yellow sheen of new wood. Reconstruction was under way.

It was the first month of 1947, over a year after the end of the Pacific War.

People were still returning to the city. During its destruction, many had left, and now it seemed that every day more returned.

During my cold, late-afternoon Ginza stroll, walking down to view Fuji in the five-thirty twilight of midwinter, I saw numerous people shuffling along the pavement. But there was no laughter and little conversation. One somehow expected festivity—there were so many people shambling along or lounging about. But there was none. And instead of shop windows there were the street stalls, each illuminated by its gas torch.

Everything was being sold—the products of a dead civilization. There were wartime medals and egret-feather tiaras and top hats and beaded handbags. There were bridles and bits and damascene cufflinks. There were ancient brocades and pieces of calligraphy, battered woodblock prints and old framed photographs. Everything was for sale—or for barter.

And around the stalls, the people. Uniforms were still everywhere—black student uniforms, army uniforms; young men wearing their forage caps, or their army boots, or their winter-issue overcoats. Others were in padded *kimono,* draped with scarves. Women still wore *kimono* or the *monpei* trousers used for farm work which in the cities constituted something like wartime dress. And many wore face masks because of winter colds. And everyone was out of fashion. In peacetime they were still dressed for war.

The crowd was very quiet. The only sound was the scuffling of boots, shoes, wooden sandals. That and the noises of the merchandise being picked up, turned over, and put down. The merchants made no attempt to sell. They sat and looked, perhaps smoking a pinch of tobacco in a long-stemmed brass pipe, staring at the black throng passing in the darkness of an early evening.

When I remember faces, I cannot remember anyone talking. I remember the quiet and the glances. A year had passed since the unthinkable had occurred, and the unendurable was still being endured. I saw a populace yet in shock.

There was an uncomprehending look in the eyes. It was a look one sometimes still sees in the eyes of children or the very ill.

And in the eyes of convalescents as well. People recuperating are people keeping quiet. Yet compared to the clatter and chatter of forty-four years later—today—Tokyo was a city of the dead. So many had been killed in the city. So many had been burned or boiled in the firebomb raids of 1945. The survivors remembered.

But at the same time, the dead were being forgotten—as they must be if we are to go on living. Every day the crowds got larger, the eyes grew brighter.

I remember a small newsstand on the Ginza run by a tough, smiling country woman. An army helmet was displayed and under it a similar-looking pot. The sign read: WE WILL TURN YOUR OLD HELMET INTO A NEW COOKING POT FOR ONLY SEVEN YEN.

I still have a photograph taken earlier in the subway corridors of Ueno Station. There, sitting or lying down, are some of the thousands of the hungry homeless. Men, women, a few children, on straw matting or on the bare concrete.

They are being inspected by two bespectacled policemen wearing mouth masks. Many of the people are dirty, and all wear remnants of what they had owned during the war—cracked shoes, torn blouses, buttonless shirts, battered hats. The most surprising thing about the picture, however, is that it is not sad.

Everyone in it is smiling—everyone except the policemen, and maybe they are as well beneath their masks. *Smile for the camera, make a good impression, best foot forward.* Even in the depths of national poverty, everyone remembered this.

Up above, on the plaza-terrace, around the statue of Takamori Saigo, there were many more, sitting on benches and embankments, some with a newspaper, some with nothing at all—all of them waiting. Waiting, it seemed, for this too to pass so that they could get on with their lives. They were like people in a train station.

The crowd had killed the grass by sitting, squatting, lying on it over the weeks and the months. And many had come and gone. The pedestal of Saigo's statue was plastered with hand-printed notices:

WATANABE NORIKO—YOUR MOTHER WAITS HERE
EVERY DAY FROM ONE TO FIVE
GRANDMOTHER KUMAGAI—SHIRO AND TETSUKO HAVE GONE TO
UNCLE SATO'S IN AOMORI—PLEASE COME
SURUKI TETSURO—YOUR FATHER IS SITTING ON THE STAIRCASE
TO THE LEFT—IF YOU SEE THIS PLEASE COME

The rains and the snows washed them away, and new ones were put up. They were like the votive messages left at shrines to invoke supernatural aid. Answered or not, they were left there until rained away or covered by notices of later misfortunes.

Tokyo back then was poor. Poverty gave it the Asian look, an appearance that prewar Japan had been at some pains to avoid. But then Asia had moved closer. And with it a kind of natural nudity.

In summer, a part of the populace was near naked. There were no more laws against going naked and so people naturally did. Being naked is more comfortable than being clothed.

I used to stand on the street corners—not perhaps those of Ginza, but certainly those of Ueno and Asakusa—and gaze at the shapely limbs, the proud bearings, the curves and angles of all this beautiful bare skin. And some not so beautiful, to be sure. Malnutrition is no beauty aid.

When people are naked, one of two things can occur. The viewer can become excited, feel sexy, and tend to view the nude as an object of desire. Or this same viewer may view the human race, finally, as it is—innocent, vulnerable, unknowing, and beautiful in that general way that insists upon the humanity of each person.

Standing on the corner I felt both, alternately, depending upon how I had slept, what had happened that day—even, for all I know, what I had eaten. But only one at a time. One cannot experience such disparities simultaneously.

I remember Tokyo moving slowly in front of me, fittingly and suitably undressed in the hot summer night, showing a beauty and innocence and naturalness that allowed me to say to myself: "Ah, this is Asia."

By then the rickshaws were gone, but the pedicabs—bicycled rickshaws introduced late into Japan—were not. These were like large tricycles. In front was a man or boy astride his bike. At the back was the two-wheeled double seat in which one reclined while being pedaled about.

They were much more commonly seen than taxis, though the taxis were more noticeable because they carried large, round tanks at the rear that in the cold of winter emitted clouds of smoke and steam.

These taxis were running on charcoal. The arrangement was apparently complicated and needed much stoking. They never went very fast and were much given to breakdowns.

There were buses, some of these also charcoal run, and after electricity was again general in the city, streetcars. There was also a variety of buggies—a few horses but more oxen. I remember seeing braces of oxen on the Ginza.

From early on, a number of attempts were made to keep occupiers and occupied apart. They were not to be allowed in the same places. We were so informed: NO FRATERNIZATION WITH THE INDIGENOUS PERSONNEL. This is what the signs said.

The local trains had their Allied Cars, broad white stripes painted on their sides. From one of these, seated in comfort, we would see into the other cars and look at the people crammed flat against the glass.

The subway (there was only one line—Shibuya to Asakusa) was off limits to Occupation personnel, as were the buses. Only the streetcars, for some reason, were allowed. In these, occupiers and occupied were permitted to promiscuously mingle.

Occupiers also could not eat in any of the restaurants still operating in those days of food rationing. Nor could they go to any of the local entertainments. No movie theaters, no all-girl dance shows—much less the *kabuki,* showing at one of the department store theaters until its own home was to be rebuilt. Instead, there were special nights when the occupiers, and only the occupiers, were invited. Thus, one by one, we got to see the *noh,* the *bunraku,* the *kabuki,* the Takarazuka All-Girl Opera, the Kokusai Gekijo All-Girl Dance Team, and other examples of Japanese culture.

The effect of such segregation was to make one want to flaunt integration. And this we all did, though penalties were enforced. For Japanese who tried to enter forbidden zones, the punishment was extreme: they were handed over to zealous Japanese police, anxious to placate outraged Occupation authorities. For the occupiers caught in a bar or all-girl opera or *kabuki* play, the penalty was severe enough. The culprit received a Delinquency Report, and if he had acquired a certain number of these, he was, it was said, sent home.

Nonetheless, the occupiers nightly flocked where they were not supposed to. The most popular of these off-limits places were not the theaters but the brothel districts. These were, discreetly, just everywhere. The largest, most famous, most lucrative was out of town, in Funabashi, which you had to have a jeep or a truck to reach: two houses, side by side—one for officers, the other for enlisted men. Here the MPs were never seen, except, of course, as customers.

Another place where fraternization was permitted was the Mimatsu Night Club, a large building directly behind Mitsukoshi Department Store on the Ginza. In the afternoon the occupied went; in the evening, the occupiers. At five the doors were closed and the Japanese customers were turned out; at six the doors opened and the Allied customers were ushered in. At nine the doors closed for good.

Dancing was permitted. That was the extent of it. MPs patrolled the premises. Under orders from a General Swing, they also carried with them a ruler just six inches long. This they would from time to time insert between the bodies of a dancing GI and his indigenous partner to make certain that fraternization was not taking place. Shortly, however, this petty custom was laughed out of existence.

The six-inch rule did not apply when the GI went to Yurakucho Station, directly behind the Dai-Ichi Building—which served as General Headquarters—and there took his pick of all that was parading up and down. I remember the whores' uniform well because it was so fetching.

The girls wore dirndl skirts, then a minor rage in the States, with limp cotton tops and lots of wooden jewelry, bracelets and necklaces and the like, all machine tooled and painted a cherry red. The hair was piled up or else frizzed in the popular "cannibal" fashion of the day. On the feet were platform shoes with cork soles, and silk stockings were often painted on—using very strong tea—with a perfectly drawn seam on the back of each leg.

The proper present was a pair of real silk stockings, straight from the PX. But equally welcome was food from the Commissary: cocktail sausages, canned stew, Ritz crackers, and, for the truly adventurous, Kraft Velveeta.

Goods were safer than money, and though the PX and Commissary rationed some items, most of us could buy what we wanted. There were, for example, no ration rules on Almond Crunch, a favorite confection of my Japanese friends.

Many—though not, I trust, my friends—sold their goods. Particularly popular were American cigarettes and whiskey, lighter flints, and Spam. All became symbols of status among the Japanese—until they became common enough that everyone had them. Lighting a Lucky was like driving a Rolls.

14 August 1947

The sun was not up and the eastern sky was still dark, and the sleeping sea was still. Walking toward the silent surf where I had walked the afternoon before, I stopped and looked, for something had changed. It was not like yesterday. The beach now held mounds of sand; where it had been scooped out were large holes.

There was a faint light now, the eastern horizon a hazy gray, and I saw that there were many of these strange holes, as though an army had dug in during the night. Each seemed occupied, as though the invasion had been that of turtles, come to lay eggs. Slowly I walked through the growing light to the nearest and looked in.

There, like a chick in its shell, lay a small boy. In the next hole too, another was curled, and in the next. The beach was pitted with holes and in each a sleeping child.

What were they doing, why were they here, I wondered, standing over this small, sleeping army. I was curious, but I had already learned not to be surprised. This was, after all, still a mysterious land—the way the world had once been.

Just the day before, on arrival from Tokyo, we had walked along this beach—Kujikurihama in Chiba—and had stopped in surprise at the sight of the fishermen.

Young or old, they were all naked as they worked at their nets, helped by half-clad wives and sisters. Each of the men wore only a headband and a narrow red ribbon around the penis. They saw us and smiled, nodded. Not at all self-conscious, they went on with their work.

—Maybe it has something to do with not offending the sea goddess.

—Going naked like that?

—No, wearing the ribbon.

—I wonder if she's Benten?

—No, this is the Garden of Eden.

And so now, the next day, I was prepared for innocent magic as I stood above the sleeping children in the promised dawn of a midsummer morning.

And as the darkness drained from the sky, I wondered what had happened. The beach now seemed a battlefield—for the war was only a year or two behind, and thoughts came easily of bodies rolling in the surf.

Then one of the bodies stirred, and a hand was thrown across the eyes. The light was now that dim gray that precedes dawn, and I heard the surf, as though it too was just awakening.

The gray turned white, and I walked across the still-cold sand, looking into the holes. The children were very young: five, eight, ten. They were still curled in their sandy nests, but now in the early light they were awakening like the newly hatched.

The surf splashed, and a head appeared over the rim of sand. Then a wave slapped and a child sat up, dark against the brightening east. Then another, and another, as though responding to a signal I could not see. Soon, they were all awake, looking eastward, waiting.

I thought I knew what they were waiting for. The sky shone as though in a like expectation, and there, in the wings of the ocean, was the sun itself. As it appeared, each child shifted and sat formally, legs beneath him—and slowly, they turned a solid black as the sun rose beyond them.

Then as the great orb rose, higher and higher, like some radiant balloon, the mysterious children stood and yawned, shook off the sand, became themselves again.

Later I discovered what had happened. It was the beginning of Obon, the feast of the dead. The departed are welcomed back to the land of the living, their former families, where they stay until they must return, three days later, to their silent land beyond the sea. There are round dances, and the altars hold flowers, dumplings, fruit. The fathers wear proper clothing—shirts and pants or summer *yukata*—and wait, facing the rising sun, for their sons. The children go to the beach to spend the night, to await the barges of the dead. When the sun appears, they go home, their invisible guests following them.

There they went, these small escorts, while the new sun shone as though for the first time. They turned and ran, like a flock of plovers, all instant accord, flying down the beach and along the shouting sea—back to family, to home.

And I, my shadow black behind me, turned to look at the sandy nests the approaching tide was filling in, one by one.

KIJIMA HAJIME

Pulling My Leg

"It's a lie."

Though I was sure of it, something icy squirmed in my small chest until my legs would no longer stay still. Not caring if I broke my neck and never once glancing aside, I dashed straight to the bottom of those stone steps.

I was perhaps five or six at the time, and my brother was ten years older. He told me this story as we climbed the steps up East Mountain.

"People call this Look-Out Mountain, but not because of the view. You be sure and face straight ahead till we get to the top, and do the same coming down. Look back and you'll turn into a stone."

He's pulling my leg, I thought. My brother squeezed my hand tight, and his voice echoed in my ears.

"Look at them all, if you think I'm lying," he added. "That's what's left of the people who turned around . . . Look, some more over there."

I was already short of breath. Dragging me along by one hand, my brother pointed with the other at the so-called human fossils that lay on both sides of the steps. His grave tone was making me afraid to look back, and soon I could barely manage to look from side to side.

One false blink might turn me to stone. I would have to spend eternity alone on this mountainside.

As if to give my disbelief the *coup de grâce,* he continued, "See that one about an inch long, off to the left? The fuller who used to live in the house behind us had a wife named Tomi. She'd climbed up to that spot one day when someone called her from below. Been there ever since."

I had never heard of this fuller's wife, or the fuller himself, but as my brother spoke, the stone he pointed to began to look like it might have been such a person. Though I was already winded, a sinking fear sent me sprinting to the top of the steps.

They led to Kodai Temple. From there we followed a winding path to the clearing where a new shrine for the Fatherland's Defender was to be built. My brother took me around the compound and eventually back to the steps.

Unbeknownst to me, his simple story of people turning into stones had settled in the deepest recesses of my mind. I still remember clearly how, though I was sure he was lying, something icy squirmed in my small chest until my legs would no longer stay still. Not caring if I broke my neck and never once glancing aside, I dashed straight to the bottom of those stone steps.

I climbed them again years later and found the shrine had grown into a magnificent structure, dedicated to the legions of dead souls. If things were as our leaders said, all those who went to war and gave their lives for the Fatherland had been deified within the shrine's walls. I clasped my hands in prayer, yet none of the people I had known came to mind.

My brother told me a number of unforgettable stories. One evening he came running home from the bathhouse and exclaimed, "I just saw a man with a tail!" I let out a whoop of surprise and started somersaulting around the room. No matter how much my mother and the rest of us scolded him, saying, "Enough of your foolishness," my brother insisted he had lifted up the man's bath towel and seen it.

"Plenty of people cover themselves up front, but this guy was hiding his behind. He kept a towel wrapped around his waist even while scrubbing, so I got suspicious and took a peek. Sure enough, there it was: a tail about this long."

When he indicated the length with his thumb and forefinger, Mother got angry and slapped his hand. I remember being overcome by an indecorous and uncontrollable fit of laughter as I imagined how humans might look with tails.

Unable to go to the bathhouse and check for myself, I couldn't be certain he was lying. I wonder if he hadn't actually seen some poor soul born with the vestige of a tail and then simply exaggerated the length.

As we walked down a crowded street one day, he whispered, "That's him, Mr. Tail. It's tucked down in those baggy pants, but he can't fool me. Take a good look at him." As I gazed, an expression of guilt seemed to emerge on the stranger's face.

Once my brother left for boarding school, I hardly saw him. Meanwhile, the war took a turn for the worse, and then not even prayers or conjuring could bring us back together. His marvelous stories remain clear even though most other memories have faded. However, I do remember his schoolteacherish attempt to make me memorize a composition and how it ended in complete failure.

Some muse inspired him to compose a song, though he had never taken a music lesson and there wasn't an instrument in our house. When both melody and lyrics were complete, he set the score before me and tried to get me to sing it.

This was before the phrase singer-songwriter became part of the Japanese vocabulary and before the tape recorder was invented. Perhaps my brother got tired of singing to himself and decided to teach me the tune in order to hear how it sounded when sung by someone else.

Instead, he taught me to hate the written note. I couldn't have cared less whether his melody was in C or G. He forced me to sing the same measures again and again until my eyes teared and the notes swam together like tadpoles. I never showed any admiration for his music, and from the start of each lesson simply waited for the first chance to escape.

At length my brother gave up on the idea of having me sing opus 1. It wasn't something that could be forced. This failure to interest me in his composition must have caused him to doubt his musicality, for he also gave up on the composition of opus 2 and whatever others might have followed.

Instead of sheet music, he came home with a book called *Chinese Poetry: An Introductory Method* and pored over it for hours, trying to string together characters into verse. I have no idea what sort of ideogrammatic things he composed. The subject was far beyond a boy of my age.

Many years have passed since my brother went away, but a stray verse from his song came back to me the other day. I was at a beach in Chiba, teaching my children to swim, as he had once taught me at Lake Biwa. Wading in the shallows, I banged my ankle on a rock, and though it hardly hurt, the wound bled profusely. Yet the blood disappeared into the seawater almost instantly, as if to demonstrate my insignificance.

I sprawled on the sand with my wound facing upwards. The sun beat down, and as I shielded my face with both hands, a melody sounded in my ears.

Lift your eyes . . . to the ocean's brim
A scale . . . rainbow

I was unable to recall the rest of the lyrics, but the meaning of this fragment seemed almost clear. A wondrous string of associations towed me along to the accompaniment of my ankle's dull throbbing.

"Ocean's brim" was the horizon, over which a "rainbow" shone with the colors reflected in fish scales. The verse bid me to look out there. Someone would appear.

My brother's troopship had sailed south and was never heard from again. Perhaps it had been hit by a torpedo or bombed by fighter planes and sunk out there, in the direction in which I now gazed.

Perhaps my brother's body had dissolved into the sea, like the blood from my ankle. One of his cells might have drifted for decades until it washed up on this shore. Perhaps it now stuck to one of these stones. Who could say for sure it wasn't so?

Or rather than a speck stuck to a stone, perhaps my brother had become a stone, as in the story he had once told me. I went so far as to pick out which one he might be. Another looked like our neighbor, Yasuhara, who had also been sunk on his way to war. One by one, the stones around me turned into the silent forms of people who had passed away. I expected that one day I too would join them, and the story that had so frightened me as a boy now seemed natural and logical.

In the wake of these thoughts, the next melodic line of the song came floating back, ethereal and void of lyrics. It rang like a heavenly summons out to sea. I didn't have a tape recorder on hand, nor did I think to jot down the notes, but even if I had, the melody's beauty would probably have faded upon a second hearing.

Elbows planted in the sand, I let my eyes wander with the music. Out on the horizon, barely visible, something leapt toward the sky, then sank beneath the waves. The creature was shaped like a sea horse, and with each jump he spun around on his tail, dancing in time to the song I had thought audible only to my ears.

Translation by Arthur Binard

Last Letters

LIEUTENANT YONETSU YOSHITARŌ TO HIS BROTHER AND STEPMOTHER

Kamikaze Special Attack Group Fugoku
Killed near Luzon Island on 13 November 1944
Native of Shizuoka Prefecture

Honorable Older Brother,

Once again, orders have come down for the attack from which we will never return. I feel not the slightest regret. Already I have grown intimate with death, the ultimate character-building passage that we human beings have to face. All that is left is to carry out the duties for which I've been trained and to fulfill the Imperial mandate. I am deeply ashamed that in the twenty-seven years of my life I have been such an unworthy son and younger brother.

I will have to leave everything up to you. It is with an untroubled heart that I fulfill the obligations for which I was born. I am merely carrying out my duties as a man.

The made-in-Manila bar of toilet soap you'll find in my things was given to me by the chief of staff. Please take good care of Mother, and take care of yourself in the coming winter.

Yoshitarō

Honorable Mother,

Please forgive the impiety of my premature departure. However, I am certain that both you and my departed mother will be happy that in serving the Emperor your Yoshitarō is becoming one of the guardian spirits of Yasukuni Shrine. Nevertheless, it pains me deeply that I am causing you sorrow in your twilight years. Please forgive me.

Yoshitarō

LIEUTENANT UEMURA MASAHISA TO HIS CHILD

Kamikaze Special Attack Group Yamato
Died 26 October 1944 in the Philippines at age 25
Graduate of Rikkyō University, Tokyo

Motoko,

You often laughed when you looked at my face. You slept in my arms, and we bathed together. Motoko, when you grow up and want to know about me, ask your mother and Aunt Kayo. I also left my photo album at home for you. It was I who named you Motoko. I thought of you as becoming a gentle, kind, and sensitive person.

I want to see you grow up to be a splendid bride, but even if I die without your knowing me, you must not grieve. When you get older and want to see me, come to Kudan and pray with all your heart, and my face will appear before you. I think you are a happy person. You resemble me very much. When people see you, they often say how much you look like me.

Your aunt and uncle treat you so well for you are their only hope. And your mother, your happiness is her whole life. Whatever becomes of me, never think of yourself as a child without parents. I too will always be watching over you. Be good, and be the kind of person others will like.

When you get older and begin to think of me, please ask someone to read this to you.

Dad

P.S. The toy doll you had as a child I took with me in my airplane as a good-luck charm—this way you are always with me. I tell you this because I think it would be wrong for you not to know.

CAPTAIN FURUKAWA TAKAO TO HIS WIFE

Killed in the sea off Kagoshima on 21 April 1945 at age 25
Native of Saga Prefecture

Recently, in calmer moments, I find my thoughts returning continually to you and our soon-to-be-born child. Please take good care of your health. When we first arrived at our base in Kyūshū, there was a sudden change in plans, and we were all ordered into special attack units. I expected to depart at any moment. Every day, as I waited for my first, and last, attack, I reread the letter you wrote the day you made the jelly and gazed at the photos of you and Sister Etchan.

Surprisingly, my heart was perfectly at peace—as though another me were gazing upon the me that was so calm.

But orders, for better or for worse, changed again, and I was assigned to another squadron and given other duties. We made two sorties to Okinawa; the first was completed without incident, and I returned without doing anything especially heroic.

Mr. Hagiwara, who visited us the other day, asked about you. Try not to be upset, but he was shot down the day after he arrived.

Now, more than ever, the fleetingness of human life astonishes me, but I have become a much stronger person. You too must be strong. Wait for me. I will return without fail. Until you've safely given birth to our child, I have no intention of dying easily.

CAPTAIN ADACHI TAKUYA TO HIS PARENTS

Kamikaze Special Attack Group No. 1 Seikitai
Killed in the Okinawa area on 28 April 1945 at age 23
Native of Hyōgo Prefecture

Honorable Mother and Father,

The difficulty of the journey you made to see me was clearly evident in your disheveled hair and in the hollows under your eyes—it made me want to bend my knees and worship before you. In the wrinkles on your brows was vivid testimony of the pains you took to raise me. Words could not express my feelings, and what little I did say was superficial in the extreme. Yet, although acutely conscious of how little time we had, I saw in your eyes and in your gaze all you wanted to say but couldn't.

When you took my hand and passed it over your chilblains, I experienced a sense of profound peacefulness unlike anything I have experienced since joining up—like being a baby again and longing for the warmth of a mother's love. It is because I bask in the beauty of your deep devotion that I can martyr myself for you—for in death I will sleep in the world of your love. Washed down with my tears was the *sushi* you prepared with such loving care, for it was like putting your love to my lips. Though I ate but little, it was the most delicious meal of my life.

Honorable Mother, even if I was never able to fully accept the love you gave me, I received so much wisdom from you. And Father, your silent words are carved deeply into my heart. With this I will be able to fight together with you both. Even if I should die, it will be with a peaceful spirit. I mean this with all my heart.

The war zone is where these beautiful emotions are put to the test. If death means a return to this world of love, there is no need for me to fear it. There is nothing left to do but press on and fulfill my duty.

At 1600 hours our meeting was over. Watching you walk out the gate, I quietly waved goodbye.

LIEUTENANT KISHI FUMIKAZU TO HIS FAMILY

Killed in the Philippines on 24 October 1944 at age 22
Graduate of Niigata Second Teaching School
Native of Niigata Prefecture

Dear Mother and Father, Brother and Sister,

End of autumn. The backyard must be filled with the cries of insects, as it is every year around this time. My heart is full to bursting with memories of the many evenings we spent talking together. I suppose you are all somewhat concerned about how I'm doing.

During my visit home in May, Sister said to me, "Ever since you joined up, Mother has been setting meals before your photograph. She's given up drinking tea, and every evening she visits the shrine to pray for you." I was so moved that I was unable to thank her. Mother really wore herself out at the farewell party the night before I left to join my unit. She was so busy preparing for my departure that she didn't sleep at all the night before. And on my sun flag, she wrote HAPPILY WAITING FOR A RETURNING CHILD. Whenever I can, I gaze at those four noble characters for the nourishment they give my soul. The fighting has become extremely intense, and there is no guarantee of my safe return. The image of all those poor school kids and everyone else singing war songs and waving a sea of flags as they saw us off to the front is burned indelibly into my mind. I firmly believe in the benevolence of the Emperor and of our parents. Mother seems to be growing weaker by the day. Brother and Sister, you will have to give her the love that I cannot.

Please forgive my impiety; I pray for the continued good health of you all. The three photo albums I sent the other day are keepsakes for Brother and Sister. Please don't worry about me. When you hear of my death, be happy for me, for I will have achieved my ambition.

Goodbye.

Translations by Nicholas Voge

KEIJI NAKAZAWA

from *Barefoot Gen*

Translators' Note

Keiji Nakazawa was six years old when the atomic bomb was dropped on his hometown of Hiroshima. Only a mile from ground zero, the boy miraculously survived, but lost half of his family in the holocaust. Growing up in postwar Hiroshima, he became a professional cartoonist and wrote sports and adventure stories for comic weeklies until an enlightened editor urged him to write about his own experience as a survivor of the bombing. The result was an autobiography in cartoon form, *I Saw It,* which described his experience in heart-rending detail. The work so impressed Nakazawa's editors that they gave him free rein to create the epic cartoon novel that would become his life's work, *Barefoot Gen.*

Barefoot Gen is a slightly fictionalized account of Nakazawa's life in wartime Hiroshima before, during, and after the bombing. It was serialized in 1972 and 1973 in *Shōnen Jump,* the best-selling boys' comic weekly, and subsequently anthologized in four volumes, becoming a hit with young readers, parents, and teachers. But even as *Gen* gained popularity as a unique resource for educating young people about the horrors of nuclear war, it provoked the ire of Japan's right wing: the story also bitterly condemned the militarist leadership that led Japan into war.

Chronicling the postwar world in which Nakazawa grew up, *Gen* eventually filled ten volumes and ended with the death of his mother from leukemia in 1966. In 1976, a group of young Japanese and Americans in Tokyo formed Project Gen, a nonprofit organization that to date has translated the first four volumes of the series into English. The pages that appear here are excerpted from the first volume of the series, which has also been translated into French, German, Swedish, Norwegian, Esperanto, Indonesian, and Tagalog. In addition, the story has been made into a three-part, live-action film, a feature-length animated film (available on videotape in the United States), an opera, and, most recently, a musical staged to critical acclaim in New York City. —Alan Gleason for Project Gen

AUG 6 MONDAY
TICK TOCK
TICK TOCK
OH, GEN- LOOK
WOW, EIKO! WHAT A BEAUTIFUL DAY- THE SKY'S SO BLUE!
EIKO... GEN- BETTER GET READY FOR SCHOOL...
O.K., MAMA
V-R-R-R-O-O-O-OM! ZOOM, ZOOM, ZOOM
KA-BOOM!
THAT'S A MIGHTY FINE BATTLESHIP GEN GAVE YOU, SHINJI!
I KNOW! -AND I SURE LOVE GEN!

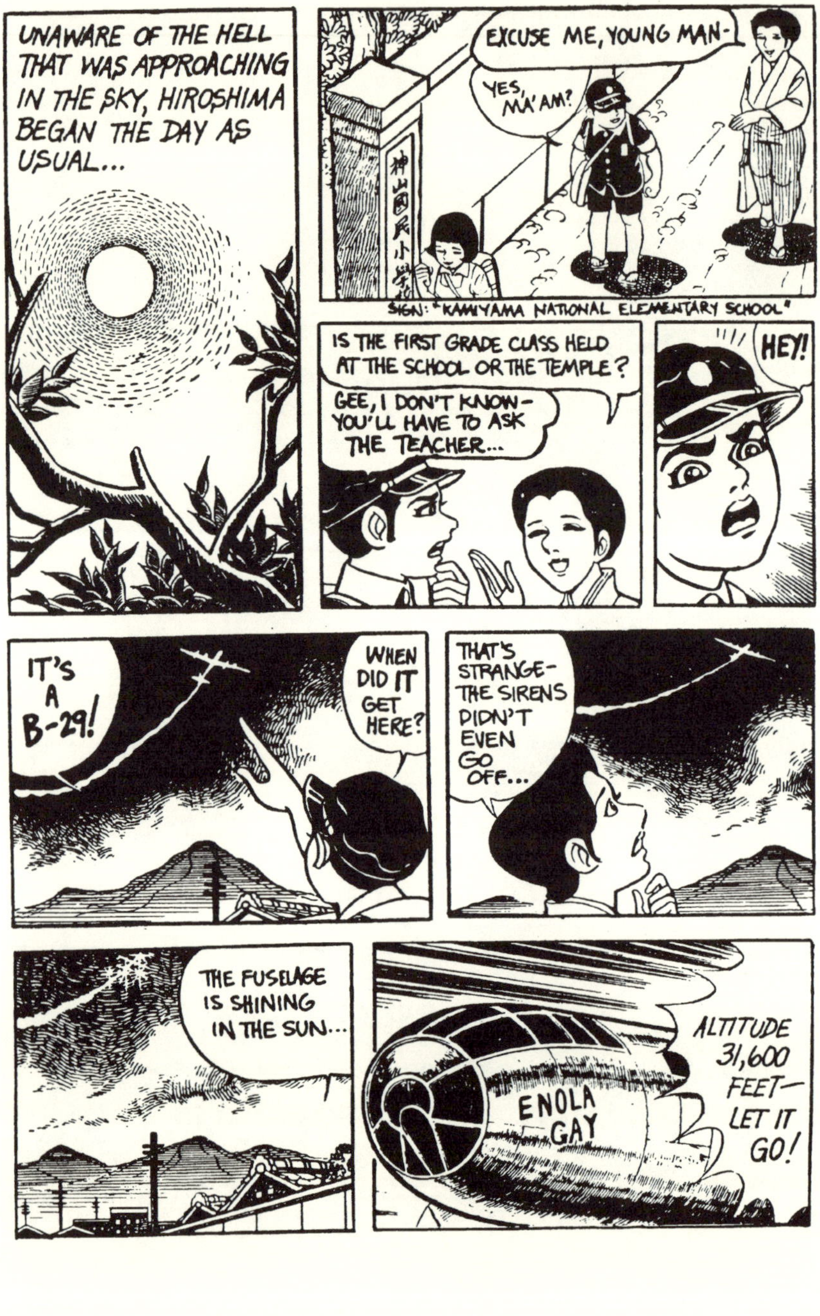
UNAWARE OF THE HELL THAT WAS APPROACHING IN THE SKY, HIROSHIMA BEGAN THE DAY AS USUAL...
EXCUSE ME, YOUNG MAN-
YES, MA'AM?
神山国民小学
SIGN: "KAMIYAMA NATIONAL ELEMENTARY SCHOOL"
IS THE FIRST GRADE CLASS HELD AT THE SCHOOL OR THE TEMPLE?
GEE, I DON'T KNOW-YOU'LL HAVE TO ASK THE TEACHER...
HEY!
IT'S A B-29!
WHEN DID IT GET HERE?
THAT'S STRANGE-THE SIRENS DIDN'T EVEN GO OFF...
THE FUSELAGE IS SHINING IN THE SUN...
ENOLA GAY
ALTITUDE 31,600 FEET-LET IT GO!

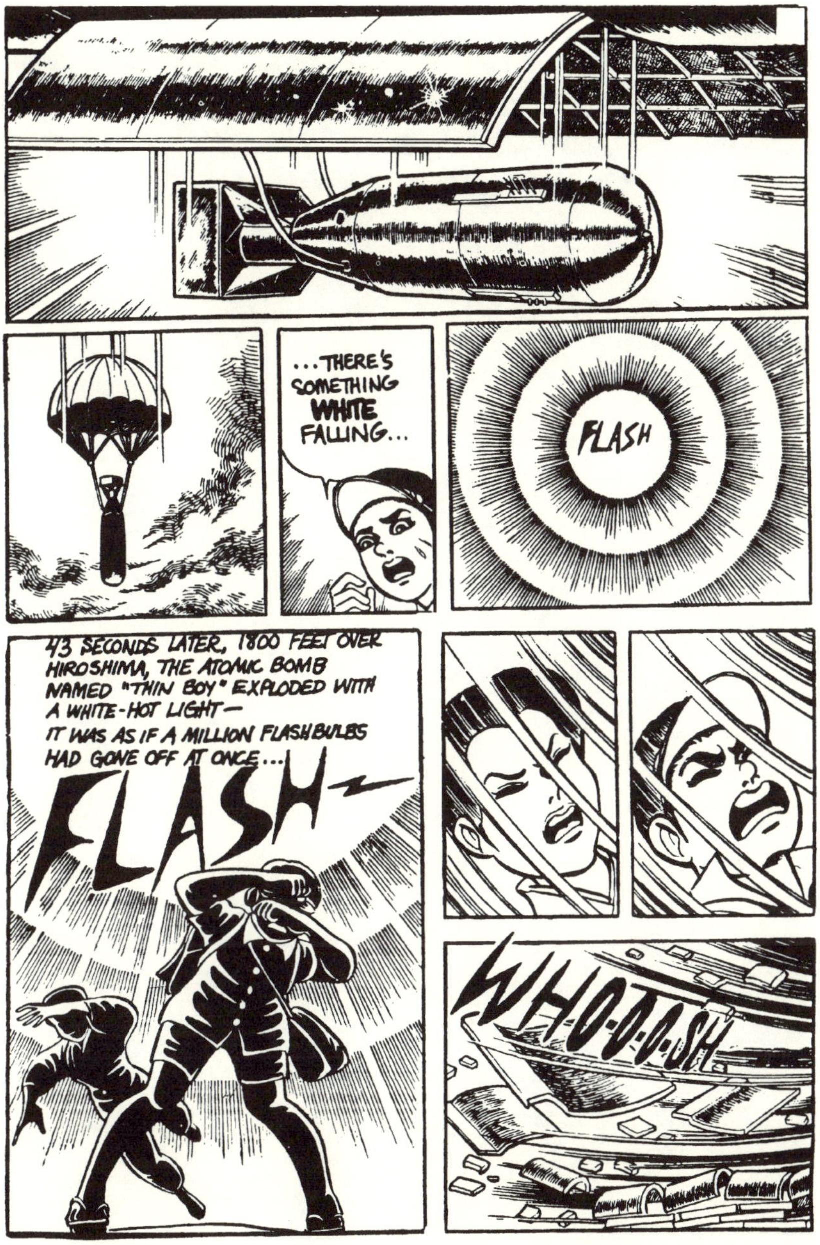
...THERE'S SOMETHING WHITE FALLING...
FLASH
43 SECONDS LATER, 1800 FEET OVER HIROSHIMA, THE ATOMIC BOMB NAMED "THIN BOY" EXPLODED WITH A WHITE-HOT LIGHT—
IT WAS AS IF A MILLION FLASHBULBS HAD GONE OFF AT ONCE...
FLASH
WH-O-O-O-SH

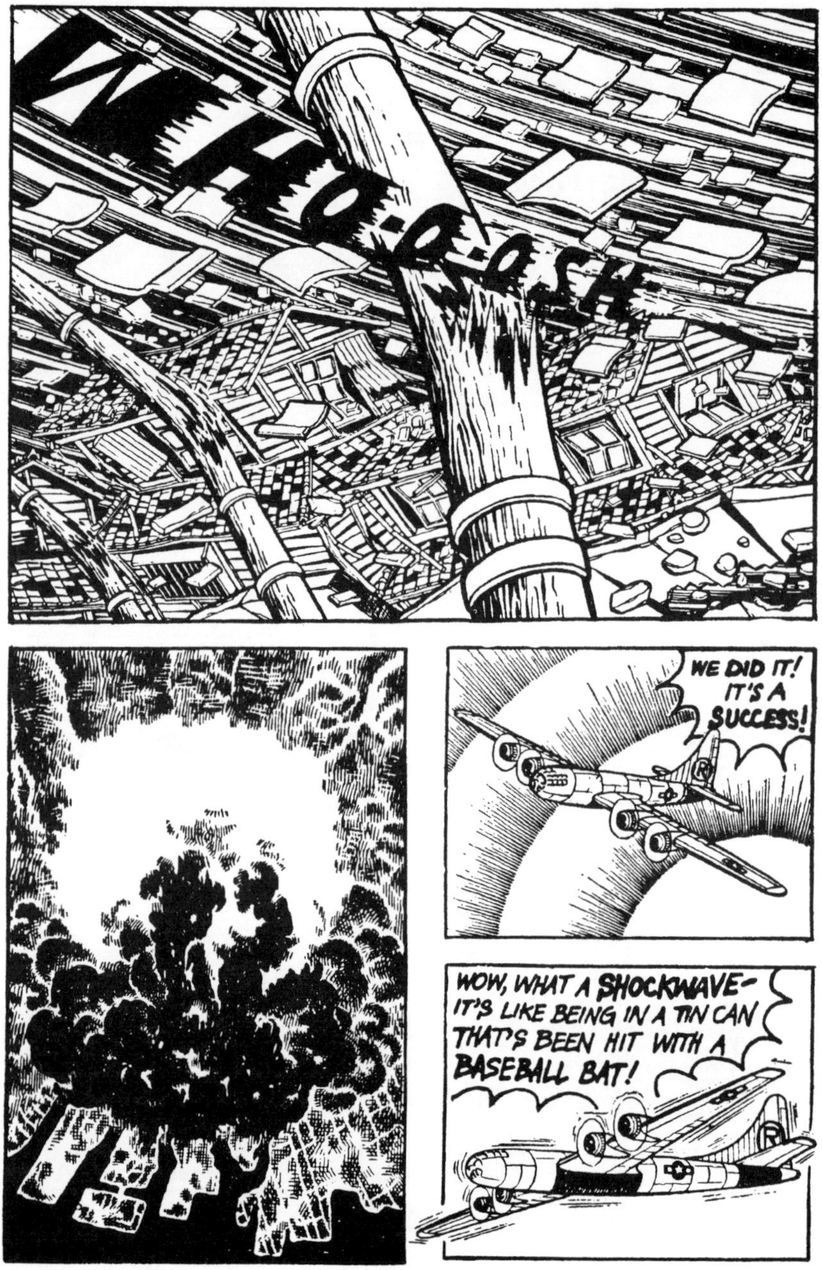
WHO-O-O-OSH
WE DID IT! IT'S A SUCCESS!
WOW, WHAT A SHOCKWAVE- IT'S LIKE BEING IN A TIN CAN THAT'S BEEN HIT WITH A BASEBALL BAT!

LIKE A WIND FROM HELL, THE ATOMIC CLOUD ROARED UP 6 MILES INTO THE SKY OVER HIROSHIMA...
UH-H-H-H..
..UH-H-H... WHAT HAPPENED? IT'S PITCH DARK!.. NIGHT ALREADY?
HOW COULD THAT BE? I WAS ON MY WAY TO SCHOOL...
SOMETHING FLASHED ...AND AFTER THAT I DON'T REMEMBER A THING...
WOW, WHAT'S WITH THIS WALL?

GASP
IT'S... IT'S THE LADY I WAS JUST TALKING TO —WHAT'S HAPPENED TO HER SKIN?
L-L-L- LADY?
SHE'S... SHE'S DEAD!
MA!!!
MA-A-A-A
...SOME-ONE'S COMING!
H-HEY! HEY, MISTER! HELP!! THIS LADY'S DEAD!
GASP

THE PEOPLE LOOK LIKE MONSTERS!
WHAT HAPPENED?
WHERE'S MY HOUSE?? EVERYTHING'S BEEN KNOCKED FLAT—

PAPA...! MAMA...! EIKO...! SHINJI...!

ARGH! WHAT DO YOU WANT? LET GO OF ME!!
SON-SONNY... BRING ME... WATER...
...PLEASE... ....PLEASE... MY THROAT IS BURNING... ...WATER..
HANG ON, MISTER, JUST HANG ON - I'LL GET SOME...
QUICK...
...QUICK..

THE HEAT OF THE EXPLOSION LITERALLY MELTED THE SKIN OF ALL WHO WEREN'T SHELTERED FROM THE RAYS... THOSE WEARING DARK CLOTHING WERE BURNED PARTICULARLY BADLY... MOST PEOPLE WERE LEFT NAKED, THEIR CLOTHING RIPPED AWAY BY THE FORCE OF THE BLAST...
WHE-HE-HE
WOW— THAT HORSE IS ON FIRE!!

I'LL USE THIS HELMET TO CARRY WATER IN...
HANG ON! I'LL WASH YOUR HANDS IN A SECOND...
WHY DID ALL THIS HAPPEN—WHY? I JUST DON'T UNDERSTAND...
MOMMY!
I CAN'T SEE!!
THE BLAST STUCK ALL THIS GLASS INTO US!!
HEY, MISTER! I GOT YOU SOME WATER!
M-M-MISTER...?
HE... HE'S DEAD!
GASP
HELP!
—THE FIRE'S SPREADING THIS WAY!
RUN!

FOR HOURS, GEN WANDERS ALONE THROUGH THE BURNING WRECKAGE OF HIROSHIMA, SEARCHING FOR HIS FAMILY...

SOMEWHERE IN THE FLAMES ARE HIS LITTLE BROTHER, HIS SISTER, FATHER, MOTHER, AND THE UNBORN CHILD SHE CARRIES...

PAPA! EIKO! SHINJI!
GEN! THANK GOD YOU WEREN'T HURT!
GEN! MY LEG HURTS- IT'S STUCK!
OH, GEN- HELP! I CAN'T EVEN BUDGE THAT ROOF...
DAMN! I'LL GET THEM OUT SOMEHOW
GEN! IT HURTS- IT HURTS!
HOLD ON, SHINJI- I'LL GET YOU OUT IN A MINUTE!
CREEAK
COME ON, GEN, HURRY! GET ME OUT- OW-W-W!
UNGGH...
UNGGGH...

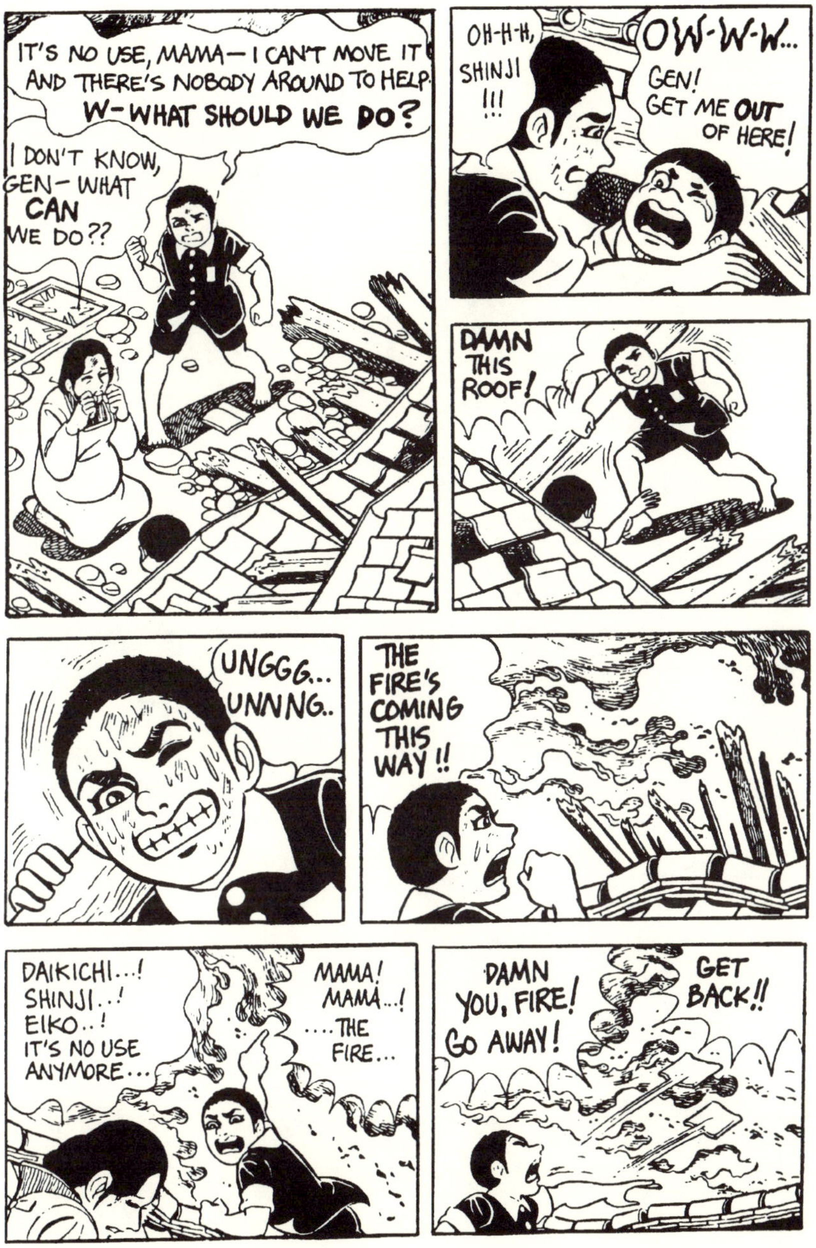
IT'S NO USE, MAMA— I CAN'T MOVE IT AND THERE'S NOBODY AROUND TO HELP. W-WHAT SHOULD WE DO?
I DON'T KNOW, GEN— WHAT CAN WE DO??
OH-H-H, SHINJI !!!
OW-W-W... GEN! GET ME OUT OF HERE!
DAMN THIS ROOF!
UNGGG... UNNNG..
THE FIRE'S COMING THIS WAY !!
DAIKICHI...! SHINJI..! EIKO..! IT'S NO USE ANYMORE...
MAMA! MAMA...! ....THE FIRE...
DAMN YOU, FIRE! GO AWAY!
GET BACK!!

COME ON, MAMA. LET'S GO— COME ON, MAMA—
No! No!
I'M GOING TO DIE WITH THEM!!
I'M GOING TO DIE WITH EVERYONE ELSE!!
CRACKLE
CRACKLE
W-W-WAAA! WA-A-A-A!! MAMA! MAMA!!

AS THEY ESCAPE THE FLAMES, GEN'S MOTHER GOES INTO LABOR, AND WITH NO ONE TO HELP THEM, THEY BRING A NEW LIFE INTO THE DYING CITY...
HANG ON, MAMA!
HANG ON!
AAAAA-AAAHHHH!
WAAAAAH
PANT PANT
IT'S BORN!
THE BABY'S BORN, MAMA!
WAAHH! WAAHH!
PANT PANT! HOLD THE BABY'S HEAD GENTLY AND WASH ITS BODY WITH WATER.
RIGHT!
HEE HEE HEE, IT'S A GIRL! MY LITTLE SISTER! GEE, SHE'S GOT A FACE LIKE A MONKEY'S!
WAAHH
WAAAHH
WWAAHH

HEY THERE, TOMOKO! I JUST BROUGHT YOU INTO THE WORLD ALL BY MYSELF – I'M YOUR BIG BROTHER, SO YOU'D BETTER LISTEN TO ME...
WA-A WA-A
HURRY AND GROW UP SO WE CAN PLAY TOGETHER!
PAPA- EIKO- SHINJI- LOOK!
WE'VE GOT A NEW LITTLE SISTER!! SEE HOW HEALTHY SHE IS? SHE'S GOING TO BE BEAUTIFUL WHEN SHE GROWS UP... SHE'S...
SH- SHE'S...
W-A-A-A-A...
...Y-YOU'LL NEVER KNOW HER...

-LET ME HOLD HER, GEN...
REMEMBER THIS, TOMOKO! THIS IS WHAT TOOK YOUR FATHER, BROTHER AND SISTER FROM US... THIS IS WAR—
WHEN YOU GROW UP, YOU MUST NEVER LET THIS HAPPEN AGAIN!!
W-A-A-A...

Testimonials

Editor's Note

The Battle of Okinawa—later called, because of its savagery, the "Typhoon of Steel"—claimed the lives of more than 200,000 people. Included among the dead were girls aged fifteen to nineteen from the Okinawa Women's Normal School and the First Prefectural Girls' High School. A total of 219 students and 18 teachers from the schools were mobilized as nurses attached to the Haebaru Army Field Hospital, and another 79 students and 3 teachers were dispatched to other medical units. More than 200 of them were eventually killed.

Adding to the tragedy and futility of their deaths is the fact that many of the girls survived the bombardment of the battle; the majority were killed after the defeat of the Japanese army was already a certainty. In the midst of heavy fighting on Kyan Peninsula and the disintegration of Japanese forces, the military abruptly disbanded the corps of nurses. On 18 June, the defenseless girls were ordered out of the caves where Japanese soldiers were hiding, but were forbidden to surrender. As a result, during the fire storm of American bombardment, reinforced by U.S. infantry with tanks and flame throwers, the young nurses were denied not only protective shelter but also rations of food and water reserved for the military. In the next five days—during which all organized resistance collapsed—most of the young girls were killed.

The Himeyuri Peace Museum was modeled after the main school building in which the girls had once studied. It contains portraits of all the young victims who died after the military's retreat to the southernmost tip of the Kyan Peninsula, panels explaining the circumstances under which they died, twenty-eight volumes of testimonials and memoirs by 90 survivors, and a life-sized diorama of Himeyuri Cave. The testimonials bring to life each phase of the battle, as witnessed by the student nurses.

The Himeyuri Alumni Association writes, "Today, memories of the battle are fast being eroded away by the passage of time. . . . We are determined all the more to do our best to tell our stories of war, and by exposing the brutality and insanity of war, to never allow it to happen again."

ITOKAZU DETACHMENT CAVE PACKED WITH THE SERIOUSLY WOUNDED

Yabiku Toshiko (now Shimabukuro Toshiko)
Then 17 and a junior, Preparatory Course, Women's Normal School
Assigned to Itokazu Detachment

It was 1 May when fifteen of us were taken from Haebaru to the Itokazu Detachment cave, now called Abuchira *gama* (cave), by our teacher, Oshiro Chizen. There were only about twenty medical personnel—including military surgeons Oshiro and Nishihira, one nurse, several corpsmen, and us—taking care of some seven hundred patients. The cave was always filled with an odious smell. The stench was unbearable, so it was almost impossible to nurse the wounded or tend to their wounds.

I can still hear the cries and shrieks of those soldiers in the throes of death during surgical operations. It was hell itself. We didn't have enough anesthetic, so doctors administered it just enough to ease their patients' tension.

One patient begged desperately, "That's enough! Doctor, kill me! Just kill me now!"

"Shut up! You can't put up with this much pain?! You're a Japanese soldier, aren't you?!" the surgeon shouted at him.

By mid-May, you could tell the condition of the patients had gotten really bad. All of them were smeared with pus, and lice crawled all over their bodies. The number of brain-fever and tetanus patients rapidly increased. Completely deranged, brain-fever patients were really terrible. They'd suddenly stand up and start walking, trampling seriously wounded soldiers lying in the cave.

"Take this madman somewhere else!" panicked soldiers would shout. Medical corpsmen would rush to the scene and take him further into the cave. "Where are you taking him to?" somebody would ask, but the corpsmen never replied.

Tetanus patients developed cramps in their legs and arms, finally getting lockjaw. When they reached that point, they could no longer even eat the cream of rice gruel. Such patients were taken to a narrow isolation ward enclosed by wooden shutters. They kept their eyes wide open and just stared at us as if to implore us to get them out of there.

Starved almost to death, soldiers shouted and screamed for something to eat. "You had that sergeant's arm or leg! Cook it, broil it!" Of course they were talking about amputated arms and legs. Horrible even to imagine. But that's war.

LIMBS AMPUTATED WITHOUT ANESTHETIC

Kishimoto Hisa (now Kohatsu Hisa)
Then 17 and in her first year, Regular Course, Women's Normal School
Assigned to Second Surgery Unit

As fighting got heavier, the Internal Medicine Unit was abolished and renamed the Second Surgery Unit. Our job was to hold down the arms and legs to be amputated from soldiers. For pain, a patient was given just a sniff of ether. I held down the arm a doctor was going to cut off and encouraged the patient to endure. That was really frightening. The amputated hand still clutched my hand.

"*Akisamiyo!*" I shouted and desperately tore it off my hand. Such arms and legs were still warm even after being cut off, and we would wrap them in rags and hurriedly throw them into waste containers.

For an operation on the shoulder, a soldier was told to sit in a chair. He was a sergeant who'd been shot through his shoulder. He was operated on without any anesthesia. His muscles were cut about three centimeters deep and ten centimeters long, with a special pair of scissors, in about ten cuts. He didn't scream, but his brow was sweating and tears streamed down his face. I tried to hold his hand, but he wouldn't let me. Instead he held his own hand to bear the pain. I bet it hurt him to death.

"DON'T BOTHER ABOUT THE PATIENTS—GET OUT!"

Shimabukuro Tomi (now Nakamoto Tomi)
Then 18 and in her second year, Regular Course, Women's Normal School
Assigned to First Surgery Unit

On the eighteenth [of June], when I arrived at Ihara Cave, the first news I heard was about the "demobilization orders." Nakasone-*sensei* was talking to the group about it. We didn't know what he was saying at first. We listened to his talk absentmindedly.

The doctors then shouted at us to leave the cave as soon as possible.

It was then that I realized we had to vacate the cave. There was a pile of rice sacks near me. I scooped with my hands the unpolished rice from one of the bags and gave it to all the members of the student corps. I also distributed among them some amount of dehydrated *miso* seasoning. When we were ready to leave, it was already daybreak, and reconnaissance planes were flying over us. While we were waiting for our departure, there rushed into our cave two of our teachers assigned to other units, Yonamine-*sensei* and Uchida-*sensei*.

They told us that the Second Surgery Cave had been "straddled" and attacked, and some were wounded or killed. The surviving members had left the cave in twos and threes to join us. So we told them, "*Sensei!* they've disbanded us. Teachers and students all left the cave. Only the seriously wounded students are here."

"Is that right?" they asked, evidently shocked. But presently, they went to see the wounded students and comfort them.

My classmate Chinen-*san*, who couldn't move and was lying on the floor, grabbed at my pants and said, "Don't go away! Don't leave us here alone." I didn't know what to do, so I gathered water trickling from the wall into a bowl and gave it to her, when a surgeon bellowed, brandishing his sword, "Get out or I'll cut your heads off! I'll take care of the patients! You'll all be killed if you stay here!" He was furious.

Ishikawa-*san*, Kanda-*san*, and Uezu-*san* lay there. They couldn't move but were still conscious.

We hesitated at the cave entrance, going out and coming back in again. Then vice-principal Teruya, who had left the cave earlier, came back, blood dripping from his face and arms. He'd been hit by a mortar shell. I followed him into the cave, trying to talk to him, but the doctor again shouted at me, "Leave him alone! Get out!"

Well, we plucked up all our courage and dashed out into the open with Yonamine-*sensei* and Uchida-*sensei*, not knowing where to go but just following other people.

FATHER AND SON DRIVEN OUT OF THE CAVE

Miyagi Toyo (now Tomimura Toyoko)
Then 20 and in her second year, Regular Course, Women's Normal School
Assigned to Itokazu Detachment

Two soldiers happened to pass by, so we told them we were looking for refuge and asked if they could take us to a cave.

"Yes," they said, "wait here for a while." They went away and then came back to take us to a large hole under huge coral rocks overgrown with pandanus plants. It was filled with refugees.

When we got there, an Okinawan man and a boy about fourteen or fifteen, apparently his son, were sitting at the entrance of the cave. Suddenly, one of the soldiers started shouting at the father and son, brandishing his sword at them.

"Anyone who does not obey military orders, I'll cut him down," he growled. In other words, he was trying to drive them out of the cave in order to make room for us. The four of us were really frightened and said to the soldier, "Please, soldier, we don't want to get in the cave by driving them out!"

But the frightened father and son jumped out of the cave and ran away before we knew it.

EXECUTED AS A SPY

Ginoza Hiroko (now Shinzato Hiroko)
Then 16 and in her fourth year, First Prefectural Girls' High School
Assigned to Tama Unit Accounting Section

It was around midnight. There were many people, civilians, and soldiers hiding in the pandanus grove, but nobody made any sound. All of a sudden, I heard a young woman screaming, "Father, Father!"

I asked a soldier next to me what was going on. He told me that a soldier had overheard the woman's father talking about the deployment of Japanese troops, so the soldier had arrested him as a spy and was taking him away for execution on charges of leaking classified military information. I heard some people hustling away somebody, and the young woman was screaming, "Father, Father!" I couldn't see anything, but I could hear the voices and noise. I gathered the man was being executed. By that time, the Japanese forces had been completely routed by the enemy and there was little discipline among them, but they carried out such executions nonetheless.

"Never talk about the military. Absolutely not!" the two of us whispered to each other. Everybody else also kept their mouth shut. Indeed, it was a terribly frightening time for us. The two weeks we spent in that cave at Kyan Point seemed terribly long and were filled with many painful experiences. At night the only sound we heard was the monotonous lapping of the waves, and that nearly drove me out of my mind. I was also so lonely that the only hope I had was seeing my family before I died.

About that time, there was a seriously wounded soldier who'd somehow managed to get to Kyan. "I'm wounded like this and can't even walk anymore and I can't go out to look for food. I want to die, but I don't have the guts to kill myself, so please kill me," he said to his fellow soldiers. I later heard that one of the soldiers had shot him in the temple and put him to rest. Days later, winds carried the sickening odor of rotting flesh to us. That soldier's body was rotting out there, I thought, and this made me feel miserable.

And there was an old couple. The man had died and the woman wouldn't leave him, saying she wanted to die beside him. It was really pitiful.

There were countless corpses lying around at Kyan Point, and Americans were burning them with flame throwers.

ARASAKI BEACH, THE END OF THE WORLD

Kaneshiro Kikuko (now Miyagi Kikuko)
Then 16 and in her first year, First Prefectural Girls' High School
Assigned to Tama Unit Accounting Section

The tanks were after us, and Yoza-*san* was instantly killed. We lay her body on the roadside and ran away. It was daytime. The fierce attack had started early in the morning. The road was littered with corpses. Tripping many times over corpses covered with maggots, we ran desperately. That was the worst day. If you raised your head a little, you heard bullets hitting the ground around you. Soldiers were covered with blood, their uniforms tattered, and everywhere there were wounded soldiers crawling on the ground.

The enemy burned pandanus groves with flame throwers and smoked out people hiding in them. We stuck to Taira-*sensei* and kept on fleeing along the shore. By then our group had been reduced to twelve. Enemy ships would come close to the shore, broadcasting calls to surrender: *Americans will protect you. Come aboard as soon as possible. Those of you who can't swim, please walk toward Minatogawa Village during the daytime. Never move during the night.* We could see their faces clearly. That made us even more scared. Tanks were approaching with flame throwers. I felt more dead than alive.

We continued to flee along the shore of Kyan Point, wading across jagged coral reefs when the tide was low and clinging to the walls of wave-eroded recesses at the base of the cliff, like crabs when the tide was high. Below, waves were pounding the cliff, and spray whirled around us. I was scared to death. Totally exhausted in mind and body, we were talking about committing suicide. Third-year students were especially impatient.

"Taira-*sensei*, let's die before it's too late!" some demanded.

"*Sensei*, let's do it immediately!" others prodded the teacher.

Taira-*sensei* looked quite disturbed because he, as our teacher, had the responsibility to protect our lives and was determined to do so. I had a hand grenade he had given me.

"It's all over. So let's sing a song," someone said.

Taira Sadako, Miyagi Tomiko, Itarashiki Yoshiko, and I started singing our favorite song, "Furusato" (Our native place), all of us looking toward the sea. Our voices were hoarse, so we could hardly sing. As we sang, our singing turned into sobbing.

"I want to see my mother!" Itarashiki-*san* said in tears. "I wish I could walk freely again under the blue skies with no bombs dropping!"

Upon hearing that, everybody started crying loudly. It was too sad to accept that we had to die after being cornered in such a wretched place, we all thought.

On the morning of 21 June, we found a little cave and tried to squeeze ourselves into it, but it was too narrow, and three of us—Taira-*sensei,* Higa-*san,* and I—were left outside. So we sat there near the entrance, leaning against the rock wall. The enemy had stopped attacking, so there was no bombardment—merely an eerie silence. There were countless enemy ships offshore, ominously silent, while numerous soldiers and civilian refugees, gripped with fear, huddled silently under rock ledges and in crevices and caves along the shore.

Then that dreaded broadcasting resumed. The frightening voice calling for surrender reverberated in the area: *We won't kill you. Raise your hands and come out.* Hearing this, one soldier stood up, raised his hands, and started walking in the water toward the ship. We all watched him in surprise. Then came a bang. Some soldier hiding under a rock ledge had shot him from behind. He fell down in the water and floated, his blood turning the water around him red. Frightened, nobody said a word.

The silence seemed to last forever, and then a blood-covered soldier tumbled toward me. He said he had thrown a grenade toward a group of Americans and they had shot back and seriously wounded him. "Enemy!" he screamed.

At that instant, Taira-*sensei* dashed into the inner part of the cave where nine classmates were hiding. Higa-*san* and I rushed into the next cave, where Yonamine-*sensei*'s group hid. Almost instantaneously an American appeared and started firing at us point blank. A deafening sound it was. *Bang! Bang! Bang!* Next to me, Ashitomi-*san* groaned and fell against me. Both Nakamoto-*san* and Uechi-*san* were instantly killed. The sergeant to my right was also killed instantly and fell on my face. Shimabuku-*san,* Higa-*san,* and Ōganeku-*san* were seriously wounded.

Just about that time, Taira-*sensei,* who had dashed into the cave where nine classmates were hiding, committed suicide with a hand grenade. When Higa-*san* and I ran into the cave, we found it splattered with blood, and ten persons were lying in a pool of blood. Taira-*sensei* was lying in the center, his intestines blown out. The third-year students had been the most badly wounded, some of them mangled almost beyond recognition. Lying a little apart from the group, Higa-*san* and Seragaki-*san* were also dead. Futenma-*san* died after a few groans. Strangely, the fourth-year students looked relatively untouched—just tiny red spots on their faces—though they too were dead.

We stood there, petrified and mute. That was the ugliest scene we'd ever seen. In an instant, four were killed and ten others had committed suicide. It was hell itself.

"NURSES, NO USE DYING FOR THE EMPEROR AT THIS TIME"

Arakaki Setsu (now Ameku Setsu)
Then 18 and in her first year, Regular Course, Women's Normal School
Assigned to First Surgery Unit

When I woke up the next morning, I was amazed to find so many American ships on the water in front of me. Some of them were broadcasting surrender instructions to us. *Come out of hiding. Detekoi,* they repeated. Now the nine of us had to make up our minds—to commit suicide or surrender.

We had two hand grenades among us. We all agreed to commit suicide with the grenades. Then someone said if we had one grenade each, we could all die without fail, but there was no assurance all nine of us would die with only two grenades.

"I've no objection to suicide, if you only let me hold one of the grenades," someone said. "Otherwise, I'd rather stay alive without any wound."

"Don't be rash," another said.

"Have you forgotten what you've been taught?" another retorted.

"What have we been taught? Like what?" another said.

"Like never to suffer the disgrace of being captured."

Senior students got into a dead-serious argument over the matter. Junior students wouldn't say a word. Perhaps they thought they had no choice but to abide by whatever decision the seniors reached. They remained silent and just listened.

Then a noncommissioned officer who was listening to our argument said suddenly, "You student nurses, this is no time for you to die for the Emperor. If you die now, what will happen to Okinawa in the future? We are soldiers, but we don't even have hand grenades. Young girl students like you shouldn't carry such dangerous things. I'll give you some crackers to eat, so let me have those grenades."

He admonished us for a while not to do anything rash. Finally, I handed the grenades to him. He did all the talking because he wanted them for himself.

After he got the grenades from us, he told us to go out and surrender to the Americans. Of course, we didn't want to do that and argued against it, but finally he talked us into going out. The Americans were now just behind us.

"DON'T TAKE OFF MY CLOTHES!"

Yabiku Toshiko (now Shimabukuro Toshiko)
Then 17 and in her third year, Preparatory Course, Women's Normal School
Assigned to Itokazu Detachment

"I'm not afraid of dying. Kill me now, please! You may kill me," I said, bringing the muzzle of the rifle to my chest.

"No! No!" the American soldier said.

He was trying to tell me something with his gestures. Then he started to cut my uniform with his scissors. I was sure he was going to strip me of my clothes, so I hollered at him and bit his hand as hard as I could.

"Why do you take my clothes off? I'm telling you to kill me! You can't kill me, so you're trying to put me to shame!" I shouted at the top of my voice.

But the American soldier, standing beside me and watching me like I was mad, was just smiling.

I tried to bite him again.

"Oh, no, no . . . ," he said and started cutting one of my trouser legs lengthwise from the bottom up to the thigh, where I had a gash. Then he turned his scissors crosswise and cut off the pant leg, making it look like a pair of shorts. He poured some kind of disinfectant onto the maggot-infested wound and out came many wriggling worms.

After treating the wound, he took a stick of chewing gum from his pocket and offered it to me. I refused to take it. He then showed me a canteen and drank water from it.

If they were going to kill me anyway, I might as well drink the water and die, I thought. And I drank from his canteen.

FINALLY THE SUNSHINE, ON 22 AUGUST

Tokuyama Masako (now Arasaki Masako)
Then 17 and in her fourth year, First Prefectural Girls' High School
Assigned to Accounting Section

The Americans let loose a barrage of shots like fireworks from their bivouac positions. And soon an unconfirmed report came to us that Japan had been defeated. There were seven people in the cave, including us.

People at the sugar-mill site where we used to get together to exchange information said with a troubled look on their faces that such a thing could never have happened, and they would not believe the report. The Americans were celebrating their victory, firing guns and cannons, but people thought it was a *kamikaze* attack.

On that night, Komatsu-*san* said to us, "You are women. You'd better go out and surrender." But we didn't listen to him because we decided we would rather die than be taken prisoner.

An officer from Yama Unit, a short distance away, volunteered to go to a nearby U.S. camp to confirm the report. When he came back, he said it was true and that everybody should be ready to leave the cave to surrender on the twenty-second.

Around ten o'clock that morning, a soldier from Yama Unit came to our cave to see if we were ready. Three soldiers reluctantly left the cave. We could not make up our minds. No soldier had asked us if we would follow him, so we were just watching. Some of them were packing their belongings in the darkness of the cave, and one soldier was shaving himself.

There were two seriously wounded soldiers we had been taking care of in the cave. Apparently they'd heard what Komatsu-*san* and we were talking about. One of them insisted to us, "You shouldn't surrender. You'd better stay here."

Hiroko-*san*, my classmate, told me that we should leave but that the seriously wounded soldiers were counting on us for their survival. She added, "If you decide to stay, then I will too."

But I decided to leave as she had first suggested. I decided so because I didn't want to die in the darkness of the cave and thought that if I were going to be killed anyway, I would rather die in an open field, under the bright sun. I assumed the Americans would not spare my life once I was captured.

Outside the cave, I couldn't open my eyes. The sun I saw for the first time in many weeks was too bright. As my eyes got used to the light, I looked around, but the people were all strangers to me, though I had lived with them in the cave for about two months. They looked at me strangely too. They used to call us Masa-*chan* and Hiro-*chan*, but now they didn't seem to know which of us was Masa-*chan* and the other Hiro-*chan*. Of course, we couldn't tell which of them was the sergeant we had been taking orders from.

While we were staring at each other with stupid looks on our faces, the seriously wounded soldiers who'd said they would remain in the cave crawled out. They hadn't been able to move even to get their daily food rations. Now, with all the strength left in them, they'd crawled out of the cave to survive and were drying themselves in the hot sun.

The sun was bright, and it stung our eyes.

Translations courtesy of the Himeyuri Peace Museum

LISA OTTIGER

In My Absence

I never knew my grandfather, a man who more than fifty years ago went to the Philippines, married my grandmother, volunteered to serve in World War II, and died. All my life, he was a mystery, someone we talked about with awe, the symbol of a glamorous and tragic past. And he remained a myth to me until I was given a packet containing letters he had written to my grandmother during the war, along with other letters, photos, and documents.

I knew I needed to write his story, for many reasons, but really for only one that's important. This is a love story.

Someone's Grandfather

Across the sea, corpses in the water.
Across the mountain, corpses in the field.

Japanese war song

During World War II, 140,000 Allied soldiers were imprisoned by the Japanese in Southeast Asia. About one-third of those men died in captivity. One of those men was my grandfather, a casualty of Japanese aggression in the Philippines. Reading the letters given to me by my grandmother, I have come to understand the effect of one man's death on many lives: his wife and child, his parents, his best friend, his uncle, fellow officers. I try to imagine this one loss magnified by the thousands, by the tens of millions of civilians and soldiers who died in the war.

The Package

When I untied the bundle of brown envelopes held together by rusty paper clips and string, I found letters from my grandfather to my grandmother written while he was in various Japanese POW camps in the Philippines, letters from his mother to his wife after his death, and letters from friends refusing to believe that he had died. The paper was brown and brittle, the ink faded to a purplish color. Most of my grandfather's letters were written on precious scraps of paper he had managed to obtain in prison. I had known that these letters existed, but I hadn't known how many there were. Until her health began its final turn for the worse, my grandmother never showed them to my mother; nor did she talk about her husband. Then she gave the letters to my mother, and my mother gave them to me.

When I was growing up, there was only one picture of my grandfather: in it, he wears a white dinner jacket and is leaning against a bar. The photograph was in my grandmother's living room, which we used once a year, at Christmas, to open presents. The photo was displayed only after the death of Grandma's second husband, in 1972; as a result, my mother saw no pictures of her father when she was growing up. Suddenly I had photos of him on polo fields in Shanghai and Manila; a studio portrait taken at age twenty-four, just before he sailed for Shanghai in 1932; a picture of him as a toddler on a front porch in Columbus, Mississippi—sent to my grandmother by the town's bank manager after my grandfather's death. There were wedding pictures, too, in which my grandmother looked very young and very happy. In one photo, the bride and groom are descending a flight of marble stairs, and my grandmother's face is alive with joy. In a slightly out-of-focus picture, they are dancing and her laughing face is tucked against his chest.

It was said my grandfather was so handsome that when he entered a room, men and women both turned to look at him. There was a glamour about him. In his photos he appears surprisingly boyish, though in profile he looks older, with curly black hair and large, round eyes, which were either brown or green, depending on who was describing them. He was fairly tall and had a tendency to slouch, to lower his chin and gaze up, wide-eyed, at the camera. He seems unassuming, even nice. Something about him reminds me of my own father, though they look nothing alike. His smile and expression of surprise make me think of my brother.

In most of the photos, he is dressed either in riding clothes or a dinner jacket. In one photo of a group of party guests on a terrace—perhaps at the Manila Polo Club—the men are all in dinner jackets and the women have marcelled hair and slinky evening gowns. My grandmother is seated in a circle of women, holding a martini; my grandfather stands next to another man behind her, holding a cigarette. It is a very formal world.

Grandma stole most of these pictures from my grandfather's parents after the war, then had them copied. She had lost everything of her own; she didn't even have wedding photos.

Learning to Listen

My grandmother always said exactly what she thought. Once, when I was eleven, she asked me what I wanted to be when I grew up. When I replied that I wanted to be a writer, she said that I didn't have enough imagination. At the time I was hurt, but now I know that you need other things—even more than imagination—in order to write.

A Perfect Childhood

My grandmother was born on 13 July 1911, and grew up in a grand house in Manila with her sister, Mary, and two brothers. Her father, Frederick Cadwallader, was a Texan, a sculptor who had given up his art to follow his brother to the Philippines. There, he made and lost a fortune in lumber and developed a lifelong habit of drawing on tablecloths. In a silver-framed photo of him as a young man, he is standing, smiling, next to a half-finished, life-sized marble statue of a woman. Another photo, found among my grandmother's papers and taken near the end of his life, shows him bearded and stern.

Grandma's mother, Doña Florence—whom we called Grandma Dos—was the daughter of a mestiza woman and a Pennsylvanian packed off to the Philippines by his family to cure him of his gambling habit. Grandma Dos claimed she could see the dead. Her children, my grandmother among them, were raised by a Chinese *amah*, Ah Yee, whose dream was to save enough money to go home to China to die. Ah Yee went to China several times to die, but kept returning to Manila very much alive.

Apparently, my grandmother and her siblings were terrible children. In a series of photos of the family gathered in the garden, my grandmother is a skinny, long-limbed little girl, and her brother, Fred Junior (called "Little Man"), makes faces at the camera: sticking out his tongue, putting his fingers in his ears, crossing his eyes. Their father looks bemused; Grandma Dos looks thunderous. In the final picture, Fred is wailing while my grandmother and Auntie Mary, her sister, look on with delight. In an earlier photo, all the Cadwallader children, dressed appropriately in devil costumes, are piled into a car that appears to be a Model T; Grandma is the littlest fat-faced devil in front, sticking out her tongue.

The Wedding

Grandma was smart and funny and beautiful, but she didn't marry until she was twenty-nine. One of her suitors grumbled that she was waiting for a knight on a white horse. That knight was William Harrington, a young Mississippi lawyer newly arrived from Shanghai, who—in one account—rode up to her apartment building on his white polo pony as the Cadwallader sisters were taking their evening cocktails and watching the sun set over Manila Bay. In fact, they met at a party on his first night in the city. And then she had to wait four more years: he explained to her that he couldn't afford both a wife and a polo pony, and that in four years the pony would be old, but she would still be young.

They married on 27 September 1940. The headline in the *Manila Bulletin*'s society pages read RUTH CADWALLADER BECOMES BRIDE OF W. B. HARRINGTON IN SOCIETY WEDDING. Grandma is described in the newspaper article as a "Manila girl."

My mother was born on 12 August 1941. A few months later—a little more than a year after the wedding—William Harrington went to war.

Leave-taking

Japanese planes bombed the U.S. Naval Station at Cavite, south of Manila, around three A.M. on 8 December 1941—minutes after the bombing of Pearl Harbor, which lay across the international date line. Nine hours later, at a quarter past noon, the Japanese wiped out America's largest assembly of warplanes overseas; the planes had been lined up on the ground at Clark Field, north of Manila.

When my grandfather quickly reported for active duty in the naval reserves, Grandma was very upset. Though he was determined to go, he waited for her to tell him that it was all right. The day he left, he filled the bathtub with sweetpeas, her favorite flower.

His letters to her after his capture two months later, in February 1942, show how much faith he had in his new wife and in the belief that he would return to her and their infant daughter.

From the letters, it's apparent that everyone called him Bill, except for his parents and his uncle, Hunter Walker. They simply called him Son.

"Pretty"

> Promulgating new regulations governing the movement and employment of enemy nationals in the Philippines, the authorities of the Japanese Military Administration yesterday warned these nationals to behave themselves properly in due appreciation of the generous attitude shown them by the Imperial Japanese Forces. Regret was expressed over the fact that among enemy nationals released on the permanent and conditional basis, not a few took action disappointing to administration authorities and embarrassing at the same time to other law-abiding third power nationals.
>
> *Manila Bulletin*, 16 January 1943

When the Japanese army took over Manila in January 1942, they registered all Allied civilians before interning about four thousand of them on the grounds of Santo Tomás, a three-hundred-year-old university founded by Spanish Dominican friars. Grandma, her two brothers and their wives—and my mother, who was six months old—were among those interned. Grandma's Residence Certificate, issued by the Defense Commanding Officer-in-Chief of the Greater Manila City, was among the packet of papers I was given. It lists her as thirty-three years old. Folded up with the paper was an I.D. photo of her: she looks much older; her mouth is tight with strain. A photo of my mother is attached to the certificate: a fat, smiling baby in a *camiseta* to ward off prickly heat rashes. Grandma told her that her father always called her Pretty; this had to be proof of a parent's blind love because my mother was very funny looking. Her baby pictures are startling: at age one she looks exactly as she does now, though full of a child's uncomplicated happiness. She had to grow into her face.

Santo Tomás

Dated 10 May 1943, a letter from the commandant of the Santo Tomás Internment Camp instructs internees:

> You may bring with you into the Santo Tomás Camp essential personal effects, single bed of the folding or camp cot type, bedding, mosquito net and dishes. Your hand baggage should be limited as much as possible or to the equivalent of two suitcases per person, because there is no storage accommodation for extra baggage.

Life in camp was spare and strict. My grandmother and mother lived in a wooden shanty built by one of Grandma's brothers. Young as she was, my mother remembers my grandmother's terror when, one day, my mother wandered off before morning roll call. She got almost to the main gate before she was stopped and brought back at bayonet point by a guard.

She also remembers that they weren't supposed to look at the sky. The Japanese feared that the prisoners would somehow be able to signal American planes; the punishment for looking was to stare at the sun until going blind. One day she looked up and saw a falling American plane.

As a child, my mother didn't think spending the first years of her life in an internment camp—and later in a bombed-out apartment building—was strange at all. Perhaps it was because she was so young, perhaps because my grandmother encouraged a child's faith in make-believe, telling my mother stories about fairies and dolls coming alive at midnight. At Santo Tomás, my mother had a Raggedy Ann doll, and one night she decided to stay awake until midnight to see her come alive. She filled a jar with fireflies and set it by her bed to help her see, but she fell asleep. When she woke up, it was morning and the fireflies were dead.

Letters

These are some of my grandfather's wartime letters, arranged in chronological order. They are the only record we have of what happened to him. When I started to read them, I was surprised because they didn't talk about what I expected: his fear, perhaps, or the conditions in the camps where he was imprisoned. Instead, the first of them are full of relief "now that the hostilities have ended." He is referring to the surrender of the Americans and Filipinos to the Japanese. History tells us it is after this surrender that things got bad: the Bataan Death March, the terrible dying in the POW camps in the first few months of captivity. There is none of this in his letters. Instead there are a sense of his optimism and good humor, his confidence in a safe return to his family, and his absolute faith in my grandmother's ability to come through in his absence.

I keep thinking that my grandfather must have been shocked by what was happening to him. This seems an obvious thing to say—even now, many of the acts carried out then are incomprehensible—but William Harrington was a man who had been loved and admired his whole life, and genuinely liked. His life began as an arc of promise that led him out of a Mississippi town to the glamour of Shanghai and Manila. He was blessed, lucky, golden. He was, to use an old-fashioned word, a gentleman, though not a saint—he smoked too much and drank like a fish. But he seems to have possessed a sure moral center, a quiet sense of "fair play." While in college at Washington and Lee, he made sure that a Jewish friend was accepted into his fraternity—this at a time when such a thing was simply not done. In Manila he was among the founders of the Tamaraos Polo Club, formed because the Manila Polo Club did not accept Filipino members. These are small acts, kind rather than heroic, but I think he must have been baffled by the cruelty of his last days—the collapse of the rules of the game as he knew them.

The following letter was probably written around mid-April 1942 from a prison camp on the island of Negros—one of the islands between the northernmost Philippine island, Luzon, and the southernmost, Mindanao, which are collectively known as the Visayas. It is addressed to my grandmother care of Grandma Dos; in the confusion of the American surrender, and after being transported hundreds of miles away, William Harrington did not know that all U.S. civilians in the Philippines, including his wife in Manila, had been interned. The letter was in a Manila Elks Club envelope stamped MAIL OF PRISONER OF WAR.

My darling,

I have thought of you and Mary Patricia [the baby] constantly over the last long months. With the end of hostilities here my anxiety for your safety and health has decreased and I hope some peace of mind has now come to you. Now I live for the day we three will be together again. Give our daughter my love and tell her I think of her birthday every month as it rolls around—and how many there have been and how beautiful a young lady she must be by now.

Devotedly,
Bill

Writing paper soon became a precious commodity among POWs. The letter below was dated July 1942 and written on a piece of paper stamped OFFICIAL USE ONLY—like the Elks Club envelope, a precious scrap.

My darling,

The greatest comfort to me over the last long months has been my confidence in the goodness of your family and this has been added to by my faith in your own level head and courage. It is hard to realize that Mary Patricia is a big girl of eleven and a half (almost) months with teeth coming and probably [learning] to talk and walk. You two are constantly in my thoughts and the happiest of these thoughts is of the day we three will be together again.

Please don't worry about me here. We are comfortably quartered and well treated. Our prison has ample grounds for exercise and includes a volleyball court and an indoor ball diamond. In addition to the sports I have a small (very) garden of my own from which I derive much pleasure and I hope eventually to derive a few vegetables. Every third day I am on duty as camp cook and will show you some fine points in that art when I see you. In addition to my uniforms I have several shirts and pairs of slacks. [Also] in addition to a pair of huge army shoes I have my black navy oxfords so you see I am well fixed for clothes. Am healthy and tan and now streamlined down to 155.

While all of our necessities are cared for if the Japanese authorities would permit it I wish you could send me about twenty pesos a month, three cartons of Rosita cigarettes (Tabacqueria) and some pictures of the baby (I have a newspaper photo of you at our wedding which I found but none of Mary Patricia). And more than all please write as often as you may.

All my love,
Bill

Another letter, dated August 1942:

My darling,

This opportunity to write you is a pleasant surprise furnished by the kindness of a Japanese officer. Now that I have the opportunity there is little to say except that I am in the best of health and being treated with courtesy and kindness. When I come home (and that is a wonderful word) you can practice law and I can stay home and cook for every third day I am camp cook. In my spare time, of which there is an ample sufficiency I study Spanish and work my little garden neither of which is showing great progress. If you could send me a copy of the Philippine Civil Code or the Penal Code (there are many in my old office) it would help me a lot. Once again I am most anxious to return to the law.

The pictures of M. P. are simply grand, I am amazed that we have such a beautiful daughter. Funny I am so glad now we had a daughter instead of a son and the fact that I have you to return to is my biggest support. I spend literally days at a time thinking over the happy times we have had and picturing good days to come.

Give my love to all there and keep a heart full for yourself.

Devotedly,
Bill

Three years later, at war's end, my grandfather did not come home with the other POWs. Friends and family tried to find out what had become of William Harrington. A little of the chaos of the world comes through in their letters: the urgency of finding one man among the many lost. What most struck me in reading them was that no one really believed that my grandfather would not come back: it was impossible that he, of all people, would not survive.

Maybe it is human nature not to believe in the possibility of your own death or the death of a loved one. I keep thinking of a recent airplane crash: two hundred souls falling for thirty thousand feet, probably believing until they hit the water that they might still make it. I imagine my grandfather's life speeding up in those last months, his falling, unbelieving.

My mother speaks of the incredible strength of my grandmother. Was she always so strong, or had William Harrington made her that way? Grandma lost her husband, her home, all her belongings, even her wedding ring, which she sold to a Japanese soldier in the camp for milk. Had my grandfather recognized something in this slight, pretty, laughing woman that would allow her to survive the loss of almost everything?

The following letter, dated 20 March 1945, was sent to my grandfather's uncle in Connecticut by a military commander.

> Dear Mr. Walker,
>
> Your letter of the 15th instant reached me this morning and I am indeed glad that I can give you some information regarding your nephew.
>
> I was well acquainted with Bill as he and I were together from the time we left Corregidor 22 February 1942 until he left Bilibid as a member of a draft of war prisoners being transferred to Japan on 13 December 1944. We also served at Cavite before the war.
>
> We were both members of a detachment of naval officers sent to Cebu in February 1942 for duty with the army Visayan-Mindanao force. Upon evacuation of Cebu, 11 April 1942, I went to Mindanao while Bill was taken a prisoner in the Cebu-Negros area. Later I was taken prisoner on Mindanao. We both arrived at the prison camp at Davao, Mindanao, on the same boat in October 1942 and were together at that camp until 6 June 1944, when we were transferred to Manila, Bill going to Cabanatuan and I remaining at Bilibid. In September 1944 Bill was sent down from Cabanatuan to Bilibid as a member of the last draft of officers and men the Japs were transferring to Japan. I saw him the morning they were marched out to board the steamer on 13 December 1944. There were about 1800 officers and men in the draft.
>
> W. H. Bicknell, Commander (SC) USN

Another letter, dated 12 April 1945 and printed on United Press Association stationery, kept the family's hopes alive:

> Dear Mr. Walker,
>
> The information you have about your nephew, Lieutenant "Bill" Harrington, is correct. He was sent to Japan on 13 December 1944.
>
> You, no doubt, have heard that the ship was bombed on the 14th. We know definitely that 300 men were considered missing and 63 considered casualties. However, Bill's name did not appear on either list and so we are quite sure that he reached Japan safely. So far as we know, none of these prisoners was sent to China proper. However, a part of this draft may have been sent to Manchuria.
>
> While in Washington some time ago, I was told by a high-ranking officer that every effort was being made to get a complete list of prisoners from the

Japanese. I don't know what success has crowned the efforts of the War Department along these lines. I am sure that you will be notified immediately when news is received from Japan.

Thanks a lot for your well wishes and I hope the above information verifies that which you have.

Sincerely,
Franz Weisenblatt

Beyond Hope

After I had read through all the letters twice, I found a scrap of paper that looked like it had been torn off an envelope. In pencil—in writing that doesn't look like my grandmother's, but whose else can it be?—was the following, copied down from what I believe was a radio broadcast, "Free Philippines," and dated Monday, 26 February 1945:

> Washington—Eight hundred American prisoners suffocated in the packed holds of a Japanese prison ship which left Manila last December, according to a navy officer who escaped. About 1,600 prisoners were herded into the tiny holds of the ship on the night of 13 December and were held there at the points of rifles for 36 hours. The vessel was sunk by an American bombing attack on 15 December.

Hellship

Time does not heal all wounds;
it buries them in very shallow graves.

American POW

The ships the Japanese used to transport POWs from camps across Asia to Japan were known as hellships. Men were crammed into holds without food or water, many dying of starvation and suffocation. However, most died when these ships, which were unmarked, were torpedoed by American submarines or bombed by American planes. The Japanese estimate that twenty-five transport ships were bombed or torpedoed. More than ten thousand POWs—one in three of all POWs who died in the Pacific War—were killed by friendly fire at sea. And more Americans died from the sinking of one ship, the *Arisan Maru,* than during the Bataan Death March.

On 13 December 1944, the last healthy prisoners of the old Spanish prison Bilibid, my grandfather among them, were marched out at 10:30 A.M. in columns of four to a pier where a ship was waiting. A truck followed behind to pick up men who could not finish the march. The final transport ship out of Manila, the *Oryokko Maru* loaded 1,619 prisoners. Almost two-thirds of the prisoners were officers; most enlisted men had already been shipped out. The prisoners included the remaining medical officers from the Bilibid and Cabanatuan POW camps and combat-unit commanders from Bataan and Corregidor. In addition, the ship had a crew of one hundred, including thirty guards; about seven hundred Japanese nationals, mostly women and children; and a thousand seamen taken from ships sunk in Manila Bay. There were three holds. The aft and forward holds were overcrowded; men started to faint, and by the middle of the night many were screaming for water and air. Thirty were dead before the ship had even gotten under way—shot by guards as they tried to climb the ladders for fresh air.

Before dawn on 14 December, the vessel left in a convoy of seven, including transports with Japanese troops, a cruiser, and several destroyers. Off Subic Bay, U.S. Navy planes attacked. There were sixteen bombing raids throughout the day. Many prisoners were wounded and the Japanese anti-aircraft gunners were dead or dying. Blood was running into the hold. During the night Japanese officers took American medical officers up on deck to administer to the wounded; they had to work by candlelight and had no medicine or bandages. In the holds that night, men started to kill each other for water, to slit each other's throats to drink blood.

The morning of 15 December, Japanese wounded and civilians were unloaded at Olongapo Naval Station in Subic Bay. When American planes returned and bombed the forward hold, 150 prisoners died and a fire broke out. A Japanese guard announced that the prisoners would have to swim the half-mile to shore. Those that could swam while the rest—dead and wounded Americans and Japanese—went down with the ship. The prisoners in the water were machine-gunned by the Japanese. The surviving 1,341 prisoners were rounded up; 386 had been killed or were missing. That evening, the survivors were confined in a tennis court. They hadn't eaten since the day before. Many had burns and were covered in oil.

On 20 December, the prisoners were marched to the town of San Fernando, Pampanga. The most badly wounded were removed and killed. On the twenty-fourth, the remaining prisoners were loaded into freight cars. The sick and wounded were tied on top of the cars and ordered to wave to the American planes if the train was attacked. After thirty-six hours, the prisoners arrived in San Fernando, La Union on Lingayen Gulf. They were marched to a schoolhouse and fed, then marched to the beach. Two days later, the POWs were moved to a pier where Japanese landing boats waited to transfer them to two freighters standing offshore and bound for Takao, Formosa. The water was rough, and there was a twenty- to twenty-five-foot drop into the landing boats. Those reluctant to jump were pushed. The freighter *Enoura Maru* was loaded with 1,070 prisoners, and the rest were loaded on the *Brazil Maru*. Both ships had been carrying livestock in the holds below the main deck where the men were confined. The flies were beyond description.

The voyage to Takao took five days; en route, bodies were thrown overboard. In port, the prisoners were kept in the holds for a week, then all the men were moved to the *Enoura Maru*. During a bombing raid, the *Enoura Maru* was hit; 200 prisoners died in the forward hold. Japanese doctors went aboard but did little. Dysentery was widespread, and only three American doctors were active. The corpses were hauled off with cranes and buried with simple funeral services in a mass grave near the beach.

On 13 January, the survivors—now fewer than 600 of the original 1,619—were transferred to the *Brazil Maru*. The next day a convoy left for Moji on Kyūshū Island, sailing by night to avoid submarine attacks. The decks were covered in ice and snow, and men continued to die in the holds during the two weeks it took to reach Japan. Soon the prisoners were too weak to lift the dead up to the deck; no funeral rites were held. Arriving in Moji at dawn on 29 January, the ship unloaded fewer than 500 prisoners. Between Manila and San Fernando, 629 had died; between San Fernando and Takao, 493. Within a month of reaching Japan, 150 more died in prison camps.

Liberation

> *Rape and bayonet were the order*
> *of retreat. House to house it was said*
> *they fought, and the family remembered.*
>
> Alfred Yuson, "Manila: 23 February 1945"

As the final months of the war were unfolding in the Philippines, the American liberating forces landed on the southern island of Leyte on 20 October 1944. Moving up the archipelago, they reached Luzon, coming ashore one hundred miles north of Manila at Lingayen Gulf, the spot where the Japanese had landed in 1941. The First Cavalry armored division entered Manila on 3 February and liberated Santo Tomás; it took until March to free the rest of the city. In the house-to-house fighting, 100,000 civilians died.

Death Notice

A telegram containing William Harrington's death notice and a synopsis of his war record was sent to Grandma at the bombed-out Boulevard Apartments, where they moved after liberation. An official letter from James Forrestal, Secretary of the Navy, followed on 4 September 1945, by which time Grandma had gone to California.

The three-line letter states that William Harrington was "known to have lost his life on 15 December 1944" and extends the hope that my grandmother might "find comfort in the thought that his sacrifice was made in order that the freedom of his country might be preserved." An elderly survivor of the *Oryokko Maru* remembers only one W. B. Harrington on board, a lieutenant commander. When the ship was beached, he had swum ashore at Olongapo.

As a child, my mother had a recurring nightmare. A slender island rose out of the sea. Waves beat against it. On the island stood a line of Japanese soldiers with fixed bayonets. Men in uniform were in the water; as they tried to climb out, they were pushed back or bayoneted. My mother knew nothing of her father's death, yet she dreamed this until she was ten years old. She now believes he was one of those who died trying to swim ashore.

His remains might be just a few hours north of where we are living now.

The Wrong Ending

My grandfather was thirty-seven when he died. I keep thinking of that surprised expression on his face in certain photographs, so like my brother's, and see his body floating in the water. I wonder why they didn't know that he was special, that he was not to be harmed. I wonder if he was as healthy and hopeful as he sounded in his letters until the last, when he seemed to know it was all over. It is hard to reconcile the brutality of the camps described in POW accounts—the beatings, torture, overwork, disease, and lack of food and medicine—with my grandfather's careful letters about losing weight, learning to cook, planting a vegetable garden, studying Spanish and law. Pictures of American POWs in the Philippines show some skeletal, weighing less than a hundred pounds, others grotesquely swollen with beriberi.

I think of that Japanese officer who was kind to him. And I think of a friend's words to my grandmother: *May life be kind to you hereafter.*

Aftermath

Having just lived through a war, my grandmother forbade my mother from watching war movies. One day after school, the nuns were showing movies, and my mother, aged seven, was allowed to go. But the movie turned out to be *The Fighting Sullivans,* the story of five brothers who go off to war together and then die when the ship they are on is sunk. The last scene is of the five brothers marching arm-in-arm to heaven. My grandmother arrived to pick up my mother and found her distraught on the side of the road.

SONE YOSHI

Half a Century

For years and years you have been a skull.
NISHIGORI FUJIKO

"We had to break the piles of frozen bodies
hardened like dead trees,
and carry them to the frozen sea
and dump them quickly,"
the man who has returned from Siberia is saying.
It's so strange
that on a hot summer night
in the slight sound of the air conditioner
the man is there on the TV screen
definitely alive.

On the yonder side of the flow of half-a-century's time,
a man who expired in the frozen land
had an artificial eye in his skull,
glistening,
fiercely staring at the sky, he says.

Though a skull,
he was able to come back to his wife,
thanks to his artificial right eye.

Translation by Koriyama Naoshi

AYUKAWA NOBUO

Three Poems

MAN ON THE BRIDGE (1942)

Man on the bridge resting your elbows on the high parapet
casting a shadow in the clear sky.
The weeping trees, or
black stream flowing far beneath
the endless roofs of the town made of stone
do you really feel
the prow desperately advancing,
plowing through heavy stagnant time
striking at vanity with its oars?

Man on the bridge watching the fireworks
you came to the far bridge
to look down on the image of yourself—
abandoning the abominable wall
sighs flickering on useless paper.
Turning away birds
fatigued by artificiality
to their late gloomy branches
on the faraway bridge
you look up at the fireworks of midday.

Man on the bridge with a parched spirit,
in the quiet ebb and flow of the sleeping wave
the faces of mother, father
friends, too, are wavering.
Is there much deeper toil than this smooth cave?
Even if the pure green calls to you from the grave mound,
the surface of the water refuses to move.

Man on the bridge who is dreaming—
the day when this mud-soiled stream
will someday flow to the sea with a thunderclap

and spill out to the horizon joined to the sky,
the day when this bridge will either drift out to sea
or become a blue figure alive with motion
crying in a natural voice . . .
will that day ever come?

Man on the bridge with an earnest brow
you become one with the hazy mist,
making sure that the footprints around your life are disappearing.
What are you thinking at sunset?
The thousand steps coming and going across your back
are descending towards the same labyrinth
just walking the stairs to oblivion
holding the wooden rail
listening to the swell of polluted underground water.

Pick a moment when anger can be quelled easily,
as if there were means on Earth to cure only the flesh.
Man on the bridge with distant eyes,
nobody would believe you would lie down
trembling under the sunset sky
and smile forever to the words of the drifting wind
blowing on black water.

Leaving the dim edge of the abyss,
it's possible that people flow in time unchanging like a narrow river.
But man on the bridge,
no matter where you go
the silence of the pale river
trails after the ticking of the clock
that carves out the soul
preventing your advance like a succession of doors,
making your body into a shadow like the corridor of afternoon.

Why did it take you so long to remember
that you yourself are one small room,
and here and there are also just an illusion?
Man on the bridge. At the end of beauty,
there was no direction
there were no fireworks or dreams
no wind blowing.
Sustained by the dark blue,
gazing at the other bank
you're still cold
aren't you,
man on the bridge.

1948

"1886" read the whiskey label.
That was the year
my agony began.
Once I walked in Singapore,
far from here
with a license to kill in my pocket.
Under the blue sky
the young man who taught Pascal
died in battle
and yet, we couldn't believe we survived.

Once a German writer who hated war
showed me a painted plate.
On it was painted "1850."
That's the year I became *un étranger*
not caring where I went.
One day I took a boat
and thought of Peppercorn
committing suicide.
Toba Lake was calm.
The oars gave me a whole body
and the power bound judgement and intention tightly to my legs.
There were no birds, much less the shadows of humans.
The other side is always quiet, like a dead country.
I knew that
the evening sun threw red dye on my jacket shoulder,
and the moonlight that would make this world cold
shone on my forehead . . .

Speeding through the outskirts of Manila,
I used to laugh.
At Keelung Harbor in the rain,
I might cry
In a corner of Tokyo,
I deny all that I am.
1948
is not a label,
nor a scene on a painted plate.

Hey! Miserable black hat,
smoke from the cigarette in my yellow fingertips,
    fragile illusion!
Born out of crime—
thriving on hatred, deception, humiliation—
even though this long century

which should collapse in the dark daybreak
is almost over
today, once more
the river climbs up over the mountain
and in the city
the foul salmons of civilization
crowd together to sing those old familiar songs.

ARMY COMRADES

Hey! I haven't seen you for a long time.
I thought you'd forgotten.

Have twenty years passed?
Don't look at me with that faraway glance.

Come on, let's shake hands!

What a cold hand for a living being!
Don't you remember
the bloody straits of Johore
the scorched hills of Bukit Timah?
Can't you hear
the echo of destruction after destruction
the song of the guns roaring
in the last moments of the navy port?

Don't pretend to ignore me by hanging your head,
you foxes who hide things in keyholes, within books!
We're the ones who can meet only in the past.
Are there any secrets left?

After orders came,
that conviction—with which we immediately fell into formation
making a forest of black bayonets
and a mute sortie on the enemy,
becoming white bones in the morning—
where did it go?
That incarnation of purity rushing straight to the horizon
believing in the glory of the motherland
and the love of our brethren—
where did it disappear to?

This morning again, at the sink
you spat out green toothpaste mixed with blood.
Courteously choking your neck with a thin tie

loading your body—
still hot with the warmth of bed—
into the streetcar,
you went reluctantly to work
"I have to get just a little something
for the children
tomorrow and the day after tomorrow, too."

If you can answer me, please do so,
comrade with the white chest of a bridegroom,
how big was our defeat, how small was your victory?
What alms did you receive from the enemy,
what reparations did you make
and what did you do for the miserable victims
who lost eyes, ears, arms, or legs?

Hey, comrade! Why do you keep silent?
Looking straight this way, you don't see a thing.
You said you hoped every order would be at your level:
love of security,
retreat into idleness.
Counting on the infinite possibility of compromise,
is that all you got?

Fighting for corrupt interests
your cronies, who are so good at mimicking, sing in chorus:
Perhaps it's the age that's responsible.
They complained to the lonely bar hostess
that water doesn't change into liquor,
desire doesn't become greater consumption.

The good old boys hiding behind a tree trunk
sleeping with their gray-flecked heads touching—
pleasantly dreaming of a kingdom
where they can fill their pockets with slumber.
Though the storm never judges,
fate judges you by its momentary light
and I'm looking forward to
the end of this world!

Goodbye, comrades.
This is our first real parting
but I don't want the kiss of Judas . . .
so
goodbye.

Translations by Oketani Shogo with Leza Lowitz

KO ŬN

Six Poems

HEADMASTER ABE

Headmaster Abe Sudomu from Japan:
with his round glasses: a fearsome man,
fiery-hot like the spiciest peppers.
When he clacked down the hallway
in slippers cut from a pair of old boots,
he cast a deathly hush over every class.
In my second year during ethics class
he asked us what we hoped to become.
Kids replied:
"I want to be a general in the Imperial Army!"
"I want to become an admiral!"
"I want to become another Yamamoto Isoroko!"
"I want to become a nursing orderly!"
"I want to become a mechanic in a plane factory
and make planes to defeat the American and British devils!"
Then Headmaster Abe asked me to reply.
I leaped to my feet:
"I want to become the Emperor!"
No sooner were those words spoken
than a thunderbolt fell from the blue:
"You have formally blasphemed the venerable name
of His Imperial Majesty: you are expelled this instant!"
On hearing that, I collapsed into my seat.
But the class master pleaded,
my father put on clean clothes and came and pleaded,
and by the skin of my teeth, instead of being expelled,
I was punished by being sent to spend a few months
sorting through a stack of rotten barley
that stood in the school grounds,
separating out the still useable grains.
Every day I was imprisoned in a stench of decay
and there, under scorching sun and in beating rain,

I realized I was all alone in the world.
Soon after those three months of punishment were over,
during ethics class Headmaster Abe said:
"We're winning, we're winning, we're winning!
Once the great Japanese army has won the war,
you peninsula people will go to Manchuria, go to China,
and take important positions in government offices!"
That's what he said.
Then a B-29 appeared,
and as the silver four-engine plane passed overhead,
our Headmaster shouted in a big voice:
"That's the enemy! They're devils!" he cried fearlessly.
But his shoulders drooped.
His shout died away into a solitary mutter.
August 15 came. Liberation.
He left for Japan in tears.

YI YONG-AK

He left us the most painful and lovely of all
the modern poetry written in our land,
he left us the most painful and truthful of all.
In the 1930s when we were under Japanese rule
he would stand, hungry,
in the center of Seoul,
waiting for anyone he knew to come by.
Soon after Liberation in 1945,
So Chong-ju published a volume of poems, *Nightingale,*
in praise of long journeys to Western realms
and went out to the publication party
dressed in a fine silk shirt.
Yi Yong-ak turned up at the party
and drew him into a corner:
"Chong-ju, a word in your ear."
Then he pulled a knife from his belt
and slashed the fine silk shirt,
spat, "You hopeless bourgeois,"
and walked out.
If he was sent salted fish roe from home
far north in Hamkyong Province,
he would ask someone to look after it
and savor it little by little as he wandered about.
In the chaos of the late 1940s,
the days of chaotic poetry,

days when only flowers of sorrow bloomed,
he turned his back on every kind of vice—
every kind of trickery,
every kind of wickedness.
Those were days he could not endure.
With the Thirty-Eighth Parallel
cutting across our land's rivers and hills,
how could he remain safe?
Such was his destiny.
He left a few lines of poetry, then
went to China, and farther, to the wild far north, to Russia,
or so his elderly neighbors reckoned—
to dreadful places anyway.
A man of poetry who knew no lies,
he shines out, a distant lamp
down a long night road.

OH SONG-RYUN

A revolutionary can't live by his own name alone.
In each place he goes, he's someone else.
But certain revolutionaries
in the end earn a particular name
as their destiny.
Among comrades, each with many names,
the revolutionary Oh Song-ryun had five names.
The name he was known by was Chon-kwang,
but he had four other secret names.

Political advisor second grade to the Chinese Communist Party's
northeast anti-Japanese force,
then chief administrator of the Workers' Army,
he went into active service
and fought against the Japanese.
He fought in more than a hundred combats,
expanded the category of arms to include ideology.
The enemy was his target
and his comrades too.
In the end, one boy fighter was heard to cry out:
"Leader Chon-kwang is my ideology!"

In the so-called Kwandong suppression of Red guerrillas,
he disgraced himself by finally surrendering
to the Japanese search parties.
That was in the winter of 1941.

In the North Manchurian plains
and in Canton—
at Shanghai,
Beijing—
back in the South Manchurian plains—
his commune,
his hit-and-run attacks,
his ideological infiltrations,
his revolution—all was finished.
He betrayed as few of his companions as he could
and the revolution as much as he could.
The Second World War came to an end.
After the revolution, he was executed
in the name of the motherland
he had wandered in search of
in the days of his youth.

His baby son died of malnutrition.
His wife went missing.
Missing persons
are part of our land's traditions,
between revolution and counterrevolution.

SPIRIT SHRINE

We pray for a safe journey
by throwing a stone at the spirit shrine.
That was not something I learned from Dad
but by the time I was three I was already throwing stones.
Throwing a stone at the spirit shrine,
we pray that things go badly for those we hate.
We pray that they suffer a loss.
But we do not pray for their death.
The farmers' old-style curses
extend just so far;
no matter how wretched one may be
the curses extend just so far.
But near the end of the Japanese era
when stomachs were empty
and people were beside themselves,
very often a stone was thrown,
and people ventured to pray:
"May the kids of rich so-and-so die,
may rich so-and-so's father neither live long nor rest in peace."

The pile of stones at the spirit shrine kept growing higher.
The wife of Pak Tae-kon
told the rich people in the big house
about such prayers
and the rascal Su-dong who had said such a prayer
was summoned to the yard of the house of rich Kaneoka
where he got beaten with clubs
by the household serfs
and the owner's oldest son, Kaneoka Taro.
Soon after that, the rascal Su-dong
threw a stone late at night at the house of rich Kaneoka.
Instead of the spirit shrine,
instead of throwing a stone then praying,
in the guise of a ghost
he threw stones at the paper covering the door
of the owner's bedroom.
He was at once put in the police-station cell.
He did a month inside
then he came out.
He kept crying.
The dogs barked.

TEARS OF BLOOD

My youngest son . . . if you want to be remembered by posterity,
you must serve your country now.

Those words are spoken by Old Man Ch'oi
in the early modern novel *Tears of Blood.*
Yet its author, Lee In-jik, went to Japan on a scholarship,
learned Japanese, then served as an interpreter for the Japanese army
during the Russo-Japanese War.
Later, he was a newspaper's editor-in-chief, then its chairman,
before becoming secretary and interpreter to Lee Wan-yong;
as such, he was the official who sold our nation
with its twenty million people to the Japanese
for a mere thirty million *wŏn.*
Lee Wan-yong's enemy, Song Pyong-jun, had said the Japanese
should pay at least one hundred million,
but eager to gain credit for the annexation
he offered a closing bargain,
slashing the hundred million to a mere thirty.
In later years, Lee In-jik failed to get a single decoration.

He wrote occasional columns for the *Maeil Sinbo* paper,
then died, leaving *Tears of Blood* behind him.
He was cremated Japanese-style at Aogae Crematorium.
The four hundred and fifty *wŏn* the Japanese authorities
paid to cover his funeral expenses were his sole reward
for having administered the annexation.
He was the main pioneer of the modern Korean novel;
after him tower the figures of Ch'oi Nam-son and Lee Kwang-su.
Ah, scribblers of Korea, get down on your knees in awe.

MAN-SUN

Her face was a mass of freckles,
as if she'd been liberally sprinkled with sesame seed,
but her brows were fine, and her eyes so lovely
they made breezes spring up from the hills and plains.
Her shadow falling across the water
was like nothing else in this world.
Near the end of Japanese rule, after she had picked
and handed in the castor beans,
she left, wearing a headband stamped with the Japanese flag,
to become a comfort woman.
A woman from the Mijei Patriotic Wives Union took her away,
saying she was off to earn money at a factory
making airplane tails.
She took her away with the Japanese flag flying.
Then, *ho-ho,* a bottle of liquor
and a ration ticket for rice arrived at her family's house
from the local township head.
"*Ho-ho,* what have we done to deserve such a favor?"
After Liberation, when everyone came back,
not a word was heard from Man-sun . . .
though white campanulas blossomed
and cicadas sang.

Translations by Brother Anthony, Gary G. Gach,
and Kim Young-Moo

Fifty Years of Silence

Translator's Note

On 12 July 1999, a delegation of former comfort women and volunteers from Taiwan arrived at Haneda Airport to prepare to take legal action against the Japanese government. All were wearing T-shirts bearing the slogan 50 YEARS OF SILENCE. After meeting with members of Parliament the following afternoon, they gathered in the evening at Tokyo Women's Plaza to speak to about seventy interested people. These are three of the comfort women's stories.—M. M.

Gao Baozhu

In 1938, when I was seventeen, a man from the government office came to my house and told me to go to Guangdong to work for the Japanese military.

Guangdong was a battlefield. I wondered what I would do there. I was hungry. The place where they took me in a covered truck was Kinzan-ji, a temple. When I looked up, I saw a sign that said COMFORT STATION.

I could never have imagined it. But I had gotten a Japanese education, so I obeyed, thinking I had to do what the government told me to. When they said it was for the country, we had to go along.

After six months in Guangdong, I was taken to Hong Kong and put on a boat. There were three boats, but one was torpedoed and sank. The noise from the explosion was horrendous, and ever since, I've been deaf in one ear.

We went to Burma via Singapore. The soldiers took us in a military truck into the mountains, deep in the jungle, where they put us into a shack. The men stationed there belonged to the Tatsu Unit. I was there for about three years. Then they took me to the city.

I didn't know when Japan was defeated, but finally one day I was told that the war was over and peace had come. The officer in command gave me a pass to go home, but since I didn't have any money, I had no idea how I'd get there. I was at my wits' end when a kind soldier asked me if I wanted to go back to Taiwan. He took me as far as Viet Nam, where I tried to get on a boat. But then we were captured by French soldiers and thrown in jail. The Japanese soldier I was with told them I was Chinese, not Japanese, so they let me out and gave me a French I.D. card.

I still had no money, though, so I stayed in Viet Nam for a while doing people's laundry and things to earn my fare home. But just when I was about to get on a boat for Taiwan, all my money and clothes—everything I had—were stolen and I was left with nothing but my underwear.

Finally I managed to get to Taiwan, but I still didn't know how I'd get home. Luckily, I met someone nice enough to send a telegram for me, and my older sister came and got me. That's when I heard that none of the money I'd sent home had reached them.

Back in Taiwan, I was so ashamed of having been a "comfort woman" that I didn't want to show my face outside. People hire me for jobs that can be done in the house, and so somehow I've managed to live for the last fifty years.

Before I left Taiwan, I adopted a daughter and left her with my sister. She doesn't want to see me now, and neither do any of my relatives; the only one who visits me is my sister. I take solace in drink, and so it's gone for fifty years.

When someone from the Women's Relief Foundation told me about this movement [to sue the Japanese government], I was finally able to walk freely outside. For a year now, the Taiwanese government has been giving each of us a welfare payment of fifteen thousand *gen* a month, and that's what I'm living on now.

But I was born a Japanese, and I listened to what the Japanese government said in the same way I listened to my own parents. When they told me to go to Guangdong, I went. I did whatever they told me to do. What I want you to understand is that I did it as a Japanese.

Japanese men died for Japan. I, too, left my home and went far away for Japan. Japan is now a peaceful country. The least she can do is have some sympathy for our past lives, filled with suffering and hardship. Taiwan no longer belongs to Japan, but I wish you would take a little more interest in us.

In Guangdong, the soldiers called me "Chink." I wept as I worked "for the country," and continued to suffer after I came home, and yet the Japanese government has done nothing for me. Now I have come to see if the Japanese government has a conscience.

Of the eighteen of us who left Taiwan together, only four came back, and now only two of us remain. We are getting old. I hope the Japanese government will think of us with a human heart.

Chen Tao

I was born in 1922. When I was nineteen, I was told to work as an assistant nurse, and they took me away for what was supposed to be two years. We set off from Kao-hsiung on a cargo ship on 4 June 1941. There were eighteen of us young girls. We stopped first in Saigon, and it wasn't until we arrived at our final destination that we learned we were to work at a comfort station. We all made a big fuss, protesting that they'd lied to us, but there was nothing we could do. We were on an isolated island, one of the Andamans, so there was no hope of escape.

The comfort station was a wooden shack built by the military. Partitions separated the rooms, which had only a wooden bed and a wash basin. Above the doors were numbers from 1 to 18. I was number 3. We were called not by our names but by our numbers. The men were from the navy—the Ishikawa Unit.

After a year and two months, I was taken along with four other girls to a comfort station in Singapore. There were twenty or thirty comfort women there—from Korea, Japan, and Guangdong. Most were from Guangdong. Only Japanese soldiers came to the comfort station. The military doctor issued us condoms and antiseptic. We had to sleep with no fewer than ten men a day—and on some days more than twenty. Some of the Japanese soldiers gave us tips, and I deposited more than eighteen hundred *yen* in my military postal-savings account.

Once when I physically could not stand it anymore, I ran away and hid in the mountains, but the warden came looking for me and dragged me back. Finally, the head nurse at the field hospital helped me get on a Red Cross ship, and I came back to Taiwan. After a week of treatment at the naval hospital in Kao-hsiung, I went to my brother's place in T'ai-pei. My father was already dead.

Within two months of my return, Japan lost the war. People from my hometown offered to find a husband for me, but I refused. For a month I looked for a job in T'ai-pei but didn't find one, so when a friend from T'ai-tung asked me if I wanted to learn to sew, I said yes. For a while I supported myself making clothes.

A man I'd known when I was young came to see me in T'ai-tung, and in the end I married him and we moved to Yan-shui. I couldn't have children, so my mother-in-law tried to throw me out. My husband didn't know about my past, or why I wasn't able to have children. He died ten years ago.

Since then, I've been living alone, going from place to place in Taiwan, cooking or doing laundry for other people. I don't have a home and am now living in a warehouse in the marketplace.

Lu Manmei

I come from Hsin-chu in Taiwan. My Japanese name is Mitsuko. I only went to the third grade in school.

I was seventeen then. A Japanese policeman came to me and said, "Since your family's so poor, why don't you work as a nurse for just a year and make some money?" He put me on a military boat in Gaoxing. We landed on Hainan Dao. There I was put to work at a comfort station. I couldn't go home no matter how much I wanted to. You couldn't leave without a pass from the military.

I had to sleep with twenty men a day. If I didn't, the warden would get mad at me. I had no relatives on Hainan Dao, and I didn't know anyone. I didn't even have a clear idea of where I was. There was nothing to do but grit my teeth and stay there in the comfort station.

I got pregnant, but I was forced to work even when my stomach got big. When I was in my eighth month, they finally sent me back to Taiwan. In the end, I was on Hainan Dao for about a year and a half.

My baby died of malaria thirty-eight days after it was born.

Back in Taiwan, people talked about how I'd been a "comfort woman," so my marriage didn't work out. I'm seventy-four now, and I've been alone most of my life. The Taiwanese government gives me a welfare payment of fifteen thousand *gen* a month, but nearly half of it goes for rent, and life isn't easy. I ask all of my Japanese friends to try to influence the Japanese government. Thank you very much.

Translation by Margaret Mitsutani

OGATA KEIICHI

Hiroshima through Light: From Light to Silence, Silence to Light

CINEPOEM ON URBAN SPACE

In August 1995, London was in a festive mood, celebrating the fiftieth anniversary of the Allied victory in World War II. But in Trafalgar Square, a Sprechchor of NO MORE HIROSHIMA was raised by people who'd gathered there from all over Europe.

The name of the city was not written with the Japanese characters to which I was accustomed, but in the Roman alphabet: HIROSHIMA. And so I wondered if it was really the same city, or something else.

Then I saw a party of Japanese tourists pass quietly by the demonstrators. The square for them was no longer an ideal sightseeing spot, but a space with an entirely different meaning. At about the same time, the French government began nuclear testing in a place far removed from the criticism of other nations.

I'd never been to Hiroshima in my life, nor had any urge to go. What I set out to do was trace my own interior journey from Europe to the Hiroshima in my mind. This is my attempt to see Hiroshima.

PART ONE: INTERVENTION OF LIGHT

[Image of film projector mechanism; black-and-white clip from Godard film panning across hills in Japan. Lettering: TU N'AS RIEN VU A HIROSHIMA*]*

On 28 December 1995, a TV documentary, *A Century of Cinema*, was shown around the world. I saw it in Tokyo. In it, Jean-Luc Godard said something that spoke directly to me, erasing the distance between France and Japan: "You saw nothing in Hiroshima."

[Film-projector beam aimed into the camera; projector noise in background; fade to black]

A hundred years ago, a source of luminosity began to flash in a dark basement of a small café in Paris. Few people could foresee just how popular these moving images would later become. After all, they were just illusions projected into the dark. And yet this new intervention of light and shadow was to have untold influence on the occurrence of human perception and psychology in space.

[Black-and-white Japanese film clip: three schoolboys at play, pretending to be soldiers; cut to black-and-white clip of French woman's face]

Soon the technology of film was imported to Japan. Light came first. The "Genesis" of Japanese films brought us images of happy, if impoverished, homes. This was a landscape of happiness. Films also showed us what life could be in the far West, in the lands we dreamed of.

[War footage: Japanese Zero *attacks enemy warships]*

However, Japan began to intervene, unilaterally, in the West. And the reappearance of light and shadow became a medium for force and oppression, a way to distort reality.

[Clip from The Life of Muhomatsu: *two men in a foot race; a crowd cheering; close-up of a little boy and a woman cheering]*

Two years before the end of the war, a film called *The Life of Muhomatsu* was released. The story was about the delicate communication established between a poor rickshawer and the widow of an army officer who was raising a small child alone. The military censors cut the film to pieces. They said it was not proper to show a romance between a common rickshawer and an officer's widow, even if it was platonic.

[Film clip of actress Keiko Sonoi smiling and laughing]

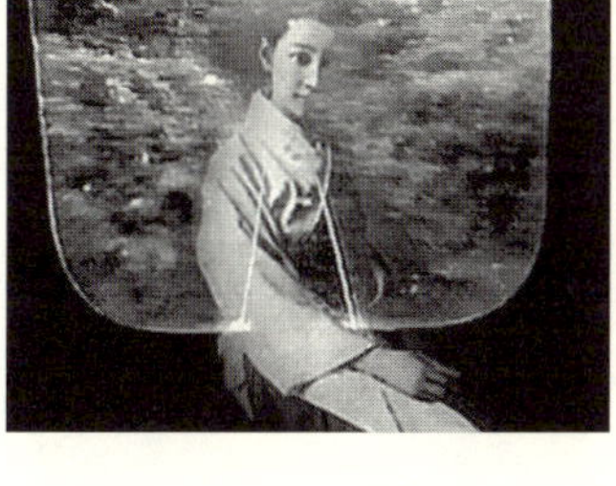

So audiences had to imagine the man's feelings, with only indirect images to go on. The actress who played the widow was thirty years old. She decided to stay in the film industry. But the difficult transition from stage acting to the new medium of film forced her to postpone indefinitely any opportunities for romance or motherhood in her own life.

[Black-and-white photograph of actress Keiko Sonoi]

During the war she toured the country with her films, to promote the attraction of this use of light and shadow.

[Image of atomic explosion]

She arrived in Hiroshima on 5 August 1945. The next day, she encountered another light there. The sixth of August happened to be her thirty-second birthday. She disappeared with the city.

[Image of a white map of Hiroshima; dissolve to Sonoi's smiling face]

Four of the five films she appeared in are lost. However, as long as we project light through the one remaining film, her image will not be erased from our memory.

[Image of film projector; soft background music plays]

One hundred years ago, a new art form was born from the intervention of light and shadow. No one knew then how powerful a medium this fragile illusion would become.

[Image of river in Hiroshima: a bridge in ruins; buildings, houses turned to rubble]

Fifty years after that, a movie actress disappeared into the darkness of the city through another intervention of light.

[Image of wasted, blackened Hiroshima; remains of domed building in foreground]

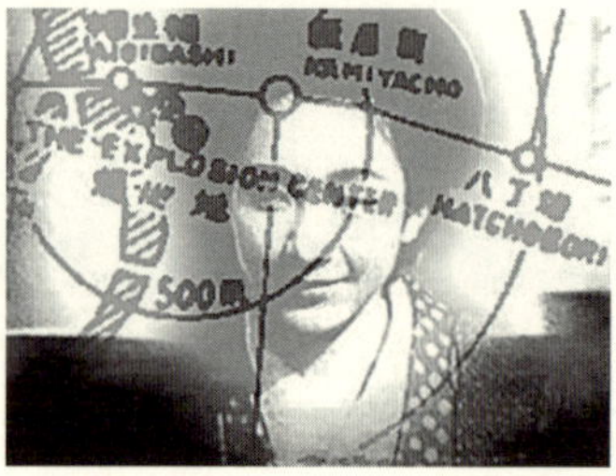

Now the meaning of the light and shadow she tried to represent in that city speaks directly to me, pulling me back to my original landscape of the Hiroshima of fifty years ago, in a search for the city's real identity.

[Fade to heading]

THE ACTRESS: KEIKO SONOI, 1913–1945

[Fade to black]

PART TWO: THE REALITY, FROM SILENCE TO LIGHT

In the beginning there were nine seconds of brightness. Then darkness and silence covered the whole city.

[Fade to white map of Hiroshima]

When the dark lifted, the flash of light could be seen to have bleached the city.

[Reconstructing Hiroshima]

For the city, the past no longer existed and the future could not be seen. Eventually, amid the black rain and the radiation, people began silently to work to rebuild a city from the *tabula rasa*. They walked about, looking for sites that resembled their memories of the place before it was crossed with light. At first, they put up temporary dwellings, not meant to last. These anonymous architects traced a new city on the white ground.

[Image of the mother's shadow]

The intervention of light left ownerless shadows here and there on the white map. The shadows were silent at first. But they took on new life in the imagination of survivors who used their memories to recreate the missing. One girl believed a shadow on a set of steps was her mother.

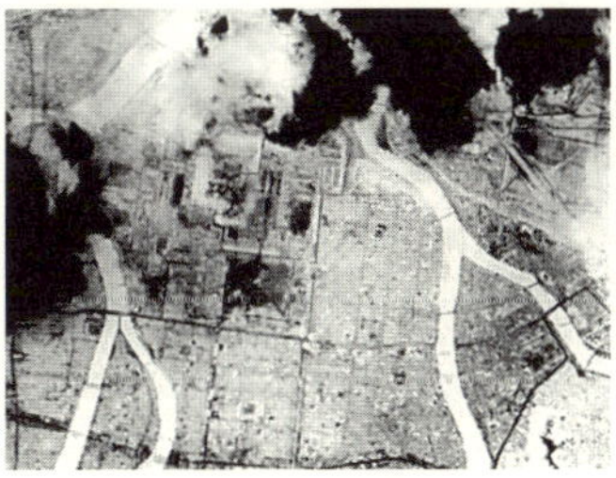

[Image of the soldier's shadow]

One mother was sure a soldier's shadow on the wall was her son. And the image of the actress became a shadow on the translucent celluloid of film. In the minds of particular individuals, these traces were transformed into images that were real.

[The Atomic Dome and sunlight]

Now I am bathed in the light of Hiroshima, where I have never been before. But now I know why this building is alive, even after losing its shadow and its function.

[The digital clock showing 8:15 A.M. at Kamiyacho crossing, in the center of Hiroshima]

The passage of time in the modern city is measured by the clock. But a clock only shows the moment; it cannot show the lapse of time.

[Kamiyacho crossing, with people walking busily about]

Ordinary life goes on now in the center of this city, as it does anywhere else in Japan. But here, with only memories of words and images of Hiroshima to go on, I am confused, and unable to link these to the scene at hand. It's as if the present is rising up suddenly in my mind, after a momentary absence occurring fifty years ago.

[Image from the window of a streetcar]

They say that the first thing that the people of this city wanted to rebuild was the streetcar. Fifty years later, I look through the window of a streetcar, and the composition of light and shadow cast by the buildings tells me the city is a different place every day.

[Construction site that stands on the place where the actress vanished]

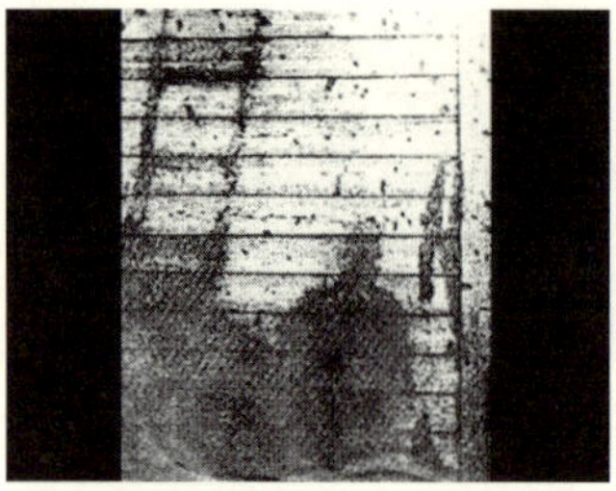

Looking for an image of the actress, I followed my map to the place where she met the light. But the place has been torn down and rebuilt over and over. Her public image as an actress is as still as a shadow.

[Sumitomo Bank building]

And in 1972, the building with the stone steps was demolished and rebuilt, taking the mother's shadow from this street and cutting off the communication between a mother and daughter.

[The Peace Museum]

The shadow was displaced, and froze, without receiving a name.

[View from the thirty-third floor of the American Hotel]

Looking out over the city, I am reminded of Merleau-Ponty's words: "This aerial view, with everything it encompasses, will fall at a certain date of the calendar; I will assign to it a certain point of apparition on the earth and in my life. One has to believe that time has continued to flow on beneath and that the earth has continued to exist."

[View of the city]

Ever since the light glinted, vanishing points have been appearing in Hiroshima.

[Encountering an old man by the river Ota]

I met a man who was looking at the river Ota. He said to me, "I've worked on construction sites all over the country over the years. But no matter what, from time to time, I come back and watch this river as it flows." There are people like him who form shadow-parts of architecture. He also said, "I've never seen any building I worked on, once it was completed."

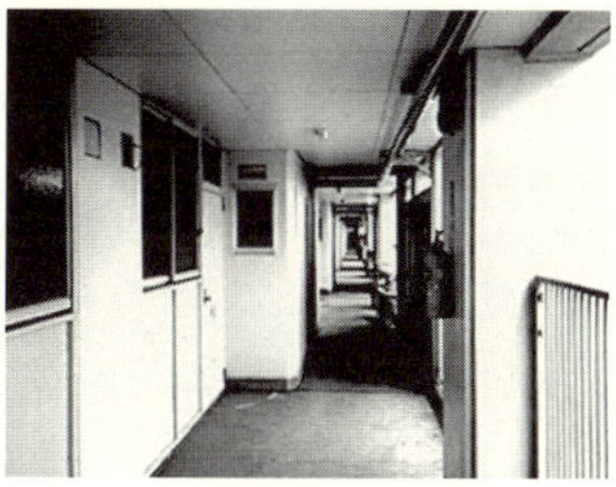

[View from a boat on the river Ota]

In contrast to the demonstrators, who raise their voices, the people who rebuilt this city are contained unobtrusively in their white concrete boxes, keeping their silence. For me, their invisible white silence embodies the absence that marks the modern city. Is "peace" really so concrete a word?

[Corridor in a housing facility for survivors of the atomic bomb]

From the outside, I can't hear any voices. And there's no way for me to enter these buildings. But the facades seem to speak of the survivors' silent despair at being the only ones to have lived through the city's rebirth.

[Light playing on the surface of the river Ota]

One hundred years ago, people understood the intervention of light into darkness as representing the creation of an entirely new interior space. Those provisional moving images then led people's stream of consciousness outward from inside, toward urban space.

Fifty years ago, another light flared in Hiroshima. Like an eclipse, it lasted only a moment. In that time, the city disappeared. But people continued to discover the areas of light amid the shadows left in the city.

The light I see falling now is gently scattering the vanishing points over the breadth of the modern city. The shadows and lights are not fixed, but shifting. This speaks of the modern city's paradoxical tension between physical concretion and fragility.

This scene may slip away from my memory, but my perception will let me retain the meaning of this luminous residue and the name of the city.

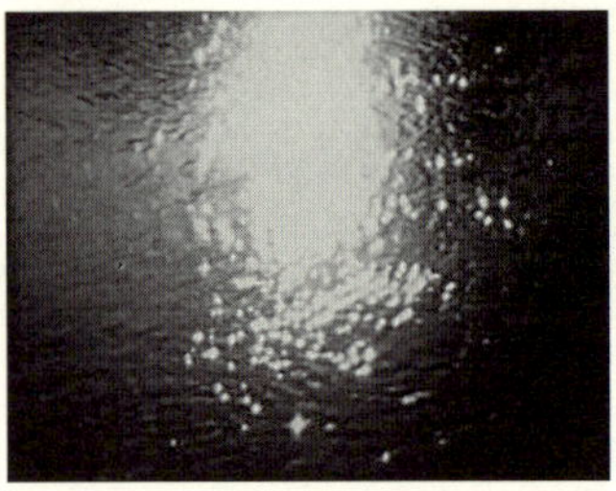

[Image of the actress superimposed over a night view of the city]

In the beginning was light, followed by dark. The city was frozen in an instant. But when light is given again to the images, they can be released from silence and begin to breathe. A vision of light projects my own perception of Hiroshima onto the screen of memory that appears in an urban space sunk into darkness.

Hiroshima was reborn from shadows. And its future will be determined by our awareness of light.

People in Hiroshima prefer to remain silent until they face death.

Kenzaburo Ōe,
Hiroshima Notes

Like you, I wanted an inconsolable memory, a memory of the shadow on the stone.

Marguerite Duras,
Hiroshima Mon Amour

A public work must resist not only the ravages of daily life, but, just as importantly, collective indifference.

Jean Attali

Light to silence, silence to light.

Louis I. Kahn

Translation by Ingrid von Essen and Elizabeth Floyd Ogata

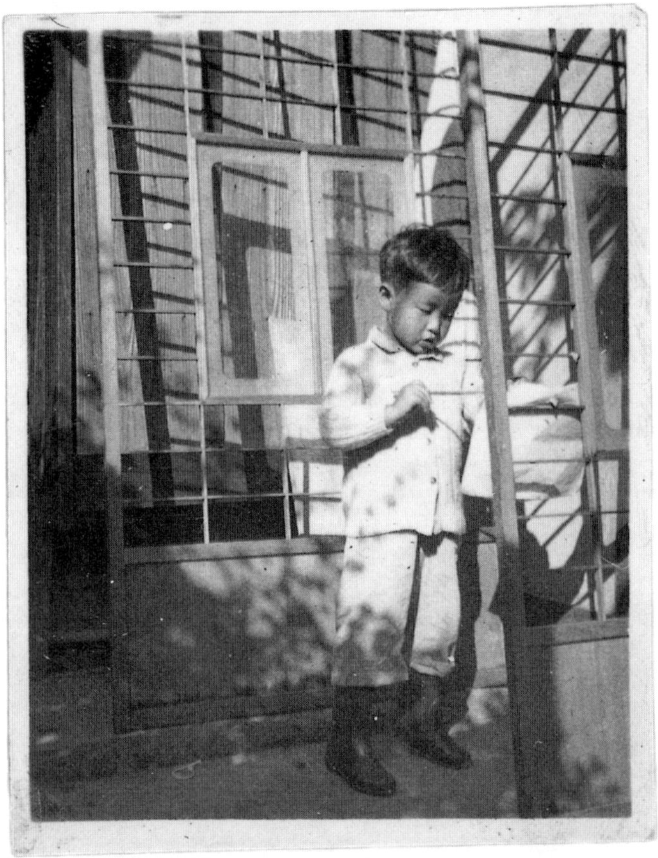

Shuzo Uemoto helping to paper sliding doors, Japan

YOKO OGAWA

The Man Who Sold Braces

Things my uncle made, whatever they were, fell apart in no time. My precious model plane; the brace of his own invention (so he claimed) that was supposed to make you taller; and his coat, which he gave me to remember him by.

Every time I saw him, my uncle was engaged in a different occupation. The job at a hat-maker was followed by an assistantship for a photographer. Then he became, in succession, the manufacturer of the braces, an instructor of table manners, a butler, and, finally, a caretaker of a museum. Maybe the assistantship came after making the braces; I forget now. He married three times, shacking up twice with someone in between marriages. He frequently took up with somebody new, though at the end of his life he lived on his own, without anyone to look after him.

In short, my uncle was someone who repeatedly cast off whatever job or life he had built up, going back to zero each time.

One thing admirable about him—at least it was admirable to me—was that, when what had been in his possession started falling apart, he didn't look sad at all. He wouldn't click his tongue or look sullen; he would calmly watch it fall apart. You could even detect a faint smile.

When the police called to ask me to come and collect my uncle's body, they had already finished the autopsy. Apparently he knew no neighbors and had no friends, and they had a lot of trouble locating his few relatives. I was back at my apartment when they called, preparing for my French class the next day.

"What did he die of?" I asked.

"Smothered to death," the person at the other end of the telephone answered.

"You mean somebody killed him?"

"No. Your uncle was pinned under the garbage he'd spread all over his room."

The respectful manner in which the stranger talked about my uncle's death consoled me a little.

My uncle and I were not blood relations. He was supposed to be my mother's older brother, but he was in fact my grandfather's oldest son from his previous marriage. He was therefore much older than my mom, and at no point had they lived together. When I was a kid, Mom would sometimes explain to me in what way they were related, but I could never really figure it out.

Nevertheless, my uncle visited us often. He would just appear without advance notice, stay for several days, and then disappear again.

He was an unwelcome guest—even a kid of my age could see that. When he came over, my mother grew nervous and restless, my father crabby. My uncle, though, didn't seem to notice; he ate and drank a lot, cheerful all the time.

I didn't care how my parents felt. I always looked forward to my uncle's next visit. He always brought me something special.

"Well, let's see if you can find where I've hidden it," my uncle would say and lift me up. Then he'd rub his cheek against mine. His stubble would tickle me and I would squirm, which amused him even more, and then he would rub his face all over mine. Finally escaping his embrace, I'd set out to find where he'd hidden his present for me, putting my hands all over his body. Then it was his turn to be tickled and to squirm.

Chocolates from abroad appeared in his hat; a miniature car in the sleeve of his jacket. Once I found a jackknife hidden inside one of his socks. Until I started school, I was convinced that my uncle conjured them up by magic.

There were some semiprecious stones embedded in the hilt of the jackknife, and the whole thing was quite heavy. It was a beautiful object, and just looking at it thrilled me. My mother discovered it later and took it away from me.

"He's really crazy, buying such a dangerous thing for a child. No discretion at all."

No discretion at all—that was what my mom said every time she talked about him.

Even though he was an unwelcome guest, our dinner menu improved a bit when he stayed with us. He sat with his legs crossed, and I sat in the space between his legs. "Mind your manners," my mom would scold me, but I wouldn't listen. Though his legs felt bumpy, it was somehow comfy sitting there.

Most of the time, only my uncle talked. My dad didn't drink at all, was by nature a glum person, and wasn't very good at holding conversations. My uncle talked about his latest job, described strange things he'd seen while traveling, and gossiped about our relatives. He would add a lot of gestures, mimic their voices, and laugh heartily, feeding me bits of food from time to time. My dad just wore a polite smile, never saying anything or asking questions. Mom simply kept going back and forth between the kitchen and dinner table.

Eventually, Dad would say stiffly, "You must excuse me. I have to wake up early tomorrow morning," and leave the table. I was told to change into my pajamas, and Mom would start clearing the table. But my uncle would remain where he was.

When I got up in the middle of the night to pee, I would find my uncle still there, drunk from whiskey. His hands moved uncertainly, and his back was awkwardly hunched. He would mumble to himself, as if talking to something invisible hanging in the air, and laugh aloud, as if we were still there.

During the day, he didn't do anything much except hang around in the living room. If Mom asked him to do something that required a man's physical power, he was only too happy to oblige her: carrying upstairs a parcel of books sent to my dad, opening the tight lid of a bottle. But such opportunities didn't turn up very often. Mom didn't seem to imagine that my uncle could be of much help.

When he was bored, my uncle would come to my room.

"All right, I'll build that model plane for you," he said one day.

The plane was a birthday present from my dad, and I'd promised him we'd build it together the following Sunday. Though I didn't worry about the promise too much, the idea of my uncle building the plane somehow made me nervous. My uncle, though, didn't seem aware of my concern. He tore open all the small plastic bags containing the plane parts.

"Let me do it too," I said.

"No. This is awfully tricky. Too complicated for a kid. Leave it to me," he said, not allowing me to touch anything—the propeller, the wings, or the glue.

The instructions were in fine print, and he seemed to be having trouble making them out. He shifted his reading glasses, pulled the lamp closer. He scattered the parts all over my desk, gluing together this part and that, only to separate them, turn one upside down, or experiment with some other part. All the while, he mumbled, "Well, this sure is tricky."

"Are you sure you can do it?" I asked, beginning to feel distressed.

"Sure, just wait a little bit longer. Yes. Sure. This is a wonderful plane," he said, nodding to himself. He was perspiring at the tip of his nose.

I couldn't stand it any longer and went outside to play. At dinnertime my uncle was still working. The plane had barely taken shape.

"You can stop if you like," I suggested hesitantly. He wouldn't give up, though.

It was the next morning when the plane was completed.

"Look," my uncle said, holding it up deferentially.

"Well, thanks," I said. Although it didn't look much like the photo on the box, I didn't want to make him feel bad. His fingers were dirty with dried glue.

The plane was oddly balanced. Not a part appeared to be placed in its proper position. There were some gaps in the window of the cockpit, the wheels were crooked, and the two wings—the most important parts—were differently angled.

My uncle departed that afternoon. The moment I lifted the plane, so as to display it on the bookshelf, the right wing came off. No sooner had I said "Oh!" than the propeller came off, the wheels tumbled out, and the other wing fell at my feet. The plane looked like a fossil, damaged and decayed.

Once, my uncle brought over an odd-looking, weirdly shaped object. What looked like a dog collar was attached to the tip of a steel plate, and a wide belt was connected to the other tip.

"This is a brace that makes you taller," my uncle said. My mom and dad made no specific response, only mumbling "Oh" and "Um."

"This is how you use it," he said, trying to demonstrate it on me.

"Are you sure it doesn't hurt?" I asked. I was alarmed. He simply nodded several times and unfastened the clasp.

"Don't worry. You'd like to become taller, wouldn't you? All the girls would fall for you. Lots of people would give anything to be taller."

What looked like a collar *was* in fact a collar, and this he fixed securely on my throat. The steel plate was placed along my spine, and the belt was fastened around my stomach.

"Well, what do you think?" My uncle proudly spread his arms. Dad glanced at me. Mom narrowed her eyes.

I had trouble breathing. My neck was constricted, and it was impossible to turn or bend. If I tried to move just a little, my backbone gave a squeak. All I could move freely were my eyes.

"If you wear this brace only half an hour every day for six months, it will make you taller by two inches. By fixing the neck and the waist properly, it stretches the muscles, stimulates the bones, and encourages the secretion of growth hormones."

"I have to wear this *half an hour?*" I was almost in tears.

"Just half an hour, and it turns you into a tall, handsome young man. You should be grateful."

"But it hurts. I can't breathe."

"You can't? Well, maybe the collar's too tight."

He fumbled with the clasp.

"This is just a trial product. I can still make improvements. I've decided to sell them by mail. This will sell, I tell you. I'm making arrangements with a factory to have them mass-produced, and I'm going to advertise in newspapers and men's magazines. I've had the product endorsed by the government as a medical instrument. Look."

From the inside pocket of his jacket, my uncle took out something that looked like an official document and waved it in front of my eyes.

"Well, that's nice," my dad said uncertainly. My mom poked the steel plate on my back with her forefinger.

"Oh, please," I said. "Take it off. I can't stand the pain any longer." I was in tears.

Soon after, my uncle did start a mail-order business. I don't know whether he really made modifications to the collar, but I saw ads in magazines. A half-naked male, oil spread all over his muscles, was wearing the brace on his back and posing proudly. The thing had felt so tight and constricting when I wore it, but it appeared to be in perfect harmony with the man's body. It looked as if it had been there ever since the guy was born.

The trial product remained in our closet for a while. None of us dared to use it. It just lay there, like the discarded shell of a strange reptile. The surface of the steel plate rusted.

On the day nonburnable trash was collected, my mother picked up the brace, aiming to get rid of it. Immediately, a screw that had been attached to the plate came off, and the collar and belt fell away too. Everything came apart.

"The belt is burnable. We have to keep it for the burnables day," my mother said.

Apparently, my uncle sold very few of them. I couldn't tell whether it was because they fell apart easily or because they didn't make you taller, as he'd advertised. Eventually my uncle was arrested for fraud. The government endorsement turned out to be forged.

We didn't hear from him for some time. It was four years after the arrest that we finally saw him again. I was in junior high at that time.

Looking back on it, I think those were my uncle's most prosperous days. He brought me expensive presents, and the quality of his clothes improved. He used French eau-de-toilette, smoked cigars, and came to our house by limousine. Before, he had walked from the station nearby.

I was told that he was working as a butler and living in some rich people's house. But Mom said he was just a handyman.

The house was owned by two old ladies who were twins. They had inherited a lot of money from their father, a man who had made a fortune in the coal business. The twins were traveling abroad most of the time, so my uncle's main job was to look after their house.

I remember our relatives whispering to each other that the two ladies shared my uncle sexually. I had trouble imagining what that meant. But they looked disgusted when they said this, so I could see it had to be something repulsive.

"They look exactly alike," my uncle said, "like two peas in a pod. Their height, voice, taste in clothes, makeup, even their wrinkles—exactly the same."

"Do you confuse them sometimes?" I asked.

"No. Never. A could be B, B could be A—makes no difference at all. They are one person together."

"What does a butler do?"

"I am a bit different from most butlers," he said, boasting as always. "My most important job is to look after the Bengal tiger."

"The Bengal *tiger?*" I blurted.

"Sure. The ladies keep him in the courtyard. They once traveled to India, and they brought him home. He was a baby tiger then."

"Is he a grownup now?"

"A real giant. You can't wrap your arms around his waist, his legs are extremely strong, and he can chew off anything with his fangs. When he runs around in the courtyard, you'd think there was an earthquake."

"Aren't you scared?"

"I am. He never trusts me. He's always ready to attack anyone. His body is tense all over, and that creates a particular type of beauty. His glittering fur reflects the sun, and his back arches beautifully. Threatening growls keep coming out of his throat. He stays alert from head to toe. His body is right in front of you, but it has a kind of magnificence that's simply untouchable."

My uncle closed his eyes, seeing the tiger in his mind's eye.

"Initially, the old ladies were interested in torture," he said, his eyes still closed. I didn't know what to say, so I kept silent.

"They traveled all over the world, buying torture instruments. It's also my job to take care of them."

"You certainly are an unusual butler."

"Just throwing somebody into the courtyard with the tiger—that's torture enough. And there are a lot more things: an ankle-breaking axe, a lip-tearing mouthpiece, a skin-peeling knife . . ."

He named a lot of instruments, but I couldn't picture any of them. All I conjured up was the brace that was supposed to make you taller.

"Actually, the biggest problem in looking after a tiger is not fear. It's smell. A thick, almost suffocating smell that rises from a big mass of life. It even sticks to your hair, and that's extremely hard to get rid of. That's why I always use eau-de-toilette. Old Lady A gave it to me when she returned from one of their trips—or maybe it was B. In any case, it's a luxury item."

My uncle thrust his chest against my nose. I couldn't escape.

"See? Smells nice, doesn't it?" My uncle waved his handkerchief to spread the smell. He lived in the house of rich people, but hadn't become rich himself. Still, he acted as if he had, in a flashy way.

I inhaled deeply. I couldn't tell whether the smell was of the eau-de-toilette, or of the Bengal tiger.

The clearest memory I have of my uncle is his departing from our house: the way he looked from behind. None of us knew where he was going. No one asked. My parents just said, "Well, so long," and not very warmly.

He never had any luggage. He never owned a briefcase or suitcase. I wonder what he did with underwear and such. He may have shoved them somewhere in his clothes, just as he did his presents for me.

"Well, I've had such a wonderful time," my uncle always said, as if he really meant it. "Be a good boy," he would say to me. "Study hard. Some of the stuff you learn may seem stupid to you, but you must pay attention. It will be useful for something someday. No matter what, it's never a waste of time to study. Life is like that."

And he would lift me up, rubbing his cheek against mine once more. It prickled, and I would wriggle my arms and legs, messing up his hair, which had just been fixed with hair oil. But he didn't care.

"Thanks for everything," he would say, bowing to my parents and smoothing his hair.

"When are you coming back?" How innocent a child can be. I *really* would want to know when he was returning.

"Well, we'll see." He was a man who never could make any kind of promise.

The last time he visited us, the twin ladies were dead and their house had been turned into a torture museum. It had been entrusted to his care. I was too big for cheek rubbing by then.

The limousine came to pick him up. There was not a speck of dust on that shiny, black, impressive car. My uncle almost stumbled on the steps of our porch. When I reached out to help him, he said, "Much obliged," in a husky voice. He smelled of his favorite eau-de-toilette.

I was taken aback. Had he grown so old in such a short time? If I'd pushed him just a little, he would have easily fallen. The body I'd searched all over for my presents had been suppler, firmer. I had always thought of my uncle as a tall man, but when I looked now, I realized he was smaller than I was.

It occurred to me that I didn't know his age. I had somehow felt as if he were ageless.

"Say hi to the Bengal tiger for me," I said, leaning into the limousine. My uncle simply nodded. I wasn't sure if he'd heard me or not.

"Say hi to the Bengal tiger for me," I repeated. The tiger was the only thing that had been willed to him.

He waved. It was a theatrical, flashy wave: one from a king surrounded by subjects who were sad to see him go.

The limousine began to glide away. I could see his back through the rear window. It looked puny and fragile, and as I blinked, it grew smaller and smaller.

"So," my dad said, going inside.

"Well, at last," my mother said, sounding relieved and following him.

I was the only one to stay outside until the car could no longer be seen. My uncle never looked back.

The funeral didn't take much time. Only a handful of people attended, and no one wept. They just sat there, in front of the altar. They didn't seem to be sad; rather they looked as if they were wondering why they were there.

I heard people whispering to each other.

"Weird—suffocated to death, but not murdered."

"I guess he was pretty weak. Maybe the wardrobe or something fell down on him, and he couldn't move."

"I still think someone murdered him. Lots of people had grudges against him."

"Anyway, they found his stomach empty—he was starving. Destined to die one way or another."

Things had begun to go wrong for him after he was suspected of indecent conduct. A neighbor reported to the police that my uncle took a girl, a minor, into the torture museum and engaged in obscene behavior with her. Indeed, it was a fact that an eighteen-year-old apprentice at a beauty salon frequented the museum and apparently had some kind of relationship with my uncle. The girl didn't file a complaint, so the case never went to court.

No one knew what kind of "relationship" the two had.

"He tortured her," my dad said. "What else? He tortured the beautician."

"Why?" I asked, surprised.

"There were torture instruments all over the house. What else can you do?"

Not long after that, he was arrested again, this time for appropriating the old ladies' money. It seems that he had spent a considerable part of their inheritance. Perhaps this is what the police had really been interested in all along. My uncle went to jail.

The museum closed permanently while he was in jail. He had no place to go when he was released.

Again and again, my uncle had implored me to visit the museum, and though I'd promised I would, I never did. There was no particular reason. I didn't detest the museum, and I didn't want to shun my uncle. I was simply too busy with my studies and club activities.

Every year, he sent me a Christmas card with a photo on it. He was always posing in front of the exhibits.

Standing proudly, he had on a bow tie and smiled pleasantly. His white shirt was impeccably ironed, and there were no smudges on his leather shoes. His right palm pointed toward the exhibits. A pearl glowed on the sleeve cuff.

"Well, what do you think? Real torture instruments, I tell you," he seemed to be saying.

The last time I saw my uncle was on a day in February, some time after he had been released on parole. Clouds hung low in the sky, and a cold wind blew incessantly. I shoved my hands into my trouser pockets, hunched over to brace myself against the wind, and looked for the apartment building my uncle lived in. It took me a long time to find it.

It was a shabby, dreary building. An oblong box with two rows of windows, completely bare. No flowers at the window, not even clothes hung to dry. The outside walls were covered with stains, the gutter had come loose at several places, and the handrail by the front steps was warped. A cat was mewing behind the weeds. I didn't hear anything else.

I checked the postboxes to make sure this was the right place. Under "201," my uncle had written his name with a felt-tip pen. The handwriting was clumsy and shaky and had been smudged by rain.

I peeked into the box. There was not a postcard, not a flyer in it. Just a dark, gaping hollowness.

"Hello, Uncle," I called, opening the door to room 201. I was at a loss as to what to say next. "Uncle, it's me."

I was sure there was someone in the room. I could hear somebody breathing intermittently somewhere. But I couldn't see anyone. I started taking off my shoes, aiming to get into the room, but couldn't even find a spot to put my foot. I just stood there. The place was entirely filled with junk.

I'm not sure "junk" is the right word. It seemed that not everything was unusable. But there was no order whatsoever; it was a totally anarchic, chaotic, oppressive jumble of things.

"So it's you—how nice of you to come." An extremely faint voice reached me through the tiny openings among the objects. It took me some time to become convinced that it was my uncle's voice.

"Well," the voice said, "don't just stand there. Come and let me see you."

"I'd like to, but it seems if I make a wrong move, things might start tumbling down . . ."

"No, it's all right. Just move along the refrigerator, step over the radio, and pass behind the wardrobe."

I entered the huge mass of junk, following my uncle's instructions.

Frayed socks, a barbecue kit, a set of encyclopedias, a dismantled clarinet, cans of cat food, a frying pan without a handle, a dried-up soap bar, a microscope, puppets, moldy breadcrumbs, a stuffed marten . . . At first I tried to make out each item, but I soon got dizzy and gave up. The entire floor was covered with objects lying on top of one another. The windows were completely hidden, and the tallest parts of the monstrous mass reached the ceiling. I made a great effort to get to the source of the voice.

"It's really you. I'm not dreaming. You've come. Come closer, I want to see you better. My eyes are not what they used to be."

Near the middle of the room, my uncle was lying down, having squeezed himself into a small open space. He stretched out his hand, shakily, toward me.

"Hi," I said, gripping his hand and putting it to my cheek.

"Oh, I remember this. Your soft hand. Feels so nice. Hasn't changed a bit."

My uncle had become extremely thin. Wrists, neck, shoulders—they were nothing but bones. I couldn't let go of his hand.

"Thank you for your card," I said.

"I sent it only to you. You were the only one I wanted to see."

After hesitating a bit, I pushed away the junk around his head and knelt down.

"How are you?" I asked. I should have questioned him about the condition of the room, but I had no idea how to put my feelings into words.

"Not bad, though my neuralgia has been bothering me a bit. It's hard when it's cold for days like this."

His bedclothes, which he had wrapped tightly around himself, were nothing but a thin blanket made of toweling. It had become so grimy that you couldn't tell the original color. As far as I could see, there was no heater in the room. But it wasn't all that cold. It seemed as if warm air was seeping out of the huge mass that surrounded us.

"It's been a long time," I said.

"Yeah. I should have been released earlier, but there were some complications. There are so many dumb people around these days."

"Are you eating enough? You should eat, you know."

"So you are old enough to worry about your uncle, huh? You were such a kid just a little while ago."

"I go to college now, Uncle."

"What are you studying?"

"French literature."

"That's marvelous. That's truly marvelous."

My uncle closed his swollen eyelids and gripped my hand. He looked as if he were fighting back tears.

"Oh, I almost forgot," I said. "I brought you a present. Let's see if you can find where I hid it." I didn't want to see his tears, so I forced myself to be funny. My uncle let out a sound a bit like a cough, a bit like a laugh. I took a box of chocolates out of my windbreaker.

"I remember you liked chocolates," I said.

"Yes. That's really nice. I never thought I'd be given presents by you."

With great care, I put the box on a pile consisting of a toaster and a tricycle. It became part of the mass in no time, part of the landscape.

When you looked carefully, you realized that though everything seemed as if it had randomly been put on top of something else, each item possessed its own contour and maintained its own balance. They were all broken, soiled, but collectively, they had a weird kind of beauty.

Things that lay directly around my uncle were mostly gadgets of some kind. Wood, metal, leather—all were combined into bizarre shapes. For a while I thought he had picked them up at a factory, but then I realized they were the museum exhibits.

A belt that was probably supposed to tie a wrist had become misshapen, its clasp ready to come off; a chain intended to tear limbs apart was now deformed; the handle of a whip was broken; a weight meant to crush knee bones was all rusty. None of them suggested its original purpose. It was as if *they* had been tortured and, limp with fatigue, were now waiting for death to come.

I glanced around my uncle's feet. The space was occupied by braces. The memory of how it hurt when I wore one came back immediately. I also remembered the wet feel of the collar around my neck and the hardness of the steel plate.

The unsold braces lay on top of one another, creating an especially dense mass. They clung so closely to each other that it seemed impossible to pull them apart.

"You still have them," I said. I only pointed, but my uncle knew what I meant without shifting his eyes.

"So you remember. Yes, it was a great invention, though very few of them were sold. I still get New Year's cards from customers who became taller thanks to the brace. I'm their savior, they tell me. Every time I see these braces, I feel my life hasn't been a complete waste."

My uncle pulled his thin blanket up to his chin and made himself into the tiniest ball possible. His eyelids remained half-closed. Sometimes he coughed, probably from phlegm. Each time he did so, the muscle on his throat twitched as if in spasm.

Still blowing hard outside, the wind rattled the windows. Suddenly, something, a rat or cockroach, skittered at the edge of my view, disappearing into the mass of torture instruments. It made a ruffling noise for a while, then became quiet.

"Take one home if you like," my uncle said. "There are plenty. You can have one. It's not too late for you yet."

"Yes, thank you," I said.

The back of the room appeared to lead to the kitchen, but I could detect no trace of cooking. Small empty bottles, every one the same kind, filled the sink: containers of eau-de-toilette.

"What happened to the Bengal tiger?" I asked.

"He died in the museum courtyard," my uncle answered. "He simply died of old age, peacefully went to heaven . . ."

For some time, we didn't say anything, didn't move. Just listened to the wind. My uncle stretched out his hand from under the thin blanket. I cupped it with both of mine. It felt as if we were praying for the tiger together.

"I think it's begun to snow," my uncle said.

"How do you know?"

"The sound of the wind has changed."

"You don't have any more blankets? You should keep warm."

"I don't need any. I'm fine this way. *You* should keep warm, though. You have to be outside. Here, put this on. It's extremely warm."

There were so many things around, but my uncle reached into the pile by his head and in no time located what he was looking for. It was a fur coat.

"What a great coat," I said. "Use it as a blanket. I'm OK."

"No, no—take it, please. This is just about the only thing I can give you now."

"OK, sure. Thank you. I'll treasure it."

My uncle closed his eyes again, looking satisfied. Eventually, I heard him breathing regularly. He was asleep.

I was surprised to find that the snow was so deep. The world was white everywhere you looked. My uncle was right. The wind had stopped, and large snowflakes were falling out of the night sky.

Not a soul was to be seen, and the cat that had been in the weeds was gone. I stepped gingerly onto the unblemished snow. I turned back to look at room 201, but I couldn't see anything in the windows.

Thanks to the fur coat, I didn't feel cold at all. The coat was soft, so soft that you wanted to rub your cheek against it. It was as if I were completely embraced by strong arms.

The coat smelled of my uncle. His eau-de-toilette. Each time I took a step, I smelled the scent and heard the sound of tiny icicles being crushed.

I had thought I'd simply go back the way I had come, but the snow had completely changed the landscape. There was nothing I could do but walk on. Snow fell on my coat, slid into the fur, and dissolved instantly. I turned back for the last time. I could no longer see the apartment house; I only saw my own footsteps, stretching into the dark beyond.

Suddenly, I realized that the left sleeve had come off the shoulder. I picked it up quickly. I saw loose thread dangling. There were grimy stains on the back.

The moment I let loose a cry, the other sleeve came off. The cold was suddenly beginning to invade me. Holding the two sleeves in my hands, I was determined to walk on. Then the seams began to fall apart at the armpits, the collar tore loose, and the pockets ripped.

In the snow light, the tiger's fur shone, unbelievably beautiful. Smothered by the beast's smell, I knelt and picked up the fragments of the tiger scattered on the snow.

Translation by Motoyuki Shibata

Reviews

■ FICTION

Contemporary Fiction by Filipinos in America. Edited by Cecilia Manguerra Brainard. Pasig City, Philippines: Anvil Publishing, 1997. 254 pages, paper $22.95.

A couple of years ago, I asked a colleague of mine who was preparing a comprehensive anthology of world literature which Filipino writers he was going to include. He wasn't aware of any, he replied, adding that they probably hadn't been translated yet.

I explained that many of the best Filipino writers in the Philippines wrote in English, a legacy of American colonialism from 1898 to 1946. With great enthusiasm and some hope, I mentioned a half dozen that he might want to consider, including N. V. M. Gonzalez, Linda Ty-Casper, and F. Sionil José. I wasn't surprised, however, when the anthology appeared without a one.

In the United States, the Philippines has always been esteemed for its strategic importance while Filipino culture has been almost invisible. The truth is that the Philippines has a rich literary heritage, extending from the archipelago to the various other countries in which Filipinos have settled, including former colonial masters Spain and the United States. The writers who have made a name for themselves in the States—Carlos Bulosan, Bienvenido Santos, Linda Ty-Casper, Ninotchka Rosca, perhaps Nick Carbo, and certainly Jessica Hagedorn—are few, though their writing is powerful and consistently good. Hagedorn is the most honored: her nomination for the National Book Award for *Dogeaters* brought some attention to lesser-known Filipino writers toiling in the vineyards of the literary lord, such as Cecilia Manguerra Brainard. The University of Washington Press has loyally kept Santos and Bulosan in print, as well as brought Gonzalez to the attention of the American public—about as much as a small university house can do for these writers.

The anthologies of Filipino and Filipino American writing published in the States have also appeared infrequently. In 1966, Leonard Casper, a prominent critic and the husband of Linda Ty-Casper, compiled an extraordinary collection called *New Writing from the Philippines.* A few Filipino American pieces were included in the seminal 1974 Asian American anthology *Aiieee!* though the vastly different experiences of Filipinos in the States, and a wholly different literary tradition, resulted in two separate introductions to the book: one for Chinese and Japanese Americans; the other for Filipino Americans.

In 1992, Luis Francia edited the marvelous *Brown River, White Ocean,* which thrived despite the publisher's barely useable design. Francia's next contribution was 1996's *Flippin': Filipinos on America,* which he and Eric Gamalinda edited for the Asian American Writers' Workshop, based in New York. A writer's book, composed half of poetry and half of prose, it is filled with the sheer pleasure of literary achievement and remains the best Filipino American anthology available today.

Cecilia Manguerra Brainard's 1993 anthology, *Fiction by Filipinos in America,* was a low-budget collection published by New Day Publishers in Quezon City, Philippines. For it she collected a good cross-section of Filipino writers, from the little known to the more accomplished, producing a good introduction to Filipino writing in America. *Contemporary Fiction by Filipinos in America,* also published in the Philippines, covers some of the same ground: seven of the twenty-five contributors were included in the earlier collection, though it is comforting to see Gonzalez and Ty-Casper again.

Since the late nineteenth century, the Philippines has been wracked by political difficulties: its revolt against Spain in 1898, American domination, a Japanese invasion, and the Marcos plutocracy. Yet except for the hints of this situation in Gonzalez's story "Confessions of a Dawn Person," and the migrant background in Alma Jill Dizon's promising "Bride," the stories in *Contemporary Fiction by Filipinos in America* focus little, if at all, on the history of the Filipino experience in the Philippines. This is a favorite theme of at least one U.S.-resident writer who is not included here, Ninotchka Rosca, who weaves that history into the fabric of her work.

With its political legacy omitted, the Philippines is neither idealized nor demonized. As an ancestral home, the place of one's consciousness before coming to America, it becomes an "otherworldly" place: subtly powerful, vivid, and distant. Within the Filipino and Filipino American world, trials and tribulations focus the self *within* a social context, but not *on* the context. Even in Brainard's contribution, "Flip Gothic," in which an uncontrollable young woman on the verge of adulthood is sent by her family in the States to live with her grandmother in Manila, the national culture of the Philippines is subjugated to the household culture, and the homeland is affective, but amorphous.

By pulling these personal, fictional quests together, the reader indeed comes away with a varied portrait of Filipinos in America, not the expression of dark causality present in the earlier generations of writers, such as Bulosan and Santos—those fantastic conjurors of Filipino American literature—but of people cautiously settling into what they hope will be a comfortable position.

In Veronica Montes's "Of Midgets and Beautiful Cousins," a Filipino American teenager and her sister, visiting their cousins in Manila, are taken to a dance club called "Small World," where the entire staff is made up of midgets. The girl is nervous and edgy. Against a backdrop of raucous eroticism—American soldiers hoot at the torch singer onstage—her cousin introduces her to a friend of his who is a waiter there and who shows an obvious interest in her. This makes her feel even more anxious, and she panics. They leave, and as they walk through the rain to their car, the waiter comes running up with an umbrella to shelter her—a sad ending to a sad evening of Filipinos, Americans, and Filipino Americans.

So many of these stories convey loneliness, disconnectedness, and an inability to form lasting attachments. They are stories rooted in rootlessness. Dizon's "Bride" harkens back to the days before World War II, when Pinoys made up a good part of the migrant workers on the plantations of Hawai'i, California, and Oregon. Cut off from the women of their homeland, they would troll the streets for hours, seeking companionship, drifting in and out of Chinese bordellos and dance bars—pictures that Bulosan drew with pathos and lyricism. Dizon's Candido has left a family behind in the Philippines; his wife has died and his children moved away. Decades pass. Hawai'i is now a state, the gateway to America. An old man, Candido receives a letter from a cousin. She knows a young woman who might want to marry, which Candido recognizes as an obvious immigration ploy. Despite this, he agrees and they wed. She quickly becomes pregnant, an unexpected event since Candido is in his early seventies. Two months after the birth of their child, she commits suicide.

The well-worn ground of the woman in a sanitarium is Linda Ty-Casper's scenario in "Dark Star/Altered Seeds." From a lesser writer, the story might be stale, but Ty-Casper is so deft with language—a fact known to readers of literary magazines and the slim novels she has published with Readers International, Inc.—it seems fresh. The narrator's husband has left her for another woman, but his return does not cure the ills that abandonment has caused:

> Is she pretty? Was that the question that woke her up? Then why did he leave? Every nameless, faceless woman; every young and jubilant face she meets becomes that woman. She. When he holds her now she becomes her, too.

The narrator's own identity has been usurped by her husband's thoughtless exchange of women, and even the reader becomes somewhat confused by the manner in which Ty-Casper has placed her pronouns. This collection abounds with such tension.

Though *Contemporary Fiction by Filipinos in America* could benefit from the addition of a bit more humor and a few East Coast writers—such as Rosca, Gamalinda, Hagedorn, and Regie Cabico—these are quibbles. Brainard has done a fine job of bringing many little-known writers—and the edginess of Filipinos in America—to the fore.

HAROLD AUGENBRAUM

A Drink Called Paradise by Terese Svoboda. Washington, D.C.: Counterpoint, 1999. 128 pages, cloth $18.

Most of us know that the Marshall Islands, especially the atolls of Bikini and Eniwetok, were used as test sites for atomic and hydrogen thermonuclear weapons. Most do not know that the total yield of the sixty-six bombs detonated at the surface of these two tiny atolls was about one hundred ten megatons—equal to one hundred ten *million* tons of exploding dynamite, more than seven thousand times the yield of Little Boy, the bomb dropped on Hiroshima, Japan. Radioactive fallout from these blasts fell like snow over a large area of the Pacific Ocean, including several inhabited atolls. Most of us are at least vaguely aware of this, yet what images really come into our minds when we hear the name *Bikini?* Not images of mushroom clouds, radioactive fallout, thyroid cancer, or jellyfish babies, but sexy women on a beach, palms swaying in the breeze, pastel sunsets, and sailboats on the horizon. We picture a woman in paradise. Clare, Terese Svoboda's protagonist in *A Drink Called Paradise,* might remark that we picture some representation of paradise because the concept of *bikini* was the beneficiary of a much more effective and appealing marketing campaign than *Bikini.* Clare is in the ad game, searching for the perfect virgin island paradise to use as a setting to advertise a new soft drink—one called Paradise. "The drink needed an island better than where the fruit came from to shoot its ad in," says Clare.

Her determined search for paradise, we learn, is more than just Madison Avenue ambition. Clare, consciously or not, is running from a dark, wounded part of her past and hoping for the emotional escape that she believes only a paradise can provide. Her quest pushes her to the farthest parts of the world, to the atolls of the Marshalls: pristine, placid blue lagoons, swaying palms, chalk-white beaches. The first island she and her crew visit does not meet Clare's expectations, so they keep looking, Clare ultimately abandoning the crew and slipping away on a supply boat to visit one of the most remote islands on Earth: "What is one more island, one more week away by boat?" When Clare lingers too long on the island and the boat leaves without her, she comes to learn that she has indeed gone too far and that what she has been trying to escape from—that dark part of her past—is what this paradise will force her to confront.

At first, the island does not seem like such a bad place to be stranded: "a beach so white, white crayon on white paper is about right, a white that stretches—yawns and stretches—its way to the lagoon of choice, the ur-lagoon of every ad for paradise." And Clare believes that the islanders are not just humoring her when they say another boat will be coming soon, no more than another week. She is content to

> float in the amber of a good time, maybe a little lonely with nobody to sigh off into the sunset with, but I collect myself, chase children who squirt me with rubber-hose creatures that grow in the shallows, burn the continental drift into my sandy thighs, cavort with snorkel and mask in the empty lagoon.

Clare has a fellow castaway, a mysterious man named Harry who may or may not be a fugitive criminal and who seeks refuge where he knows he will never be found or even looked for. He has also found the island to be paradise but in a different way: many of the women vie for his sexual attention. For Harry, whose understanding of this island is greater than Clare's, it is a paradise that comes at a very high price, one he knowingly and willingly pays. For Clare, as the days run into weeks and the islanders' promises of another boat are revealed to be lies, the illusion of paradise soon becomes evident. She becomes a victim of the deceptions she herself has worked to create, struggling in vain to keep on dreaming of "living on a beautiful tropical island that I have made out of nothing, as advertised."

Knowing that "You have to keep on inventing or else the island closes in, goes cold with too much truth," she says:

> It is the romance of the thing I know how to write: the bent palm, the burn of a cigarette in the dark, pearls against a tawny neck, water reflections, most of what started here and was whispered, sailor to merchant to whore to chamberlain to some philosopher walking around a big lake in a cold country who made it what it is so I can remake it, wrap dollar signs around it so people can burn their lives away answering yes.

Over time, Clare's perception changes. What was once distant and surreal becomes personal and very real as a new awareness ripe with abundant mysteries dawns: why does her host keep offering her coconuts to eat, yet stays away from them as if they were Eden's forbidden fruit? What is in that locked house surrounded by curls of barbed wire? What blew all the ghosts out of the cemetery? Why do the island women give Clare the name Vagina Mouth, and who tried to rape her? What are those scars "so neatly stitched around each woman's neck"? Why are there children like Temu, ones "who aren't right, whose heads are too small or too large or wrong"? How can a baby be born with no bones, no anus? What thing is in that house "with a defeated roof"?

> [T]he house is dark and doorless, and what wafts out in the heavy, humid darkness is the smell of suppuration, of scabs picked and reopened, and what sound accompanies it is constant as a series of waves. It is not the wet weepy sound I hear from Temu that carries over the water and makes Ngarima rise but guttural and fresh like a hose tightening around someone, some peculiar sound that realizes itself, like constant pain, in the present.

No, Clare has found no paradise; the island is at best some kind of Purgatory, maybe a little too close to the border of Hell.

Svoboda writes skillfully: each word, each phrase, each sentence of this deceptively small book weaves its way into the next with the mesmerizing effect of an epic incantation. While reading, it is easy to lose track of time, as if you too, like Clare, have found yourself where time no longer matters, where love and horror never should have had to meet, where death is the avenue one must take to find rebirth. *A Drink Called Paradise* is a heady drink, one whose effects will stay with you long after you have put it down. Then you may find yourself, as I did, reaching for it again.

ROBERT BARCLAY

Salvation and Other Disasters by Josip Novakovich. Saint Paul: Graywolf Press, 1998. 203 pages, paper $12.95.

In Sarajevo in October 1993, the siege of the Bosnian capital was in its eighteenth month. The morning press briefing had been given over to statistics—by then more than ten thousand people had lost their lives, tens of thousands more had been wounded, and the city was without water, electricity, and gas—and at its conclusion I had occasion to tell John Burns, the Pulitzer Prize–winning reporter from the *New York Times,* how much I admired the way his dispatches provided a human dimension to the war. This story writes itself, he replied wearily, waving at the mountains overlooking the city, where Serbian gunners were orchestrating the siege. Nevertheless a *Times* survey showed that only nineteen percent of its readers followed his stories, which usually appeared above the fold on the front page. Burns was nearing the end of his tour—it was said the Serbs had threatened to kill him.

The wars of succession in the former Yugoslavia (Slovenia, Croatia, Bosnia-Herzegovina, and Kosovo), which dominated this decade's headlines, produced not only incalculable suffering—millions displaced, hundreds of thousands killed and wounded, thousands of women raped, hundreds of cities, towns, and villages razed—but also a great deal of inspired reporting: the first drafts of history. Moreover, several fine books of reportage (history's second drafts, if you will) were published, including Roger Cohen's *Hearts Grown Brutal,* Chuck Sudetic's *Blood and Vengeance,* and Ed Vulliamy's *Seasons in Hell;* compelling radio and television reports were aired on a nightly basis. Indeed no war was more thoroughly documented than the Third Balkan War. (The First and Second Balkan Wars, in 1912 and 1913, respectively, were just as vicious, according to a report issued by the Carnegie Endowment for International Peace.) Yet journalists heard time and again, often from very educated people, that the story was too complicated to follow—and that the media had failed to cover it properly. In fact, most Americans averted their eyes from the defining tragedy of the post–Cold War world, even when, in the spring of 2000, NATO mounted its first military campaign in Kosovo to bring the conflict to an end.

Now that an uneasy peace is at hand, we may turn to the news that stays news—to poetry and fiction rooted in this much misunderstood war. And Josip Novakovich's fine collection of short stories, *Salvation and Other Disasters,* illuminates the dark hearts of ordinary people caught up in circumstances beyond their control. Novakovich, who was born in Croatia and now teaches at the University of Cincinnati, concentrates on the conflict between Orthodox Serbs and Catholic Croats that fueled the war in Croatia and complicated the fighting in Bosnia. He subscribes to the notion promulgated by Croatia's greatest modern writer, Miroslav Krleža, that Serbs and Croats are one people afflicted with two national consciences, each defining itself against the other, sometimes with disastrous consequences. "God save me," Krleža wrote, "from Serbian heroism and Croatian culture": the martial deities of the Third Balkan War. And it is one of Novakovich's literary virtues that both hardline Serbs and Croats will find fault with his descriptions of them. For what emerges in *Salvation and Other Disasters* is a relentlessly honest vision of the human condition. A one-legged man's remark—"I've lived my life to the emptiest"—could stand as the epigraph to this book.

The characters in these sixteen stories are alternately anxious and angry, disillusioned and confused. They make poor decisions, then have to live with the consequences. In "Sheepskin," a survivor of the massacre at the hospital in Vukovar,

Croatia, meets his "old tormentor" on a train in western Slavonia. Certain he has come face to face with the man who stabbed him in the thigh with a broken wine bottle, at the next stop where they must change trains, he follows him into a restaurant. There his tormentor shows him a nude centerfold, as if to say he is not interested in a homosexual encounter, and soon after, the narrator murders him—only to realize he has killed the wrong man. On a whim, he attends his victim's funeral, and before long he has fallen for the widow, who tells him her late husband, who served on the same side as the narrator, was indeed gay. He cannot believe his luck:

> I don't know why I'm having success with her—perhaps too many men are in the army, many have been killed, and there's a shortage that may be working to my advantage. Maybe she's stringing me along, maybe she's suspecting me and investigating the case. I think my guilt gives me extraordinary confidence—I have nothing to lose. I am tempted to expose myself to her, and this temptation thrills me just as much as the erotic seduction does. I am dizzy from her images—and his—swarming in my head. I should go back to the western Slavonian fields, and gather wildflowers, bury myself in their scents and colors. Then I would not need to remember and rave on the page from a strange desire to be caught. I would live like a fox in a bush of red tea.

This from a man who believes the war might have been prevented if only his countrymen had stuck to drinking the "mellifluous teas" that cure asthma, improve memory, and fill one with tenderness.

Nor is this the only story of shifting loyalties and identities. In "Crimson," a Serbian soldier kills his commanding officer in order to save a Croatian woman from being raped—only to impregnate her himself while she is still unconscious. Something changes in him. He deserts the army and returns to his hometown in Croatia, where he meets the woman, who is carrying his child and is on her way to an abortion clinic. He proposes to her, though, as she reminds him, "Mixed marriages aren't exactly in fashion." Yet she agrees to marry him and to keep the child, a decision she will regret when she unravels her son's paternity. I will not betray the conclusion of the story, which is at once startling and true. Suffice it to say that a bolt of "cold blue lightning" streaks across these pages to reveal horror everywhere.

Interspersed in this gallery of war criminals and refugees are provincial tales of children seeing their first film (which they are told is "the Devil's celluloid tail"); of émigrés in America dispensing or learning important lessons about character; of a woman who resorts to prostitution to buy her way out of a concentration camp. Well written, exactly observed, and lined with a wicked sense of humor, *Salvation and Other Disasters* is a wise and important book—one that Americans must read.

CHRISTOPHER MERRILL

Rabbit of the Nether World by Reiko Koyanagi. Translated by Hiroaki Sato and illustrated by Monica Tamano. Winchester, VA: Red Moon Press, 1999. 62 pages, paper $12.

Rabbit of the Nether World is a unique and often compelling memoir—a fragmentary, poetic re-creation of Reiko Koyanagi's wartime childhood and its many painful events. Traumatized by air raids, relocation to the countryside, and one loss after another, a lonely girl searches for connection and comfort amidst the ruins. She finds these mainly in spirits from the netherworld: a parade of dead aunts and uncles and an odd rabbit, who keeps her company on moonlit nights.

First published by Kashinsha in 1989 as *Yomi no usagi*, this book received the Poet's Club Prize the following year. The author, who runs a Tokyo art gallery, has a highly sensitive eye: she creates a "shipwrecked two-story house" in disarray, a child's secret garden, grass-leaf soup, white bombs that fall "even into the ocean," and an uncle who looks like a "skinny European dog." The atmospheric drawings by Monica Tamano lend the text a childlike air, and Hiroaki Sato's translation is seamless. Despite its sobering subject matter, *Rabbit of the Nether World* is often charming and, at its best, evokes the humanistic work of Antoine de Saint-Exupéry.

The narrative charts the girl's loss of innocence and follows the author, as an adult, on her journey to come to terms with her painful past. It begins in 1989, when the narrator takes a train and returns, almost mythically, to the house where she grew up. Raised in poverty by a single father whose love of math is more easily expressed than love for his daughter, she suffers rejection, hurt, and anger at her father. When her mother leaves them for a lover, the girl asks, "Father, wasn't there a mathematical expression that would keep Mother's heart moored to yours?"

Ironically, it is mathematics—the "useless talent" that hurts the daughter—that transports the father away from his everyday difficulties. "When I'm in math," he says, "I can forget that I must keep you alive." They travel to her father's hometown in the countryside, to the clan in the Valley of Winds, to which he never intended to return. Attempting to steer clear of the air raids and the hideous "frying pan" bombing tactics, her father carries her to the safety of the storehouse, but it has two holes—one an entrance to the netherworld, down which the girl threatens to slip. The author imagines the girl's death, and in this rendering, the father goes to pay respects to an electronic calculator in its last moments instead of going to his daughter's bedside.

In the feverish realm of near-death, the girl speaks to apparitions of her relatives, half-human, half-smoke figures pulling her towards death. With Japan's defeat around the corner and the "fragrance of death" pervading the air, she has befriended the rabbit of death, making peace with the "enemy." By the book's end, he says to her: "It was long ago, there was a war. This town also had an air raid and was surrounded by fires. I tell you, it was terrible. Burning a small rural town like this, well, I bet the other side had an awful lot of excess bombs." Then he ascends to the heavens, honored in an imaginary festival.

Having suffered the loss of her mother, the loss of her home, and the deaths of various relatives, the young girl survives. Though Koyanagi claims that her mother "was utter nonsense to her" and that she couldn't hate her because "hatred has the power to bring people together," the emotional subtext and her anger at her father undercut this denial. In the end, the daughter's search for a numeral "that doesn't exist anywhere in the world" comes down to the search for love. It's not a quantifiable entity. It can't even be explained.

LEZA LOWITZ

Only the Nails Remain: Scenes from the Balkan Wars by Christopher Merrill. Lanham, MD: Rowman and Littlefield, 1999. 401 pages, cloth $27.95.

In the prologue to *Only the Nails Remain*, Christopher Merrill writes that he did not anticipate war when, in 1991, he made arrangements to visit fellow poet Aleš Debeljak in Slovenia. He planned to hike the countryside, meet the poets and artists of his friend's country, and drink wine in the wooded mountains of the Pohorje range and Julian Alps. When it came time to consummate those plans in August 1992, Slovenia had already fought for and won its independence, and the battlefront had moved south to Croatia and Bosnia. Merrill decided to go ahead with his excursion despite the nearness of the war. The trip went as planned, but Merrill fell victim to the unexpected. The dark beauty of the region drew him in, and he fell hopelessly in love with the Balkans. His passion led him to return to Central Europe ten times over the next four years, traveling through the former Yugoslavia, four other Balkan states, and three bordering countries. His obsession eventually led him to a Sarajevo cellar, where mortar rounds whistled overhead.

Only the Nails Remain is an account of Merrill's travels. It is a study uniquely sensitive to the rhythms and nuances of a place where writing poetry is sometimes considered a national profession and where art is valued in even its most outrageously experimental forms. Merrill captures the wild beauty and romance of the region and records its dangers and inconsistencies. He describes people given to violence, courage, generosity, and hatred—at times in quick succession—but rarely to cold-blooded indifference.

Slovenian Tomaž Šalamun is the most renowned of the poets Merrill met. Adrift in a country where melancholics account for a disturbingly high percentage of the population—and poets are nearly as common—Šalamun had grown so melancholic he had been unable to write since the war began. Too many people had complimented him on how his early works prophesied the bloodshed, and he worried that, in some magical way, his poems had caused the Balkan wars. "His was a mystical view; a single verse might unleash terrific forces," Merrill writes. The book opens with one of Šalamun's prewar poems:

> I will take the nails,
> long nails
> and hammer them into my body.

Very very gently,
very very slowly
. . . .
Then I will set fire to everything.
It will burn for a long time.
It will burn for seven days.
Only the nails will remain,
all welded together and rusty.
So I will remain.
So I will survive everything.

As a metaphor for the nationalistic rhetoric that led to the breakup of Yugoslavia, the poem describes the destruction perpetrated in Bosnia and parts of Croatia and the effects of sustained brutality on the individual psyche. It also effectively demonstrates the darkness Merrill finds woven through the souls of many of the people he meets—sometimes expressed as poetry or humor and other times as hatred and violence.

In Belgrade, Merrill discovered a culture of paranoia and propaganda: the Serbs were persecuted by the Vatican, the Free Masons, the U.S. government, CNN, much of Western Europe, and Bosnian Muslims who deviously bombed their own people in order to turn international opinion against Serbians. The propaganda was intoxicating. Not even foreigners were immune to its twisting of reality. Upon arrival at his hotel, a British filmmaker introduced Merrill to Bosnian-Serb leader Radovan Karadžić. "He thinks the way we do," the filmmaker said to Karadžić. Merrill was horrified. Karadžić, a poet and Sarajevo psychologist before the war, was Serbian leader Slobodan Milošević's man behind the ethnic-cleansing campaign in Bosnia.

Karadžić was such a bad poet that some speculate he was made mean by the near universal disdain his countrymen showed for his work. At times Karadžić's prewar verses, like Šalamun's, seem to predict the destruction that accompanied the breakup of Yugoslavia ("Take no pity let's go / kill the scum down in the city"). But unlike Šalamun's writing, Karadžić's poetry is devoid of mystical forces; the Bosnian-Serb president's poetry outlines a future he helped direct, including the destruction of Bosnia's capital.

From the gently sloping mountains that encircle Sarajevo, Serbian troops rained sniper bullets and mortar rounds on the tiled-roof houses, mosques, and cathedrals. They shut the natural-gas lines down, which forced residents to burn their books for heat. Witnesses say that when the phosphorus shells hit the national library, priceless manuscripts and historic books burned for days.

On one of his trips to the Bosnian capital, Merrill attended a concert. There was very little running water and not enough food in the city, and the performance aimed to raise the spirits of the besieged. The hall was unheated and the musicians were unable to tune their instruments, but the evening was saved by a performance artist who danced around a bathtub, fell in with a splash, and stayed under for a full minute. The scarce beauty of a bath had the wartime audience applauding wildly.

Because of the frequent mortar attacks in Sarajevo, Merrill spent much of his time there huddled in the basement of an apartment building. On one occasion, he and his neighbors debated which books were best to have on hand during a siege. Merrill would not be separated from his volume of poetry by St.-John Perse. A humanitarian worker preferred an anthology of erotica. A Bosnian woman named Mirna made her suggestion. "Marx and Lenin," she said. "They burn forever."

KAREN BLAKEMAN

About the Contributors

Brother Anthony studied at Queen's College, Oxford University, before joining the Community of Taizé in France in 1969. He lived in the Philippines from 1977 to 1980, then moved to Korea, where he became a naturalized citizen in 1994 and took the Korean name An Sonjae. He has translated numerous volumes of Korean poetry and is a professor at Sogang University.

Harold Augenbraum is director of The Mercantile Library of New York and its Center for World Literature. Among his publications are *Growing Up Latino: Memoirs and Stories* and *The Latino Reader: An American Literary Tradition from 1542 to the Present.* He is also a member of the board of directors of the Asian American Writers' Workshop.

Ayukawa Nobuo was born in Tokyo in 1920 and died in 1986. He attended Waseda University and was a founding member of the Arechi (Wasteland) group of poets. Drafted into the Japanese Imperial Army in 1942, he was sent to Sumatra, where he contracted malaria, and then home to recuperate. With the publication of his first major poems, "The Dead Man" and "America," he emerged as Japan's preeminent anti-war poet and an important literary critic who voiced the conscience of the postwar generation.

Robert Barclay is a former resident of the Marshall Islands who lives in Hawai'i and travels throughout the Pacific.

Arthur Binard graduated in English literature from Colgate University in 1990. A deep curiosity about the ideogram led him to Japan, where he now writes poetry in both English and Japanese. Among his published works are *Catch and Release, Timeless,* and *Our Cup of Tea,* a bilingual book for children. He is the Japan correspondent for *Colors* magazine.

Karen Blakeman is a journalist who covered the NATO mission to Bosnia and Herzegovina from 1995 to 1997. In 1998, she worked in Sarajevo for the Organization for Security and Cooperation in Europe, investigating incidents of intimidation of and violence against the media. She now lives and writes in Hawai'i.

Anthony H. Chambers has translated fiction by Tanizaki Jun'ichirō and Mishima Yukio, among other Japanese writers. He is a professor of Japanese at Arizona State University.

Dazai Osamu was a prolific writer of short stories who was best known for his novels *The Setting Sun* (1947) and *No Longer Human* (1948). Collected translations of his shorter works include *Self Portraits, Blue Bamboo,* and *Crackling Mountain.* Known as much for his troubled and decadent life as for his writing, he committed suicide in 1948.

Gary G. Gach was honored with an American Book Award for his recent anthology *What Book!?—Buddha Poems from Beat to Hiphop. All Ways: 3 Poems* is forthcoming from Creative Arts. He lives in San Francisco.

Samuel Grolmes has published poetry, fiction, and translations of Japanese works. A former Fulbright professor to Japan, he recently published *Tamura Ryuichi: Poems 1946–1998,* a book cotranslated with Tsumura Yumiko.

Francis and Irene Haar were invited in 1939 to Japan, where Francis opened a photography studio. That same year, his first book by a Japanese publisher, *Way to the Orient,* was issued; this was followed by *Around Mount Fuji* and other books. When World War II broke out, the Haar family was kept under surveillance by the Japanese military. In 1945, Francis began photographing for the U.S. Occupation Forces, and shortly afterwards, Irene opened Irene's Hungaria, a restaurant in the Ginza district that quickly became a meeting place for artists, writers, and actors, both Japanese and foreign. In 1960, Francis and Irene settled in Honolulu, where Francis became deeply involved in the study of Hawaiian culture. He received numerous national and international awards for his work, and his many books include the forthcoming *Francis Haar: A Lifetime of Images,* from which the piece in this issue is taken.

Hayashi Kyoko was born in Nagasaki in 1930 and spent her childhood in Shanghai during Japan's occupation of China. After returning to Japan in spring 1945, she enrolled in Nagasaki Girls' High School. On 9 August, she was exposed to the atomic bomb while working as a student recruit in a Mitsubishi munitions factory. She began writing in the early 1960s, and in 1975 received the prestigious Akutagawa Prize for her story "Ritual of Death." Today she is recognized as one of the foremost chroniclers of the A-bomb experience in Japan. Her story in this issue is from the collection *Cut Glass, Blown Glass* (1978).

Jeanne Wakatsuki Houston was born in Inglewood, California. Coauthored with James D. Houston, her best-known work is the memoir *Farewell to Manzanar,* the story of her family's experience in an internment camp during World War II. Her writing has earned numerous honors, including a U.S.-Japan Cultural Exchange Fellowship and a Rockefeller Foundation Residency in Bellagio, Italy. Her novel-in-progress, *Fire Horse Woman,* explores the lives of three generations of Japanese American women in Japan and California.

Ishigaki Chōkō is the pen name of Emiko Hannah Ishigaki, who was born in Shenyang, China, in 1931 and raised in Tokyo. Since 1990, she has published several books of *tanka,* the most recent of which is *Requiem, or An-kon-ka.* She is the dean of the graduate school and a professor of early childhood education at Seiwa

College; the mother of four children and grandmother of six, she is also the president of the Japanese Society for the Education of Young Children.

Ishii Shinpei was born in 1942 in Dairen, Manchuria, and graduated with a degree in journalism from Doshisha University in Kyoto. He has been an editor, television producer, and translator. In 1992, he won the Galaxy Award for *Songs Have No Borders*, a program for the Nippon Television Network. His numerous translations into Japanese include Ian Buruma's *Wages of Guilt: Memories of War in Germany and Japan.* He is now a freelance writer for magazines and newspapers. A portion of the essay featured in this issue was published in the September 1991 edition of the Japanese monthly magazine *Chuo Koron.*

Kijima Hajime is the editor of *The Poetry of Postwar Japan* and the author of *Little White Hen,* a modernized folktale. His most recent books are *Responses Magnetic: Selected Poems* and *Linked Quatrains: The Cycle of "fill."* He lives in Tokyo.

Kim Young-Moo graduated from Seoul National University and received his doctorate from SUNY at Stony Brook. He has published two volumes of poems in Korean and cotranslated numerous Korean authors into English. He has been a professor at Seoul National University since 1981.

Ko Ŭn was born in 1933 in Chŏlla Province, Korea, and grew up during the Japanese Occupation. When the Korean War broke out, he was conscripted by the People's Army. In 1952, he became a Buddhist monk and lived a monastic life for ten years. For his activism confronting South Korea's military government, he was imprisoned and tortured. In prison, he began an epic cycle of poems entitled *10,000 Lives,* from which the poems printed here are taken. He has published over 100 volumes of poetry, essays, fiction, drama, and translations of Chinese poetry. He now lives with his wife and daughter in a village two hours from Seoul.

Koriyama Naoshi was born on Kikai Island in Kagoshima Prefecture in 1926. With Edward Lueders, he translated *Like Underground Water: The Poetry of Mid-Twentieth Century Japan* (1995) and with Elizabeth Ogata, *Black Flower in the Sky: Poems of a Korean Bridegroom in Hiroshima,* a collection by Chong Ki-Sheok. Volumes of his own work include *Collected Poems* (1996). He lives in Kanagawa-ken, Japan.

Leza Lowitz lived from 1990 to 1994 in Tokyo, where she worked as a freelance journalist for *Japan Times* and *Asahi Evening News.* Her books of translation include *a long rainy season* and *other side river,* both anthologies of contemporary Japanese women's poetry edited and cotranslated with Miyuki Aoyama. Her own books of poetry include *Yoga Poems: Lines to Unfold By.* Among her awards are a PEN Syndicated Fiction Award, a National Endowment for the Arts fellowship, and the *Tokyo Journal* Fiction Translation Prize.

R. F. McCarthy is a writer, translator, and lyricist who resides in Santa Monica, California. His translations include *Self Portraits* and *Blue Bamboo,* two collections of short stories by Dazai Osamu; *Sixty-Nine* and *Love & Pop* by Ryu Murakami; and *Hustlers Grotto* by Yayoi Kusama. He received a National Endowment for the Arts translation fellowship in 1996.

Christopher Merrill directs the International Writing Program at the University of Iowa. His most recent works are the nonfiction book *Only the Nails Remain: Scenes from the Balkan Wars,* the poetry collection *Brilliant Water,* and the translation of Aleš Debeljak's *The City and the Child.*

Mishima Yukio wrote seventy plays, over a hundred short stories, eleven volumes of essays, and twenty-seven novels, including *Confessions of a Mask, The Sound of Waves,* and *The Temple of the Golden Pavilion.* He committed ritual suicide in 1970.

Margaret Mitsutani was born in Pittsburgh, Pennsylvania, in 1953 and received her master's degree in comparative literature from Tokyo University in 1981. Since 1991, she has been teaching at Kyoritsu Women's University in Tokyo. Her translations of Hayashi Kyoko's stories have appeared in *Mānoa* and *Prairie Schooner;* other translations include Ōe Kenzaburo's novel *An Echo of Heaven,* a collection of three stories by Tawada Yoko entitled *The Bridegroom Was a Dog,* and *A Dream Like This World: One Hundred Haiku* by Nagata Koi, which was cotranslated by Naruto Nana.

Keiji Nakazawa was a small boy in Hiroshima when the atomic bomb was dropped in 1945. He survived to create his first cartoon in 1963 and has since published over fifty book-length works based on his experiences. *Barefoot Gen* first appeared in 1973 in *Shōnen Jump.* Nearly 2,000 pages, the story has been made into live-action and animated feature films as well as an opera. A nineteen-volume anthology of Nakazawa's work, *The Peace Comics Collection,* was recently published. Now living in Tokyo with his wife and daughter, he frequently lectures to high-school assemblies and citizen groups throughout Japan on the experience of surviving the atomic bomb.

Elizabeth Floyd Ogata is an editor at Kodansha International in Tokyo and an essayist and book reviewer. She is cotranslator, with Koriyama Naoshi, of *Black Flower in the Sky: Poems of a Korean Bridegroom in Hiroshima,* a collection by Chong Ki-Sheok.

Ogata Keiichi is an independent filmmaker and screenwriter. He worked as an architect for some years before affiliating with London's Architectural Association from 1994 to 1996. In London, he made what he calls cinepoems, of which *Hiroshima through Light* is one. He is currently filming his first narrative short, *Kioku no shizuku* (The sound of memory), in Tokyo, and he plans to film *Separate Landscape* in Swindon, England, in 2001. He lives in Tokyo.

Yoko Ogawa is a novelist, short-story writer, and essayist. She received the 1988 Kaien First-Novel Award for *When the Swallowtail Breaks Down;* in 1991, she received the Akutagawa Award for *Pregnancy Calendar.* Among her other works are *The Perfect Sickroom* and *Tea That Never Cools.* She lives in Kurashiki, Okayama, with her husband and son.

Oketani Shogo is a writer and translator. He lives on the northern California coast and is working with his wife, Leza Lowitz, on a book of poems by Ayukawa Nobuo, a project for which they received a 1997 National Endowment for the Arts translation fellowship.

Lisa Ottiger was born in the Philippines and grew up in Indonesia and Hong Kong. A former reviews editor for *Mānoa,* she also assisted with assembling the collection of Hong Kong fiction published in the summer 1998 issue.

Project Gen was formed in 1976 by a group of young Japanese and non-Japanese living in Tokyo who shared a desire to spread the message of *Barefoot Gen* by translating the work of Keiji Nakazawa into other languages. They consider Nakazawa's message to be one of human triumph in the face of war's terrible consequences and to be a warning against the threat of nuclear destruction.

Donald Richie is the author of numerous works on modern Japan covering such topics as *bonsai,* film, and tattooing. His most recent work is *Memoirs of the Warrior Kumagai: A Historical Novel.* In 1992, his travel memoirs were made into the public television movie *The Inland Sea.*

Sagawa Aki published the collection *Dream Conceiving the Dead Again,* which won the Oguma Hideo Prize in 1992 and from which the poem in this issue is reprinted. Her poems have been translated into Korean, and she, in turn, translates Korean poets into Japanese. Born in Tokyo, she now lives in Yokohama with her husband and daughter.

Motoyuki Shibata was born in 1954. A translator, reviewer, and essayist, he has translated into Japanese the work of Paul Auster, Steve Erickson, Steven Millhauser, Stuart Dybek, and Ethan Canin, among others. He received the 1992 Kodansha Essay Award for his book *The Half-Hearted Scholar.* He lives in Tokyo with his wife.

Sone Yoshi lives in Maebashi, Japan, and has published four books of poems. The poem in this issue is from her latest book, *Falling Flower Petals.*

Gladys Swan is the author of seven books of fiction, the most recent of which is *News from the Volcano.* She teaches a fiction workshop in Antigua, Guatemala.

Tamura Ryuichi was born in 1923. He served in the Japanese Imperial Navy during World War II and was the founder of the postwar magazine *Arechi (Wasteland).* He wrote thirty books of poetry, including a farewell volume, which was published in 1999, the year after his death. The poem in this issue is from *Poetry of Ryuichi Tamura* (CCC Books, 1998), translated by Samuel Grolmes and Tsumura Yumiko.

Tsumura Yumiko has taught American literature at Baika Women's College and earned a master of fine arts degree in poetry and translation at the University of Iowa. Her books include *Tamura Ryuichi: Poems 1946–1998,* which she cotranslated with Samuel Grolmes.

Uda Rei is the pen name of Abe Toshiaki. Born in Yokohama in 1930, he graduated in 1951 from Tokyo University of Foreign Languages and Studies, where he majored in Chinese. His books include *The Desolation of Voiceless Places,* a biography of He qi fang; *The Philosophy of Healing in Chinese Poetry;* and the poetry collection *The Boy Who Turned into a Beech Tree,* where the poem in this issue first appeared.

Shuzo Uemoto was born in Hiroshima, Japan, in 1947 and moved to Hawaiʻi in 1953. He is a photographer for the Honolulu Academy of Arts and a lecturer in photography at Kapiolani Community College. His most recent published work is *Lessons of Aloha* (Watermark Press, 1999).

Nicholas Voge was raised in Los Angeles. In 1981, he received a bachelor's degree in Japanese from the University of California at Los Angeles. After attending graduate school at the University of Hawaiʻi, where he studied Japanese language and literature, he spent eight years in Japan. He now works as a freelance translator, interpreter, and copywriter and lives in Hawaiʻi with his wife and daughter.

Ingrid von Essen is a freelance editor living in London.

Mary Yukari Waters has published fiction in such magazines as *Triquarterly, Glimmer Train,* and *Shenandoah.* She recently won a Pushcart Prize. She lives in Long Beach, California.